iPhone® for Seniors

7th Edition

by Dwight Spivey

for
dummies®

iPhone® for Seniors For Dummies®, 7th Edition

Published by: **John Wiley & Sons, Inc.**, 111 River Street, Hoboken, NJ 07030-5774, www.wiley.com

Copyright © 2018 by John Wiley & Sons, Inc., Hoboken, New Jersey

Media and software compilation copyright © 2018 by John Wiley & Sons, Inc. All rights reserved.

Published simultaneously in Canada

For general information on our other products and services, please contact our Customer Care Department within the U.S. at 877-762-2974, outside the U.S. at 317-572-3993, or fax 317-572-4002. For technical support, please visit https://hub.wiley.com/community/support/dummies.

Wiley publishes in a variety of print and electronic formats and by print-on-demand. Some material included with standard print versions of this book may not be included in e-books or in print-on-demand. If this book refers to media such as a CD or DVD that is not included in the version you purchased, you may download this material at http://booksupport.wiley.com. For more information about Wiley products, visit www.wiley.com.

Library of Congress Control Number: 2017955654

ISBN 978-1-119-41716-3 (pbk); 978-1-119-41703-3 (epub); 978-1-119-41721-7 (epdf)

Manufactured in the United States of America

10 9 8 7 6 5 4 3 2 1

Contents at a Glance

Introduction

I f you bought this book (or are even thinking about buying it), you've probably already made the decision to buy an iPhone. The iPhone is designed to be easy to use, but you can still spend hours exploring the preinstalled apps, finding out how to change settings, and figuring out how to sync the device to your computer or through iCloud. I've invested those hours so that you don't have to — and I've added advice and tips for getting the most out of your iPhone.

This book helps you get going with the iPhone quickly and painlessly so that you can move directly to the fun part.

About This Book

This book is specifically written for mature people like you, folks who may be relatively new to using a smartphone and want to discover the basics of buying an iPhone, making and receiving phone calls, working with its preinstalled apps, and getting on the Internet. In writing this book, I've tried to consider the types of activities that might interest someone who is 50 years old or older and picking up an iPhone for the first time.

Foolish Assumptions

This book is organized by sets of tasks. These tasks start from the beginning, assuming that you've never laid your hands on an iPhone, and guide you through basic steps using nontechnical language.

This book covers going online using either a Wi-Fi or 3G/4G connection, browsing the web (Chapter 11), and checking email (Chapter 12). I'm also assuming that you'll want to use the iBooks e-reader app, so I cover its features in Chapter 16. Not to mention covering other great things you can do with your iPhone, such as taking and sharing your photos and videos (Chapters 18 and 19, respectively), and much more!

Icons Used in This Book

Icons are tiny pictures in the margin of pages that call your attention to special advice or information, such as:

TIP

These brief pieces of advice help you to take a skill further or provide alternate ways of getting things done.

WARNING

Heads up! This may be difficult or expensive to undo.

REMEMBER

This is information that's so useful, it's worth keeping in your head, not just on your bookshelf.

TECHNICAL STUFF

Maybe this isn't essential information, but it's neat to know.

Beyond the Book

There's even more iPhone information on www.dummies.com. This book's Cheat Sheet offers a list of General settings, Mail, Contacts, and Calendar settings to be aware of, and the settings you can control for browsing in Safari. To get to the cheat sheet, go to www.dummies.com, then type *iPhone for Seniors For Dummies Cheat Sheet* in the Search box. This is also where you'll find any significant updates or changes that occur between editions of this book.

Also, there are online chapters that show you a wide range of iPhone apps to make your phone more useful and fun. Go to www.dummies.com/go/iphonefsfd7e.

Where to Go from Here

You can work through this book from beginning to end or simply open a chapter to solve a problem or acquire a specific new skill whenever you need it. The steps in every task quickly get you to where you want to go, without a lot of technical explanation.

At the time I wrote this book, all the information it contained was accurate for the iPhone 5s, SE, 6 and 6 Plus, 6s and 6s Plus, 7 and 7 Plus, the iPhone 8, 8 Plus, and iPhone X, version 11 of iOS (the operating system used by the iPhone), and version 12.5 of iTunes. Apple is likely to introduce new iPhone models and new versions of iOS and iTunes between book editions. If you've bought a new iPhone and found that its hardware, user interface, or the version of iTunes on your computer looks a little different, be sure to check out what Apple has to say at www.apple.com/iphone. You'll no doubt find updates there on the company's latest releases.

1
Getting to Know Your iPhone

IN THIS PART . . .

Starting your new iPhone

Navigating the home screen

Customizing your settings

Activating special features

Chapter **1**

Buying Your iPhone

You've read about it. You've seen on the news the lines at Apple Stores on the day a new version of the iPhone is released. You're so intrigued that you've decided to get your own iPhone to have a smartphone that offers much more than the ability to make and receive calls. iPhone also offers lots of fun apps, such as games and exercise trackers; allows you to explore the online world; lets you read e-books, magazines, and other periodicals; allows you to take and organize photos and videos; plays music and movies, and a lot more.

Trust me: You've made a good decision, because the iPhone redefines the mobile phone experience in an exciting way. It's also an absolutely perfect fit for many seniors.

In this chapter, you learn about the advantages of the iPhone, as well as where to buy this little gem and associated data plans from providers. After you have one in your hands, I help you explore what's in the box and get an overview of the little buttons and slots you'll encounter — luckily, the iPhone has very few of them.

Discover the Newest iPhones and iOS 11

Apple's iPhone gets its features from a combination of hardware and its software operating system (called iOS; the term is short for iPhone operating system). The most current version of the operating system is iOS 11. It's helpful to understand which new features the iPhone 8, 8 Plus, and X (pronounced "ten") models and iOS 11 bring to the table (all of which are covered in more detail in this book).

New features in iPhone 8 and 8 Plus include

» **Splash, water, and dust resistance**: Your new iPhone is resistant to damage caused by water splashing onto it or from dust collecting within it.

WARNING

iPhone 7's warranty doesn't cover water or dust damage. *Water and dust resistant doesn't mean water and dust proof.*

Now, you don't want to take your iPhone deep-sea diving, but it's likely to survive submersion in about a meter of water for up to 30 minutes. Mind you, this number has been tested in a lab, and isn't based on real-world conditions. In other words, if your iPhone gets wet it's much more likely to survive the ordeal than previous iPhone iterations, but it still isn't something you'd like to see happen to your expensive investment.

» **An A11 Bionic chip**: No, owning a new iPhone won't make you the Six-Million Dollar Man or the Bionic Woman, but it will provide you with one really nice power boost over previous iterations. This chip has been tested and demonstrated by third parties to perform as well as some Mac laptop chips (and completely blows top-of-the-line Android devices out of the water). Your iPhone will be able to handle pretty much any task you can throw at it with ease.

» **Glass bodies and wireless charging**: iPhone 8 and 8 Plus both boast all-glass bodies, which not only look great, but also allow you the option of wireless charging. Wireless charging gives you the ability to simply lay your iPhone onto a wireless charger pad to give it an energy boost.

This wireless charging thing is no joke. Imagine being able to charge your iPhone by simply laying it on a table in a coffee shop, or an airport, or in your car, or any other place a wireless charging pad can be incorporated. You'll never need to worry again if you've forgotten your charger cable! While wireless charging isn't new to the smartphone market, Apple's adoption of it is. Therefore, you're about to see wireless charging stations in almost every conceivable place. And you'll love it — guaranteed.

» **A 12MP rear-facing camera**: The camera in iPhone 8 and 8 Plus offers such features as a larger lens aperture (which allows for more light and better nighttime photos) and optical image stabilization (providing sharper images with longer exposure than previous iPhone versions).

» **A 7MP front-facing camera**: The front-facing camera now supports a higher resolution and wide color capture, making FaceTime calls and selfies much sharper and more vibrant.

» **Stereo speakers and no headphone jack**: You can listen to audio in stereo and with deeper bass, with speakers on both ends of the enclosure. This also allows the volume to be much louder from the external speakers than before. You can also connect your Earpods (included with your iPhone 8 and 8 Plus) via the Lightning connector.

Don't worry if you have a set of headphones you prefer that use the old 3.5mm headphone jacks. Both the iPhone 8 and 8 Plus ship with an adapter for connecting 3.5mm headphone jacks to the Lightning connector.

» **The Retina HD display**: The new displays in the iPhone 8 and 8 Plus support True Tone to help match the display color to the ambient lighting, affording a more natural experience. The color gamut of the display is also wider, providing richer colors than ever before.

Apple claims to have taken the smartphone into the future with its newest premium iPhone model, the iPhone X. The X is premium in every way, including price, but for some users the cost may be small compared to the return. New features introduced with iPhone X include

» **An A11 Bionic chip**: The iPhone X also includes the new A11 Bionic chip, and that's a good thing. The truly innovative tech in X demands a processor that can handle some heavy lifting, while still being able to answer calls and retrieve email.

» **Glass body and wireless charging**: Like iPhone 8 and 8 Plus, iPhone X is comprised of an all-glass body (with a tiny sliver of stainless steel around the edges to hold it all together), allowing a beautiful appearance and wireless charging. The glass is also the most durable of that used in any smartphone ever, according to Apple.

Don't read that as unbreakable. Cases are still a good idea.

» **Edge-to-Edge display**: iPhone X is Apple's first edge-to-edge display, meaning there's nothing else on the front of your iPhone but screen. Which brings me to my next point.

» **No Home button**: That's right, the method you've used for a decade now to return to the Home screen is now a thing of the past with this iPhone model. You simply swipe up from the bottom of the screen to provide the same effect as pressing the Home button. This also means that Touch ID is a thing of the past. Therefore, there's a new recognition tool.

» **Facial Recognition**: Touch ID is being replaced on iPhone X with Face ID. Using Face ID and the front-facing camera, your iPhone X unlocks when it recognizes your face.

Any iPhone device from the iPhone 5s forward can use most features of iOS 11 if you update the operating system (discussed in detail in Chapter 3); this book is based on version 11 of iOS. This update to the operating system adds many features, including

» **Much-improved Control Center**: Control Center allows you to quickly access many of your iPhone's features by simply swiping up on your screen. Control Center has been streamlined and the new interface is simpler to navigate. You can also customize Control Center to contain only items that you use often.

» **Siri improvements**: Siri now sounds like a more natural voice, and translates into several languages.

- » **Improvements to the Notes app**: With iOS 11, Notes takes another giant leap forward. Tables are easy to add, handwriting is supported, and drag-and-drop is a great new tool. You can also use Notes to scan paper documents!

- » **Files app**: Finally, Apple has delivered a great app called Files that allows you to browse the files stored on your iPhone. You can also use it to browse and work with files you've stored on other cloud services, such as Google Drive and Dropbox.

- » **Improvements to Maps**: Maps has always been great for getting around on the road, but now Maps shines when helping you navigate interiors. New built-in maps help guide you in unfamiliar public buildings, such as airports.

- » **Store many more photos and videos than ever before**: iOS 11 is the first version of iOS that uses a new compression format for photos and videos. High-quality photos and videos take up much less storage on your iPhone.

TIP

Don't need or use all the built-in apps? You can remove them from your Home screen. When you remove a built-in app from your Home screen, you aren't deleting it — you're hiding it. The is due to security reasons that are beyond the scope of this book. However, the built-in apps take up very little of your iPhone's storage space, and they can easily be added back to your Home screen by searching for them in the App Store and tapping the Get button.

These are but a very few of the improvements made to the latest version of iOS. I suggest visiting www.apple.com/ios/ios-11 to find out more.

Choose the Right iPhone for You

The sizes of the iPhone 8 models vary:

- » iPhone 8 measures 2.65" by 5.45" (4.7" diagonally) and 7.3 mm thick.
- » iPhone 8 Plus measures 3.07" by 6.24" (5.5" diagonally) and 7.5 mm thick (see **Figure 1-1**).

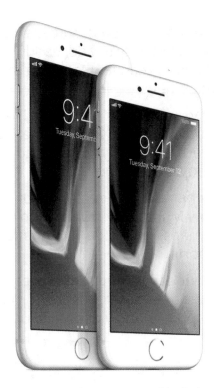

Image courtesy of Apple, Inc.

FIGURE 1-1

You can get iPhone 8 or 8 Plus in gold, silver, or space gray.

Other differences between iPhone 8 models come primarily from the current operating system, iOS 11.

iPhone 8 and 8 Plus models have a few variations:

» 3G talk time of up to 21 hours on 8 Plus and 14 hours on 8.

» iPhone 8 Plus has two rear-facing cameras, providing amazing optical zoom, Portrait mode, and other features, while 8 has a single rear-facing camera.

» Screen resolution: The higher the resolution, the crisper and brighter the phone display. The iPhone 8 provides 1334 x 750 resolution (more than 1 million pixels) and 8 Plus provides 1920 x 1080 (more than 2 million pixels).

iPhone X (**Figure 1-2**) comes in either space gray or silver and its dimensions are 2.79" by 5.65" (5.8" diagonally) and 7.7 mm thick. It also sports a Super Retina HD display with 2436 x 1125 resolution.

Image courtesy of Apple, Inc.

FIGURE 1-2

Table 1-1 gives you a quick comparison of iPhone SE, 6s, 6s Plus, 7, 7 Plus, 8, 8 Plus, and X (models currently sold by Apple). All costs are as of the time this book was written. (Some carriers may introduce non-contract terms.)

TABLE 1-1   iPhone Model Comparison

Model	Storage	Cost (may vary by carrier)	Carriers
SE	32 and 128GB	from $349	AT&T, Verizon, Sprint, T-Mobile, Virgin Mobile
6s	32 and 128GB	from $449	AT&T, Verizon, Sprint, T-Mobile, Virgin Mobile
6s Plus	32 and 128GB	from $549	AT&T, Verizon, Sprint, T-Mobile, Virgin Mobile

(continued)

TABLE 1-1 *(continued)*

Model	Storage	Cost (may vary by carrier)	Carriers
7	32 and 128GB	from $549	AT&T, Verizon, Sprint, T-Mobile, Virgin Mobile
7 Plus	32 and 128GB	from $669	AT&T, Verizon, Sprint, T-Mobile, Virgin Mobile
8	64 and 256GB	from $699	AT&T, Verizon, Sprint, T-Mobile, Virgin Mobile
8 Plus	64 and 256GB	from $799	AT&T, Verizon, Sprint, T-Mobile, Virgin Mobile
X	64 and 256GB	from $999	AT&T, Verizon, Sprint, T-Mobile, Virgin Mobile

TIP

One exciting pricing option is the iPhone Upgrade Program. You choose your carrier, get an unlocked phone so you can change carriers, and receive Apple Care + to cover you in case your phone has problems, all starting at a cost of $34.50 a month (depending on the iPhone model you select). Data usage from your carrier will come on top of that.

Decide How Much Storage Is Enough

Storage is a measure of how much information — for example, movies, photos, and software applications (apps) — you can store on a computing device. Storage can also affect your iPhone's performance when handling such tasks as streaming favorite TV shows from the World Wide Web or downloading music.

TIP

Streaming refers to playing video or music content from the web (or from other devices) rather than playing a file stored on your iPhone. You can enjoy a lot of material online without ever downloading its full content to your phone — and given that the most storage endowed iPhone model has a relatively small amount of storage, that isn't a bad idea. See Chapters 17 and 19 for more about getting your music and movies online.

Your storage options with an iPhone 8, 8 Plus, and X are 64 or 256 gigabytes (GB). You must choose the right amount of storage because you can't open the unit and add more as you usually can with a desktop computer. However, Apple has thoughtfully provided iCloud, a service you can use to back up content to the Internet (you can read more about that in Chapter 4).

How much storage is enough for your iPhone? Here's a guideline:

>> If you like lots of media, such as movies or TV shows, you might need 256GB.

>> For most people who manage a reasonable number of photos, download some music, and watch heavy-duty media such as movies online, 64GB may be sufficient. But if there's any possibility you may take things up a notch in the future regarding media consumption and creation (such as the newest grandchild being on the way soon), you should probably seriously consider 256GB.

>> If you simply want to check email, browse the web, and write short notes to yourself, 64GB likely is plenty.

TECHNICAL
STUFF

Do you have a clue how big a *gigabyte* (GB) is? Consider this: Just about any computer you buy today comes with a minimum of 500GB of storage. Computers have to tackle larger tasks than iPhones, so that number makes sense. The iPhone, which uses a technology called *flash storage* for data storage, is meant (to a great extent) to help you experience online media and email; it doesn't have to store much since it pulls lots of content from online. In the world of storage, 32GB for any kind of storage is puny if you keep lots of content (such as audio, video, and photos) on the device.

What's the price for larger storage? For the iPhone 8, a 64GB unit costs $699 and 256GB adds another $150, setting you back $849. iPhone 8 Plus with 64GB is $799 and the model tops out at $949 for 256GB. Not to be outdone, iPhone X is the priciest iPhone yet, ranging from $999 for 64GB to $1,149 for 256GB. Note that prices may vary by carrier and by where you buy your phone.

Understand What You Need to Use Your iPhone

Before you head off to buy your iPhone, you should know what other connections and accounts you'll need to work with it optimally.

At a bare minimum, to make standard cellular phone calls, you need to have a service plan with a cellular carrier (such as AT&T or Verizon), as well as a data plan that supports iPhone. The data plan allows you to exchange data over the Internet (such as emails and text messages) and download content (such as movies and music). Try to verify the strength of coverage in your area, as well as how much data your plan provides each month, before you sign up.

You also need to be able to update the iPhone operating system (iOS) and share media (such as music) among Apple devices. Though these functions can be utilized without a phone carrier service plan, you have to plug your phone into your computer to update the operating system or you may also update wirelessly over a network. You need to use a local Wi-Fi network to go online and make calls using an Internet service, such as Skype.

TIP

Given the cost and high-tech nature of the iPhone, having to juryrig these basic functions doesn't make much sense. Trust me: Get an account and data plan with your phone service provider.

You should open a free iCloud account, Apple's online storage and syncing service, to store and share content online among your Apple devices. You can also use a computer to download photos, music, or applications from non-Apple online sources (such as stores or sharing sites like your local library) and transfer them to your iPhone through a process called syncing.

Apple has set up its iTunes software and the iCloud service to give you two ways to manage content for your iPhone — including apps, music, or photos you've downloaded — and specify how to sync your calendar and contact information.

There are a lot of tech terms to absorb here (iCloud, iTunes, syncing, and so on). Don't worry. Chapters 3 and 4 covers those settings in more detail.

Know Where to Buy Your iPhone

You can't buy an iPhone (shown in a variety of colors in **Figure 1-3**) from just any retail store. You can buy an iPhone at the brick-and-mortar or online Apple Store and from mobile phone providers, such as AT&T, Sprint, T-Mobile, Verizon, and Virgin Mobile (in store only). You can also find an iPhone at major retailers, such as Best Buy and Walmart, through which you have to buy a service contract for the phone carrier of your choice. You can also find iPhones at several online retailers (such as Amazon.com and Newegg.com) and through smaller, local service providers, which you can find by visiting `https://support.apple.com/en-us/HT204039`.

Image courtesy of Apple, Inc.

FIGURE 1-3

Apple offers unlocked iPhones. Essentially, these phones aren't tied into a particular provider, so you can use them with any of the four iPhone cellular service providers. Though you save a lot by avoiding a service commitment, these phones without accompanying phone plans can be pricey. But there's a trend for providers offering cheaper plans and installment payments on the hardware.

See What's in the Box

When you fork over your hard-earned money for your iPhone, you'll be left holding one box about the size of a deck of tarot cards.

Here's what you'll find when you take off the shrinkwrap and open the box:

» **iPhone**: Your iPhone is covered in a thick, plastic-sleeve thingy. Take it off and toss it back in the box.

Save all the packaging until you're certain you won't return the phone. Apple's standard return period is 14 days.

» **Apple EarPods with Lightning connector**: Plug the EarPods into your iPhone 8, 8 Plus, or X for a free headset experience.

» **Documentation (and I use the term loosely)**: This typically includes a small pamphlet, a sheet of Apple logo stickers, and a few more bits of information.

» **Lightning to USB Cable**: Use this cable to connect the iPhone to your computer, or use it with the last item in the box, the USB power adapter. If you own an iPhone 4s or earlier, you have the Dock Connector to USB Cable, a larger, bulkier, 30-pin connector.

» **Apple USB power adapter**: The power adapter attaches to the Lightning to USB Cable so that you can plug it into the wall and charge the battery.

» **Lightning to 3.5mm headphone jack adapter**: This adapter will allow you to connect your headphones with 3.5mm jacks to your iPhone 8, 8 Plus, or X.

That's all there is in the box. It's kind of a study in Zen-like simplicity.

TIP

Search for iPhone accessories online. You'll find iPhone cases (from leather to silicone), car chargers, and screen guards to protect your phone's screen.

Take a First Look at the Gadget

In this section, I give you a bit more information about the buttons and other physical features of the newest iPhone models. **Figure 1-4** shows you where each of these items is located on the iPhone 8 and 8 Plus.

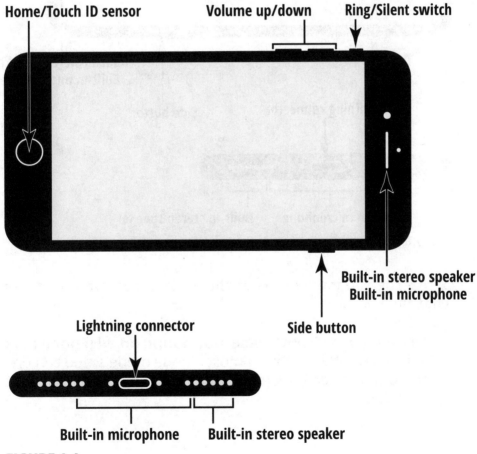

FIGURE 1-4

Figure 1-5 shows the lay of the land regarding iPhone X.

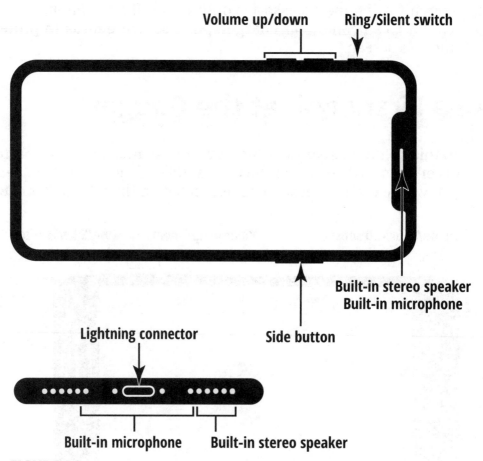

FIGURE 1-5

Here's the rundown on what the various hardware features are and what they do:

» **Home/Touch ID button/sensor (found on all iPhone models except iPhone X)**: On most iPhone models, you can press this button to go back to the Home screen to find just about anything:

- The Home screen(s) displays all your installed and preinstalled apps and gives you access to your iPhone settings. No matter where you are or what you're doing, press the Home button and you're back at home base.

- You can also press the Home button twice to pull up a scrolling list of apps so that you can quickly move from one to another (Apple refers to this capability as multitasking).

- If you press and hold the Home button, you open Siri, the iPhone voice assistant.

- With iPhone 5s and later, the Home button contains a fingerprint reader used with the Touch ID feature.

TIP

If you're a fortunate iPhone X user, you can return to the Home screen by simply swiping up from the very bottom of the screen.

» **On/Off/Sleep/Wake button**: You can use this button (whose functionality I cover in more detail in Chapter 3) to power up your iPhone, put it in Sleep mode, wake it up, or power it down.

» **Lightning connector**: Plug in the Lightning connector at one end of the Lightning to USB Cable that came with your iPhone to charge your battery, listen to audio with your EarPods, or sync your iPhone with your computer (which you find out more about in Chapter 4).

» **Ring/Silent switch**: Slide this little switch to mute or unmute the sound on your iPhone.

» **Built-in stereo speakers**: One nice surprise when I got my first iPhone was hearing what a nice little sound system it has and how much sound can come from the tiny speakers. The speakers in iPhone 8 and 8 Plus provide rich stereo sound and deeper bass than previous models, and are located on the bottom edge of the phone and at the top part near the earpiece.

» **Volume up/down buttons**: Tap the volume up button for more volume and the volume down button for less.

TIP

You can use the volume up button as a camera shutter button when the camera is activated.

>> **Built-in microphones**: Built-in microphones make it possible to speak into your iPhone to deliver commands or content. This feature allows you to do such things as

- Make phone calls using the Internet.
- Use video calling services, such as Skype.
- Work with other apps that accept audio input, such as the Siri built-in assistant.

Chapter **2**

Exploring the Home Screen

I won't kid you: You have a slight learning curve ahead of you if you're coming from a more basic cellphone (but if you own another smartphone, you've got a head start). For example, your previous phone might not have had a Multi-Touch screen and onscreen keyboard.

The good news is that getting anything done on the iPhone is simple, when you know the ropes. In fact, using your fingers to do things is a very intuitive way to communicate with your computing device, which is just what iPhone is.

In this chapter, you turn on your iPhone, register it, and then take your first look at the Home screen. You also practice using the onscreen keyboard, see how to interact with the touchscreen in various ways, get pointers on working with cameras, and get an overview of built-in applications (more commonly referred to as "apps").

Although the iPhone's screen has been treated to repel oils, you're about to deposit a ton of fingerprints on your iPhone — one downside of a touchscreen device. So you'll need to clean the screen:

» A soft cloth, like the one you might use to clean your eyeglasses, is usually all you'll need to clean things up.

» If the soft cloth doesn't work, you can try third-party cleaners and screen protectors.

Make sure that any third-party cleaners or screen protectors you purchase are compatible with your particular iPhone model. The materials used in the screens of each iPhone model may vary.

See What You Need to Use iPhone

You need to be able, at a minimum, to connect to the Internet to take advantage of most iPhone features, which you can do using a Wi-Fi network (a network that you set up in your own home or access in a public place such as a library) or a 3G/4G (LTE) connection from your cellular provider. You might want to have a computer so that you can connect your iPhone to it to download photos, videos, music, or applications and transfer them to or from your iPhone through a process called *syncing* (see Chapter 4 for more about syncing). An Apple service called iCloud syncs content from all your Apple iOS devices (such as the iPhone or iPad), so anything you buy on your iPad that can be run on an iPhone, for example, will automatically be pushed to your iPhone. In addition, you can sync without connecting a cable to a computer using a wireless Wi-Fi connection to your computer.

Your iPhone will probably arrive registered and activated, or if you buy it in a store, the person helping you can handle that procedure.

For an iPhone 8, 8 Plus, or X, Apple recommends that you have

» A Mac or PC with a USB 2.0 or 3.0 port and one of these operating systems:

- macOS version 10.9.5 (Mavericks) or newer
- Windows 7 or newer

» iTunes 12.7 or newer, available at `http://www.itunes.com/download`.

» An Apple ID

» Internet access

Turn On iPhone for the First Time

The first time you turn on your iPhone, it will probably have been activated and registered by your phone carrier or Apple, depending on whom you've bought it from. Follow these steps:

1. **Press and hold the Side button (found a little bit below the top of the upper-right side of your iPhone) until the Apple logo appears.** In another moment, a series of screens appears, asking you to enter your Apple ID username and password.

2. **Enter your Apple ID.** If you don't have an Apple ID, you can follow the instructions to create one.

3. **Follow the series of prompts to set up initial options for your iPhone.** You can make choices about your language and location, using iCloud (Apple's online sharing service), whether to use a passcode, connecting with a network, and so on.

TIP

You can choose to have personal items transferred to your iPhone from your computer when you sync the two devices using iTunes, including music, videos, downloaded apps, audiobooks, e-books, podcasts, and browser bookmarks. Contacts and Calendars are downloaded via iCloud, or (if you're moving to iPhone from an Android phone) you can download an app from the Google Play Store called Move to iOS (developed by Apple) to copy your current Android settings to your iPhone (Apple provides more information about migrating from

Android to iOS at `https://support.apple.com/en-us/HT201196`). You can also transfer to your computer any content you download directly to your iPhone by using iTunes, the App Store, or non-Apple stores. See Chapters 13 and 15 for more about these features.

Meet the Multi-Touch Screen

When the iPhone Home screen appears (see **Figure 2-1**), you see a pretty background and two sets of icons.

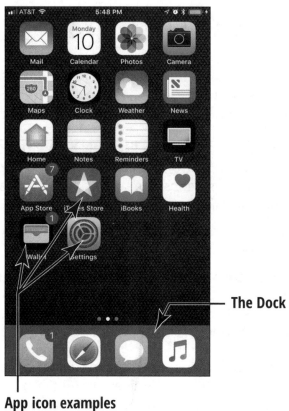

The Dock

App icon examples

FIGURE 2-1

One set of icons appears in the Dock, along the bottom of the screen. The *Dock* contains the Phone, Safari, Messages, and Music app icons by default, though you can swap out one app for another. You can add new apps to populate as many as 10 additional Home screens for a total of 11 Home screens. The Dock appears on every Home screen.

Other icons appear above the Dock and are closer to the top of the screen. (I cover all these icons in the "Take Inventory of Preinstalled Apps" task, in Chapter 3.) Different icons appear in this area on each Home screen. You can also nest apps in folders, which almost gives you the possibility of storing limitless apps on your iPhone. You are, in fact, limited — but only by your phone's memory.

TIP

Treat the iPhone screen carefully. It's made of glass and it will break if an unreasonable amount of force is applied.

The iPhone uses *touchscreen technology:* When you swipe your finger across the screen or tap it, you're providing input to the device just as you do to a computer using a mouse or keyboard. You hear more about the touchscreen in the next task, but for now, go ahead and play with it for a few minutes — really, you can't hurt anything. Use the pads of your fingertips (not your fingernails) and try these tasks:

REMEMBER

» **Tap the Settings icon.** The various settings (which you read more about throughout this book) appear, as shown in **Figure 2-2.**

To return to the Home screen, press the Home button for most iPhone models. If you have an iPhone X, swipe up from the very bottom edge of your screen.

» **Swipe a finger from right to left on the Home screen.** This action moves you to the next Home screen.

TIP

The little white dots at the bottom of the screen, above the Dock icons, indicate which Home screen is displayed.

» **To experience the screen rotation feature, hold the iPhone firmly while turning it sideways.** The screen flips to the horizontal orientation, if the app you're in supports it.

To flip the screen back, just turn the device so that it's oriented like a pad of paper again. (Some apps force iPhone to stay in one orientation or the other.)

FIGURE 2-2

» **Drag your finger down from the very top edge of the screen to reveal such items as notifications, reminders, and calendar entries.** Drag up from the very bottom edge of the Home screen to hide these items, and then drag up on all iPhone models except the X to display Control Center (containing commonly used controls and tools and discussed later in this chapter). With the X, swipe from the right corner of the screen towards the center to open Control Center.

TIP

You can customize the Home screen by changing its *wallpaper* (background picture) and brightness. You can read about making these changes in Chapter 9.

DISCOVER 3D TOUCH AND QUICK ACTIONS

3D Touch allows you to get different results depending on the amount of pressure you apply to the screen, and get feedback on your actions with taps from the screen. For example, if you open the Photos app, you can tap lightly to select a photo, press a bit harder to see a preview of that photo, and press even harder to open the photo full screen. The ability to preview such items as emails, websites, maps, and photos before opening them can save you time. The medium press is called a Peek and the hard press is called a Pop.

Quick Actions involve pressing an icon on the screen to see items you're likely to want to select. For example, if you press the Phone icon, you'll get a shortcut list of commonly called contacts. If you press the Maps app, you see a list of places you often go, such as your home, to quickly display a map of that location. Quick Actions provide a shortcut menu to your most frequently used items, saving you time and effort.

Say Hello to Tap and Swipe

You can use several methods for getting around and getting things done in iPhone using its Multi–Touch screen, including

» **Tap once.** To open an application on the Home screen, choose a field, such as a search box, choose an item in a list, use an arrow to move back or forward one screen, or follow an online link, tap the item once with your finger.

» **Tap twice.** Use this method to enlarge or reduce the display of a web page (see Chapter 11 for more about using the *Safari* web browser) or to zoom in or out in the Maps app.

» **Pinch.** As an alternative to the tap-twice method, you can pinch your fingers together or move them apart on the screen (see **Figure 2-3**) when you're looking at photos, maps, web pages, or email messages to quickly reduce or enlarge them, respectively. This method allows you to grow or contract the screen to a variety of sizes rather than a fixed size, as with the double-tap method.

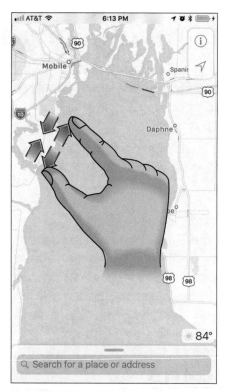

FIGURE 2-3

You can use the three-finger tap to zoom your screen to be even larger or use multitasking gestures to swipe with four or five fingers (see the "Learn Multitasking Basics" task, in Chapter 3). This method is handy if you have vision challenges. Go to Chapter 9 to discover how to turn on this feature using Accessibility settings.

» **Drag to scroll (known as *swiping*).** When you touch your finger to the screen and drag to the right or left, the screen moves (see **Figure 2-4**). Swiping to the left on the Home screen, for example, moves you to the next Home screen. Swiping down while reading an online newspaper moves you down the page; swiping up moves you back up the page.

» **Flick.** To scroll more quickly on a page, quickly flick your finger on the screen in the direction you want to move.

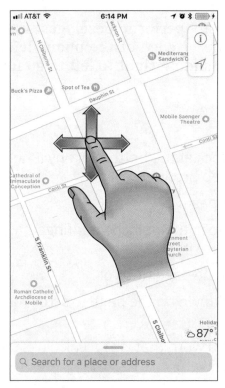

FIGURE 2-4

» **Tap the Status bar.** To move quickly to the top of a list, web page, or email message, tap the Status bar at the top of the iPhone screen. (For some sites, you have to tap twice to get this to work.)

» **Press and hold.** If you're using Notes or Mail or any other application that lets you select text, or if you're on a web page, pressing and holding text selects a word and displays editing tools that you can use to select, cut, or copy and paste the text.

TIP

When you rock your phone backward or forward, the background moves as well (a feature called *parallax*). You can disable this feature if it makes you seasick. From the Home screen, tap Settings ⇨ General ⇨ Accessibility and then tap and turn on the Reduce Motion setting by tapping the toggle switch (it turns green when the option is enabled).

Your iPhone offers the ability to perform bezel gestures, which involves sliding from the very outer edge of the phone left to right on the glass to go backward and sliding right to left to go forward in certain apps.

TIP

You can try these methods now:

» Tap the Safari button in the Dock at the bottom of any iPhone Home screen to display the web browser.

» Tap a link to move to another page.

» Double-tap the page to enlarge it; then pinch your fingers together on the screen to reduce its size.

» Drag one finger up and down the page to scroll.

» Flick your finger quickly up or down on the page to scroll more quickly.

» Press and hold your finger on a word that isn't a link (links take you to another location on the web).

The word is selected, and the Copy/Look Up/Speak/Share/Spell tool is displayed, as shown in **Figure 2-5.** (You can use this tool to either get a definition of a word or copy it.)

» Press and hold your finger on a link or an image.

A menu appears (shown in **Figure 2-6**) with commands that you select to open the link or picture, open it in a new tab, add it to your Reading List (see Chapter 11), or copy it. If you press and hold an image, the menu also offers the Save Image command.

Tap Cancel to close the menu without making a selection.

» Position your fingers slightly apart on the screen and then pinch your fingers together to reduce the page; with your fingers already pinched together on the screen, move them apart to enlarge the page.

» Press the Home button to go back to the Home screen.

The Copy/Lookup... tool

FIGURE 2-5

FIGURE 2-6

Display and Use the Onscreen Keyboard

The built-in iPhone keyboard appears whenever you're in a text-entry location, such as a search field or a text message. Follow these steps to display and use the keyboard:

1. Tap the Notes icon on the Home screen to open the Notes app.

2. Open a note to work in:

- Tap the note page.
- If you've already created some notes, tap one to display the page, then tap anywhere on the note.

3. Type a few words using the keyboard, as shown in **Figure 2-7.**

To make the keyboard display as wide as possible, rotate your iPhone to landscape (horizontal) orientation. (If you've locked the screen orientation in Control Center, you have to unlock the screen to do this.)

QuickType provides suggestions above the keyboard as you type. You can turn this feature off or on by tapping and holding either the Emoji (the smiley face) or International icon (looks like a globe) on the keyboard to display a menu. Tap Keyboard Settings, then toggle the Predictive switch to turn the feature Off or On (green). To quickly return to Notes from Keyboard Settings, tap the word "Notes" in the upper-left of your screen.

After you open the keyboard, you're ready to use it for editing text.

You'll find a number of shortcuts for editing text:

» If you make a mistake while using the keyboard — and you will, especially when you first use it — tap the Delete key (it's near the bottom corner, with the little *x* on it) to delete text to the left of the insertion point.

To type a period and space, just double-tap the spacebar.

» To create a new paragraph, tap the Return button (just like a computer keyboard).

» To type numbers and symbols, tap the number key (labeled 123) on the left side of the spacebar (refer to **Figure 2-7**). The characters on the keyboard change (see **Figure 2-8**).

If you type a number and then tap the spacebar, the keyboard returns to the letter keyboard automatically. To return to the letter keyboard at any time, simply tap the key labeled ABC on the left side of the spacebar.

» Use the Shift button (it's a wide, upward-facing arrow in the lower-left corner of the keyboard) to type capital letters:

• Tapping the Shift button once causes only the next letter you type to be capitalized.

• Double-tap (rapidly tap twice) the Shift key to turn on the Caps Lock feature so that all letters you type are capitalized until you turn the feature off.

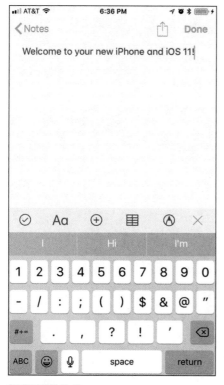

FIGURE 2-7

FIGURE 2-8

- Tap the Shift key once to turn off Caps Lock.

  You can control whether Caps Lock is enabled by opening the Settings app, tapping General and then Keyboard, and toggling the switch called Enable Caps Lock.

» To type a variation on a symbol or letter (for example, to see alternative presentations for the letter *A* when you press the A button on the keyboard), hold down the key; a set of alternative letters/symbols appears (see **Figure 2-9**).

  This trick works with only certain letters and symbols.

TECHNICAL STUFF

» Tap the smiley-faced Emoji button to display the Emoji keyboard containing symbols that you can insert, including numerical, symbol, and arrow keys, as well as a row of symbol sets along the bottom of the screen.

FIGURE 2-9

TIP

Tapping one of these displays a portfolio of icons from smiley faces and hearts to pumpkins, cats, and more. Tap the ABC button to close the Emoji keyboard and return to the letter keyboard.

A small globe symbol will appear instead of the Emoji button on the keyboard if you've enabled multilanguage functionality in iPhone settings.

» Press the Home button to return to the Home screen.

» If you own an iPhone 6s Plus, 7 Plus, or 8 Plus you can use a wide screen. Turn the phone to horizontal orientation. Tap Notes and then tap in a note to display the onscreen keyboard, which now takes advantage of the wider screen and includes some extra keys, such as Cut, Copy, and Paste.

TIP

Within the Notes app, you can display a shortcut keyboard that allows you to create a checklist, choose a font style, insert a photo, or create a drawing within your note. See Chapter 24 for more about using this feature in the Notes app.

Flick to Search

The Search feature in iPhone helps you find suggestions from the web, Music, iTunes, and the App Store as well as suggestions for nearby locations and more. Here's how to use Search:

1. Swipe down on any Home screen (but not from the very top or bottom of the screen) to see the Control Center screen, then swipe from left to right to reveal the Search feature (see **Figure 2-10**).

FIGURE 2-10

2. Begin entering a search term.

In the example in **Figure 2-11**, after I typed the word "grocery," the Search feature displayed maps and other search results. As you continue to type a search term or phrase, the results narrow to match it.

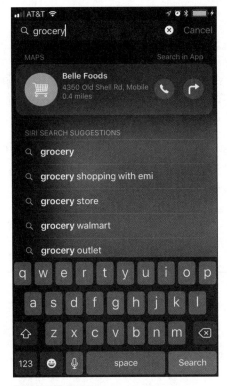

FIGURE 2-11

3. Scroll down to view more results.

4. Tap an item in the search results to open it in its appropriate app or player.

Chapter **3**

Getting Going

Now, it's time to get into some even more aspects of using the iPhone and its interface (how you interact with your device).

In this chapter, you look at updating your iOS version (the operating system that your iPhone uses), multitasking, checking out the cameras, discovering the apps that come preinstalled on your iPhone, and more.

Update the Operating System to iOS 11

This book is based on the latest version of the iPhone operating system at the time: iOS 11. To be sure that you have the latest and greatest features, update your iPhone to the latest iOS now (and do so periodically to receive minor upgrades to iOS 11 or future versions of the iOS). If you've set up an iCloud account on your iPhone, you'll receive an alert and can choose to install the update or not, or you can update manually:

1. Tap Settings. (Be sure you have Wi-Fi enabled and that you're connected to a Wi-Fi network to perform these steps.)

2. Tap General.

3. Tap Software Update (see **Figure 3-1**).

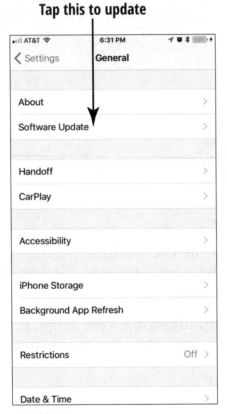

FIGURE 3-1

Your iPhone checks to find the latest iOS version and walks you through the updating procedure if an update is available.

Learn Multitasking Basics

Multitasking lets you easily switch from one app to another without closing the first one and returning to the Home screen. With iOS 11, this is accomplished by previewing all open apps and jumping from one to another; you quit an app by simply swiping upward. To learn the ropes of basic multitasking, follow these steps:

1. Open an app.

2. Press the Home button twice. The Running Apps list appears (see **Figure 3-2**).

FIGURE 3-2

TIP

If you have an iPhone X, invoke multitasking by swiping up from the bottom edge of the screen to the center of the screen, then pausing a moment until the list of running apps appears.

3. To locate another app that you want to switch to, flick to scroll to the left or right.

4. Tap an app to open it.

TIP

Press the Home button once to remove the Running Apps list from the Home screen and return to the app that you were working in. If you have an iPhone X, tap an app in the list to exit multitasking.

Examine the iPhone Cameras

iPhones have front- and back-facing cameras. You can use the cameras to take still photos (covered in more detail in Chapter 18) or shoot videos (covered in Chapter 19).

For now, take a quick look at your camera by tapping the Camera app icon on the Home screen. The app opens, as shown in **Figure 3-3.**

You can use the controls on the screen to

» Switch between the front and rear cameras.

» Change from still-camera to video-camera operation by using the slider at the bottom of the screen.

» Take a picture or start recording a video.

» Choose a 3- or 10-second delay with the Timed Photos button.

» Turn HDR (high dynamic range for better contrast) on or off.

» Tap the Flash button to set flash to On, Off, or Auto.

» Use color filters when taking photos or videos.

» Take a "burst" of photos by tapping-and-holding the Camera's button. A small photo count will display above the button to show how many photos you've taken.

» Open previously captured images or videos.

FIGURE 3-3

When you view a photo or video, you can use an iPhone sharing feature to send the image by AirDrop (iPhone 5 and later only), Message, Notes, Mail, and other options (depending on which apps you've installed). You can also share through iCloud Photo Sharing, a tweet, Facebook, or Flickr.

More things that you can do with images are to print them, use a still photo as wallpaper (that is, as your Home or lock screen background image) or assign it to represent a contact, and run a slideshow. See Chapters 18 and 19 for more detail about using the iPhone cameras.

Discover Control Center

Control Center is a one-stop screen for common features and settings, such as connecting to a network, increasing screen brightness or volume, and even turning a built-in flashlight on or off. Here's how to use it:

1. To display Control Center with most iPhone models, swipe up from the very bottom of the screen. Access Control Center with an iPhone X by swiping from the right corner of the screen to the center. The Control Center screen appears.

2. In the Control Center screen, tap a button or tap and drag a slider to access or adjust a setting (see **Figure 3-4**).

FIGURE 3-4

3. After you make a change, swipe the top of Control Center down to hide the screen.

Some options in Control Center are hidden from initial view, but may be accessed using 3D Touch that basically means pressing-and-holding (using slightly more force than a typical tap) a button in

Control Center. For example, use 3D Touch (press-and-hold) on any of the Communications buttons (Airplane Mode, Cellular Data, Wi-Fi, and Bluetooth) to reveal two more options: AirDrop and Personal Hotspot (as shown in **Figure 3-5**).

FIGURE 3-5

Other 3D Touch options in Control Center include

» Adjust the Flashlight brightness level.

» Select a device for Airplay.

» Set a quick timer.

» Instantly start recording video or take a selfie.

TIP

Try 3D Touching other buttons in Control Center to see what other options are waiting for you to discover. If you 3D Touch an item and its icon just bounces, there are no further options available for the item.

Did you notice the large amount of empty space at the top of Control Center when you opened it? That's because iOS 11 allows you to customize Control Center (one of my favorites of the new features). All that extra space is waiting to be filled by you:

1. Tap Settings.

2. Tap Control Center, then tap Customize Controls to open the Customize screen (shown in **Figure 3-6**).

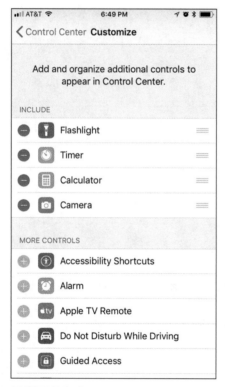

FIGURE 3-6

3. Add or remove items from Control Center:

- To remove an item, tap the "-" to the left, then tap the Remove button that appears to the right.

- To add an item, tap the "+" to the left. You'll see the item in Control Center the next time you visit it.

Use 3D Touch to find any extras for the item. If the item just bounces when you 3D Touch, there are no further options.

Lock Screen Rotation

Sometimes you don't want your screen orientation to flip when you move your phone around. Use these steps to lock the iPhone into portrait orientation (narrow and tall, not low and wide):

1. Swipe up from the bottom of any screen to open Control Center.

2. Tap the Lock Screen button. (It's the button in the top-right corner of Control Center.)

3. Swipe down from the top of Control Center to hide it.

Explore the Status Bar

Across the top of the iPhone screen is the Status bar (see **Figure 3-7**). Tiny icons in this area can provide useful information, such as the time, battery level, and wireless-connection status. Table 3-1 lists some of the most common items you find on the Status bar.

If you have GPS, 3G, 4G cellular (LTE), or Bluetooth service or a connection to a virtual private network (VPN), a corresponding symbol appears on the Status bar whenever a feature is active. (If you don't already know what a virtual private network is, there's no need to worry about it.)

← **Status bar**

FIGURE 3-7

TABLE 3-1   **Common Status Bar Icons**

Icon	Name	What It Indicates
	Wi-Fi	You're connected to a Wi-Fi network.
	Activity	A task is in progress — a web page is loading, for example.
2:30 PM	Time	You guessed it: You see the time.
	Screen Rotation Lock	The screen is locked in portrait orientation and doesn't rotate when you turn the iPhone.
	Battery Life	This shows the charge percentage remaining in the battery. The indicator changes to a lightning bolt when the battery is charging.

Take Inventory of Preinstalled Apps

The iPhone comes with certain functionality and applications — or apps, for short — built in. When you look at the Home screen, you see icons for each app. This task gives you an overview of what each app does.

By default, the following icons appear in the Dock at the bottom of every Home screen (refer to **Figure 3-1**), from left to right:

» **Messages**: If you love to instant message, the Messages app comes to the rescue. The Messages app has been in iPhone for quite some time. Now you can engage in live text- and image-based conversations with others on their phones or other devices that use email. You can also send video or audio messages.

» **Phone**: Use this app to make and receive phone calls, view a log of recent calls, create a list of favorite contacts, access your voice mail, and view contacts.

» **Music**: Music is the name of your media player. Though its main function is to play music, you can use it to play audio podcasts and audiobooks as well.

» **Safari**: You use the Safari web browser (see **Figure 3-8**) to navigate on the Internet, create and save bookmarks of favorite sites, and add web clips to your Home screen so that you can quickly visit favorite sites from there. You may have used this web browser (or another, such as Google Chrome) on your desktop computer.

Apps with icons above the Dock on the Home screen include

» **Mail**: You use this application to access email accounts that you have set up in iPhone. Your email is then displayed without you having to browse to the site or sign in. You can use tools to move among a few preset mail folders, read and reply to email, and download attached photos to your iPhone. Read more about email accounts in Chapter 12.

FIGURE 3-8

» **Calendar**: Use this handy onscreen daybook (see **Figure 3-9**) to set up appointments and send alerts to remind you about them.

» **Photos**: The Photos app in iPhone helps you organize pictures in folders, send photos in email, use a photo as your iPhone wallpaper, and assign pictures to contact records. You can also run slideshows of your photos, open albums, pinch or unpinch to shrink or expand photos, and scroll photos with a simple swipe.

Your iPhone can use the Photo Sharing feature to share photos among your friends. Since iOS 7, Photos displays images by collections, including Years and Moments.

» **Camera**: As you may have read earlier in this chapter, the Camera app is Control Center for the still and video cameras built into the iPhone.

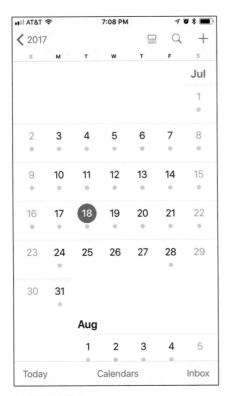

FIGURE 3-9

» **Weather**: Get the latest weather for your location and others instantly with this handy app (see **Figure 3-10**). You can easily add other locations to check for weather where you're going or where you've been.

» **Clock**: This app allows you to display clocks from around the world, set alarms, and use timer and stopwatch features.

» **Maps**: With this iPhone mapping app, you can view classic maps or aerial views of addresses and find directions from one place to another whether traveling by car, foot, or public transportation (which requires installing a third-party app). You can even get your directions read aloud by a spoken narration feature.

» **TV**: This media player is similar to Music but specializes in playing videos and offers a few features specific to this type of media, such as chapter breakdowns and information about a movie's plot and cast.

FIGURE 3-10

» **Notes**: Enter text, format text, or cut and paste text and objects (such as images) from a website into this simple notepad app.

» **Reminders**: This useful app centralizes all your calendar entries and alerts to keep you on schedule and allows you to create to-do lists.

» **News**: News is a customizable aggregator for stories from your favorite news sources.

» **iTunes Store**: Tapping this icon takes you to the iTunes Store, where you can shop 'til you drop (or until your iPhone battery runs out of juice) for music, movies, TV shows, and audiobooks and then download them directly to your iPhone. (See Chapter 15 for more about how the iTunes Store works.)

» **App Store**: Here you can buy and download applications that do everything from enabling you to play games to building business presentations. Many of these apps and games are free!

» **iBooks**: The iBooks app is now bundled with the iPhone out of the box. Because the iPhone has been touted as being a good small screen e-reader — a device that enables you to read books on an electronic device, similar to the Amazon Kindle Fire HD — you should definitely check this one out. (To work with the iBooks e-reader application itself, go to Chapter 16.)

» **Health**: This is exciting very useful app that you can use to record various health and exercise statistics and even send them to your doctor.

» **Home**: Home helps you control most (if not all) of your home automation devices in one convenient app. See Chapter 24 for more information.

» **Wallet**: This Apple Pay feature lets you store a virtual wallet of plane or concert tickets, coupons, and more and use them with a swipe of your iPhone across a point of purchase device.

» **Settings**: Settings is the central location on the iPhone where you can specify settings for various functions and do administrative tasks, such as set up email accounts or create a password.

There are also some preinstalled apps located on the second Home screen by default, including some in an Extras folder. Wrapped up in the Extras folder are some other handy tools: Compass, Contacts, Voice Memos, and others.

Additionally, on the second Home screen, you'll find

» **FaceTime**: Use FaceTime to place phone calls using video of the sender and receiver to have a more personal conversation.

» **Calculator**: Use this simple app to add, subtract, and so on.

» **Files**: New to iOS 11, this app allows you to browse files that are stored not only on your iPhone, but also files you may have stored on other services, such as iCloud Drive, Google Drive, Dropbox, and the like. It's about time!

» **Podcasts**: Before iOS 8, you had to download the free Podcast app, but now it's built into your iOS iPhone. Use this app to listen to recorded informational programs.

TIP

Several useful apps are free for you to download from the App Store. These include iMovie and iPhoto, as well as the Pages, Keynote, and Numbers apps of the iWork suite.

Lock iPhone, Turn It Off, or Unlock It

Earlier in this chapter, I mention how simple it is to turn on the power to your iPhone. Now it's time to put it to sleep (a state in which the screen goes black, though you can quickly wake up the iPhone) or turn off the power to give your new toy a rest.

Here are the procedures you use to put the phone to sleep or turn it off:

TIP

» **Sleep**: Press the Side button just below the top of the right side of the phone. The iPhone goes to sleep. The screen goes black and is locked.

The iPhone automatically enters Sleep mode after a brief period of inactivity. You can change the time interval at which it sleeps by adjusting the Auto-Lock feature in Settings ➪ Display & Brightness.

» **Power Off**: From any app or Home screen press and hold the Side button until the Slide to Power Off bar appears at the top of the screen, and then swipe the bar. You've just turned off your iPhone.

» **Force Off**: If the iPhone becomes unresponsive, for most models hold the Power and Home buttons simultaneously until the phone shuts itself off. For iPhone X, press and hold both the Side and Volume Down buttons to achieve the same result.

To wake most iPhone models up from Sleep mode, simply pick up your iPhone (this feature was introduced in iOS 10 and only works on models from the iPhone 6s and newer) or press the Home button once. Notice at the bottom of the screen the iPhone tells you to press the Home button again (see **Figure 3-11**). Do so, and the iPhone unlocks. If you have an iPhone X, simply tap the screen to wake from sleep, or press the Side button once.

FIGURE 3-11

TIP

If you have the Passcode feature enabled, you'll need to enter your Passcode before proceeding to unlock your screen after raising your iPhone or pressing the Home button. However, if you have Touch ID enabled, you only need press the Home button once and rest your finger on it for it to scan your fingerprints; the iPhone will automatically unlock.

TIP

Want a way to shut down your iPhone without having to press buttons? Go to Settings ⇨ General, then scroll all the way to the bottom of the screen. Tap the Shut Down button, slide the Power Off slider, and your iPhone will go off.

Chapter **4**

Beyond the Basics

Your first step in getting to work with the iPhone is to make sure that its battery is charged. Next, if you want to find free or paid content for your iPhone from Apple, from movies to music to e-books to audiobooks, you'll need to have an iTunes account.

You can also use the wireless sync feature to exchange content between your computer and iPhone over a wireless network.

Another feature you might take advantage of is the iCloud service from Apple to store and push all kinds of content and data to all your Apple devices — wirelessly. You can pick up where you left off from one device to another through iCloud Drive, an online storage service that enables sharing content among devices so that edits that you make to documents in iCloud are reflected in all iOS devices and Macs running OS X Yosemite or later.

Charge the Battery

My iPhone showed up in the box fully charged, and let's hope yours did, too. Because all batteries run down eventually, one of your first priorities is to know how to recharge your iPhone battery.

Gather your iPhone and its Lightning to USB Cable and the Apple USB power adapter.

TIP

Connector cables from earlier versions of iPhone or other Apple devices (such as iPad or iPod) don't work with your iPhone 5 or newer. However, adapters are available from Apple.

Here's how to charge your iPhone:

1. Gently plug the Lightning connector end (the smaller of the two connectors) of the Lightning to USB Cable into the iPhone.

TIP

If you have a hard case for your iPhone, you should remove the phone from it if you're charging it over several hours because these cases retain heat, which is bad for the phone and the case.

2. Plug the USB end of the Lightning to USB Cable into the Apple USB power adapter (see **Figure 4-1**).

FIGURE 4-1

3. Plug the adapter into an electric outlet.

TIP

If you're moving from an Android phone to an iPhone, consider downloading the Move to iOS app (which was developed by Apple). This app allows you to wirelessly transfer key content, such as contacts, message history, videos, mail accounts, photos, and more from your old phone to your new one. If you had free apps on your Android device, iPhone will suggest you download them from the App Store. Any paid apps will be added to your iTunes Wish List. By the way, when you download the app from the Google Play Store you'll be well-served not to bother reading some of the viciously negative comments made by some Android users who harbor a true hatred of all things Apple.

Sign into an iTunes Account for Music, Movies, and More

The terms iTunes Account and Apple ID are interchangeable: Your Apple ID *is* your iTunes Account, but you'll need to be signed into iTunes with your Apple ID to download items from the iTunes Store.

To be able to buy or download free items from the iTunes Store or the App Store on your iPhone, you must open an iTunes account. Here's how to sign in to an account:

1. Tap Settings on your iPhone.

2. Scroll down and tap iTunes & App Stores; the screen shown in **Figure 4-2** appears.

3. Tap Sign In (see **Figure 4-3**), and enter your Apple ID and password, then tap the Sign In button.

4. Tap Password Settings in the iTunes & App screen to bring up the screen shown in **Figure 4-4.**

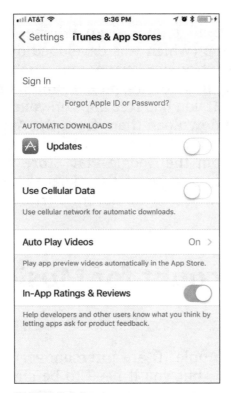

FIGURE 4-2   FIGURE 4-3

5. Select whether you'd like your password to be requested every time a download is attempted (recommended) or to allow downloads for up to 15 minutes after the password has been entered without having to reenter it. Also, toggle the switch to On or Off (depending on whether you require your password to be entered when downloading free items). I recommend setting it to On; even if an app is free, there may be some items that you just don't want loaded onto your iPhone without your permission.

TIP

If you prefer not to leave your credit card info with Apple, one option is to buy an iTunes gift card and provide that as your payment information. You can replenish the card periodically through the Apple Store.

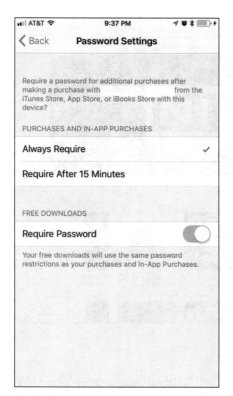

FIGURE 4-4

Sync Wirelessly

You can connect your iPhone to a computer and use the tools there to sync content on your computer to your iPhone. Also, with Wi-Fi turned on in Settings, use the iTunes Wi-Fi Sync setting to allow cordless syncing if you're within range of a Wi-Fi network that has a computer connected to it with iTunes installed and open.

There are a few steps you have to take with your iPhone connected to your computer before you can perform a wireless sync with iTunes:

1. If you're charging with an electrical outlet, remove the power adapter.

2. Use the Lightning to USB Cable to connect your iPhone to your computer.

3. Open iTunes, then click the icon of an iPhone that appears in the tools in the left corner of the screen (see **Figure 4-5**).

FIGURE 4-5

4. Click the check box labeled Sync with this iPhone over Wi-Fi (as seen in **Figure 4-6**).

TIP

You may need to scroll down a bit to see the Sync with this iPhone over Wi-Fi option.

5. Click Apply in the lower-right corner of the iTunes window.

6. Disconnect your iPhone from your computer.

TIP

You can click any item on the left side of the screen shown in **Figure 4-6** to handle settings for syncing such items as Movies, Music, and Apps. In the Apps category, you can also choose to remove certain apps from your Home screens. You can also tap the list of items in the On My Device section on the left side to view and even play contents directly from your iPhone.

After you complete the preceding steps, you'll be able to wirelessly sync your iPhone with your computer. Follow these steps:

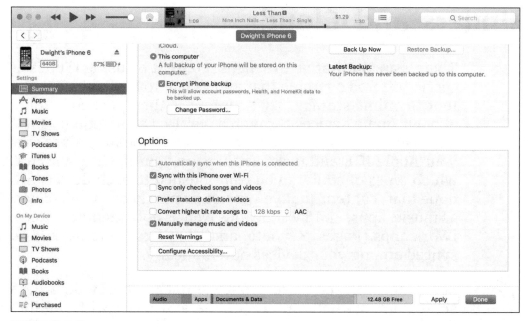

FIGURE 4-6

TIP

1. Back up your iPhone.

Chapter 24 shows how to back up your iPhone.

2. On the iPhone, tap Settings ⇨ General ⇨ iTunes Wi-Fi Sync. The iTunes Wi-Fi Sync settings appear.

3. In the iTunes Wi-Fi Sync settings, tap Sync Now to sync with a computer connected to the same Wi-Fi network.

4. If you need to connect your iPhone to a network, tap Settings ⇨ Wi-Fi, then tap a network to join.

TIP

If you have your iPhone set up to sync wirelessly to your Mac or PC, and both are within range of the same Wi-Fi network, iPhone will appear in your iTunes Devices list. This setup allows you to sync and manage syncing from within iTunes.

Your iPhone will automatically sync with iTunes once a day if both are on the same Wi-Fi network, iTunes is running, and your iPhone is charging.

Understand iCloud

There's an alternative to syncing content by using iTunes. iCloud is a service offered by Apple that allows you to back up most of your content to online storage. That content is then pushed automatically to all your Apple devices through a wireless connection. All you need to do is get an iCloud account, which is free (again, this is simply using your Apple ID), and make settings on your devices and in iTunes for which types of content you want pushed to each device. After you've done that, content that you create or purchase on one device — such as music, apps, and TV shows, as well as documents created in Apple's iWork apps (Pages, Keynote, and Numbers), photos, and so on — is synced among your devices automatically.

TIP

See Chapter 15 for more about using the Family Sharing feature to share content that you buy online and more with family members through iCloud.

You can stick with iCloud's default storage capacity, or you can increase it if you need more capacity:

» Your iCloud account includes 5GB of free storage. You may be fine with the free 5GB of storage.

Content that you purchase from Apple (such as apps, books, music, iTunes Match content, Photo Sharing contents, and TV shows) isn't counted against your storage.

The following section shows how to enable iCloud.

» If you want additional storage, you can buy an upgrade. Currently, 50GB costs only $0.99 per month.

To upgrade your storage, go to Settings, tap your Apple ID at the top of the screen, go to iCloud ⇨ Manage Storage, and then tap Upgrade next to iCloud Storage. On the next screen, tap the amount you need and then tap Buy (in the upper-right corner), as shown in **Figure 4-7**.

TIP

If you change your mind, you can get in touch with Apple within 15 days to cancel your upgrade.

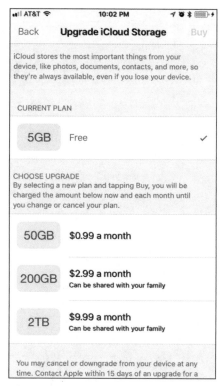

FIGURE 4-7

Turn on iCloud Drive

iCloud Drive is the online storage space that comes free with iCloud (as covered in the preceding section).

Before you can use iCloud Drive, you need to be sure that iCloud Drive is turned on. Here's how to turn on iCloud Drive:

1. Tap Settings, then tap your Apple ID at the top of the screen.

2. Tap iCloud to open the iCloud screen.

3. Scroll down in the iCloud screen and tap iCloud Drive.

4. Tap the On/Off switch to turn on (green) iCloud Drive (see **Figure 4-8**).

FIGURE 4-8

Make iCloud Sync Settings

When you have an iCloud account up and running, you have to specify which type of content should be synced with your iPhone by iCloud. Follow these steps:

1. Tap Settings, tap your Apple ID at the top of the screen, then tap iCloud.

2. In the iCloud settings shown in **Figure 4-9,** tap the On/Off switch for any item that's turned off that you want to turn on (or vice versa). You can sync Photos, Mail, Contacts, Calendars, Reminders, Safari, Notes, News, Wallet, Keychain (an app that stores all your passwords and even credit card numbers across all Apple devices), and more. The listing of apps on this screen isn't alphabetical, so scroll down if you don't see what you're looking for at first.

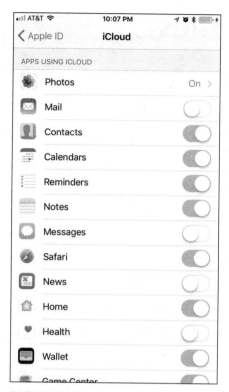

FIGURE 4-9

TIP

If you want to allow iCloud to provide a service for locating a lost or stolen iPhone, toggle the On/Off switch in the Find My iPhone field to On (green) to activate it. This service helps you locate, send a message to, or delete content from your iPhone if it falls into other hands. See Chapter 24 for more information.

3. To enable automatic downloads of iTunes-purchased music, apps, and books, return to the main Settings screen by tapping the Apple ID button in the top-left corner of the screen (refer to **Figure 4-9**), and then tap iTunes & App Stores.

4. Tap the On/Off switch for Music, Apps, Books & Audiobooks, or Updates to set up automatic downloads of any of this content to your iPhone by iCloud.

TIP

Consider turning off the Cellular Data option, which you find in the Cellular section of Settings, to avoid having these downloads occur over your cellular connection, which can use up your data allowance. Wait until you're on a Wi-Fi connection to have iPhone perform the updates.

Browse Your iPhones Files

Long-time iPhone users have pined for a way to browse files stored on our devices, as opposed to being limited to finding documents and other files only within the apps they're intended for or created by. Finally, iOS 11 introduces us to a new app called Files, which will allow us to browse not only for files stored on our iPhone, but also see our stuff that we've stored on other online (cloud) services such as Google Drive, Dropbox, and others.

You'll find the Files app on the second home screen, by default.

1. Tap the Files icon to open the app.

2. On the Browse screen (shown in **Figure 4-10**):

   - Tap the Search field to search for items by title.

   - Tap a source in the Locations or Favorites sections to browse a particular service or your iPhone.

   - Tap colors under Tags to search for files you've tagged according to categories.

3. Once in a source, illustrated in **Figure 4-11**, you may tap files to open or preview them, and you may tap folders to open them and view their contents.

4. Tap Select in the upper-right corner of the screen and then tap items to select them for an action. Available actions, found at the bottom of the screen, include

   - **Duplicating files:** Make copies of selected items.

   - **Moving files:** Move files to other sources.

   - **Sharing files:** Share files with other people in a variety of ways (Messages and Mail, for example). You can even invite them to make edits, if you like.

   - **Deleting files:** Trash files you no longer need.

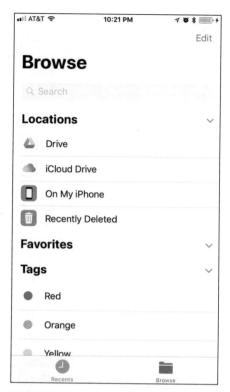

FIGURE 4-10

FIGURE 4-11

TIP

Should you like to retrieve a file you've deleted, go the Browse screen (tap Browse at the bottom of the screen if you're not already there) and tap Recently Deleted. Tap Select in the upper-right corner, tap the file you'd like to retrieve, and tap the Recover button at the bottom of the screen. The file will be placed back in the location it was originally deleted from. Please note that some services may not allow you to retrieve a file you've deleted; if you don't see the file you're looking for, contact that particular service.

2

Beginning to Use Your iPhone

Chapter **5**

Making and Receiving Calls

I f you're the type who wants a cellphone only to make and receive calls, you probably didn't buy an iPhone. Still, making and receiving calls is one of the primary functions of any phone, smart or otherwise.

In this chapter, you discover all the basics of placing calls, receiving calls, and using available tools during a call to mute sound, turn on the speakerphone, and more. You also explore features that help you manage how to respond to a call that you can't take at the moment, how to receive calls when in your car, and how to change your ringtone.

Use the Keypad to Place a Call

Dialing a call with a keypad is an obvious first skill for you to acquire, and it's super-simple.

CarPlay is a feature that provides the ability to interact with your car and place calls using Siri voice commands and your iPhone. Apps designed for CarPlay allow you to interact with controls while avoiding taking your attention from the road. Visit www.apple.com/ios/carplay/available-models to see which auto manufacturers are currently utilizing CarPlay in their products.

To manually dial a call, follow these steps:

1. On any Home screen, tap Phone in the Dock, and the app opens; tap the keypad button at the bottom of the screen, and the keypad appears (see **Figure 5-1**).

If anything other than the keypad appears, you can just tap the Keypad button at the bottom of the screen to display the keypad.

Keypad

FIGURE 5-1

2. Enter the number you want to call by tapping the number buttons; as you do, the number appears above the keypad.

TIP

When you enter a phone number, before you place the call, you can tap Add Number (found directly underneath the phone number) to add the person to your Contacts app. You can create a new contact or add the phone number to an existing contact using this feature.

3. If you enter a number incorrectly, use the Delete button that appears on the keypad after you've begun to enter a number (a left-pointing arrow with an X in it) to clear numbers one at a time.

4. Tap the Call button shaped like a telephone headset. The call is placed and tools appear, as shown in **Figure 5-2.**

TIP

If you're on a call that requires you to punch in numbers or symbols (such as a pound sign), tap the Keypad button on the tools that appear during a call to display the keypad. See more about using calling tools in the "Use Tools during a Call" task, later in this chapter.

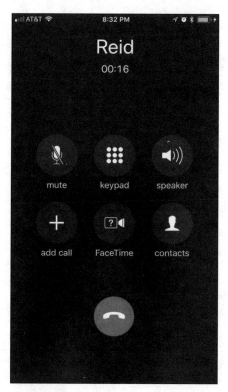

FIGURE 5-2

End a Call

In the following tasks, I show you several other ways to place calls; however, I don't want to leave you on your first call without a way out. When you're on a phone call, the Call button changes to an End button shaped like a phone receiver (see **Figure 5-3**). Tap End, and the call is disconnected.

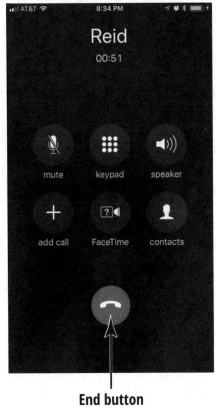

End button

FIGURE 5-3

Place a Call Using Contacts

If you've created a contact (see Chapter 6) and included a phone number in that contact record, you can use the Contacts app to place a call.

1. Tap the Phone icon in any Home screen dock.

2. Tap the Contacts button at the bottom of the screen.

3. In the Contacts list that appears (see **Figure 5-4**), scroll up or down to locate the contact you need or tap a letter along the right side to jump to that section of the list.

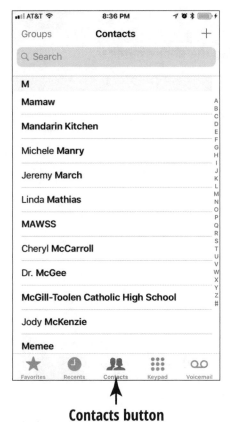

Contacts button

FIGURE 5-4

4. Tap the contact to display his or her record. In the record that appears (see **Figure 5-5**), tap the phone number field. The call is placed.

If you locate a contact and the record doesn't include a phone number, you can add it at this point by tapping the Edit button, entering the number, then tapping Done. Place your call following Step 4 in the preceding steps.

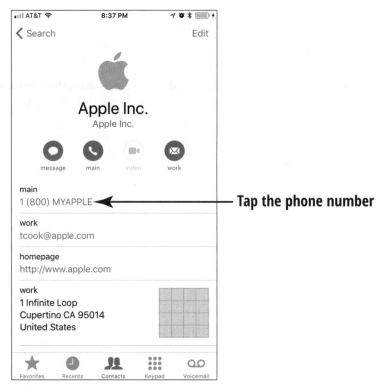

Tap the phone number

FIGURE 5-5

Return a Recent Call

If you want to dial a number from a call you've recently made or received, you can use the Recents call list.

1. Tap Phone in the Dock on any Home screen.

2. Tap the Recents button at the bottom of the screen. A list of recent calls that you've both made and received appears (see **Figure 5-6**).

   Missed calls appear in red.

REMEMBER

3. If you want to view only the calls you've missed, tap the Missed tab at the top of the screen.

4. Tap the Info icon (a small i) to the right of any item to view information about calls to or from this person or establishment (see **Figure 5-7**). The information displayed here might differ depending on the other phone and connection.

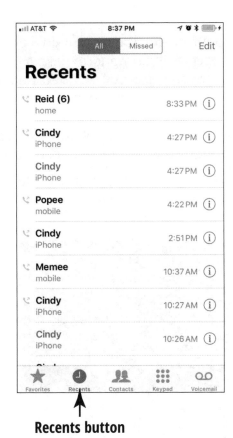

Recents button

FIGURE 5-6

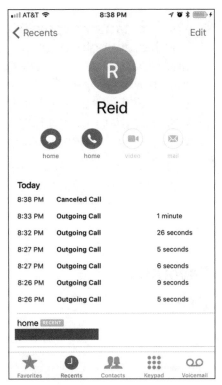

FIGURE 5-7

5. Tap the Recents button in the upper-left corner to return to the Recents list, then tap any call record to place a call to that number.

Use Favorites

You can save up to 50 contacts to Favorites in the Phone app so that you can quickly make calls to your A–list folks or businesses.

1. Tap Phone on any Home screen.

2. Tap the Favorites button at the bottom of the screen.

3. In the Favorites screen that displays (see **Figure 5-8**), tap the Add button.

4. Your Contacts list appears and contact records that contain a phone number are bolded. Locate a contact that you want to make a Favorite and tap it. Next, in the menu that appears, tap Call or Video, depending on which type of call you prefer to make to this person most of the time (see **Figure 5-9**). Tap the arrows to the right of Call or Video to choose other options for the contact, such as alternate phone numbers. The Favorites list reappears with your new favorite contact on it.

5. To place a call to a Favorite, display the Phone app, tap Favorites, then tap a person on the list to place a call.

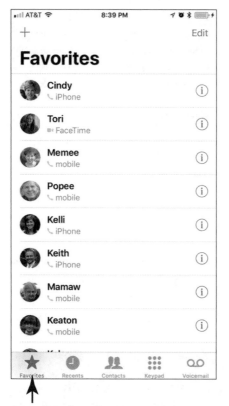

Favorites button

FIGURE 5-8

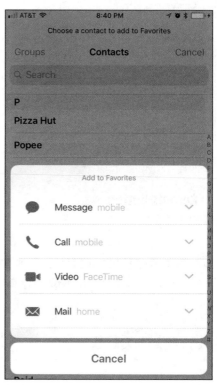

FIGURE 5-9

TIP

If you decide to place a FaceTime call to a Favorite that you've created using the Voice Call setting, just tap the Information icon that appears to the right of the favorite's listing and tap the FaceTime call button in the contact record that appears. You can also create two contacts for the same person, one with a cellphone and one with a land-line phone, for instance, and place one or both in Favorites. See Chapter 7 for more about making FaceTime calls.

Receive a Call

There's one step to receiving a call. When a call comes in to you, the screen shown in **Figure 5-10** appears:

FIGURE 5-10

» Tap Accept to pick up the call.

» Tap Message to send a preset text message without picking up. Select the message in Settings under Phone ⇨ Respond with Text.

>> Tap Remind Me to have iPhone send you a reminder to return the call without answering it.

>> If you tap Decline or don't tap either of the other buttons after a few rings, the call goes to your voice mail.

TIP

There's another quick way to send a call to voice mail or decline it: Press the Sleep/Wake button on the top of your phone once to send a call to voice mail or press the same button twice to decline the call. You can also press the Volume button once to perform the same task, if it's more convenient.

With the Handoff feature, if your iPhone is near an iPad or Mac computer (2012 model or later) and a call comes in, you can connect to the call via Bluetooth from any of the three devices by clicking or swiping the call notification. All devices have to be signed into the same iCloud account and have enabled Bluetooth and Handoff under Settings.

Use Tools during a Call

When you're on a call, whether you initiated it or received it, a set of tools, shown in **Figure 5-11,** is displayed.

Here's what these six buttons allow you to do, starting with the top-left corner:

>> **Mute:** Silences the phone call so that the caller can't hear you, though you can hear the caller. The Mute button background turns white, as shown in **Figure 5-12,** when a call is muted. Tap again to unmute the call.

>> **Keypad:** Displays the numeric keypad.

>> **Speaker:** Turns the speakerphone feature on and off.

TIP

If you are near a Bluetooth device and have Bluetooth turned on in your iPhone Settings, you will see a list of sources (such as a car Bluetooth connection for hands-free calls) and you can choose the one you want to use.

FIGURE 5-11

FIGURE 5-12

» **Add Call:** Displays Contacts so that you can add a caller to a conference call.

» **FaceTime:** Begins a video call with somebody who has an iPhone 4 or more recent model, iPod touch (4th generation or later), iPad 2 or third-generation or later, an iPad mini, or a Mac running macOS 10.7 or later.

» **Contacts:** Displays a list of contacts.

TIP

You can pair your Apple Watch with your iPhone to make and receive calls using it.

Turn On Do Not Disturb

Do Not Disturb is a feature that has iPhone silence incoming calls when iPhone is locked, displaying only a moon-shaped icon to let you know that a call is coming in.

1. To access the feature, tap Settings.

2. To enable the feature, find and tap Do Not Disturb, then toggle the Do Not Disturb switch to On (green).

TIP

When you turn on the Do Not Disturb feature, calls from Favorites are automatically allowed through by default. You can change that setting by tapping the Allow Calls From option in Settings⇨Do Not Disturb.

With iOS 11, Apple introduces a new addition to the Do Not Disturb feature: Do Not Disturb While Driving (shown in **Figure 5-13**). This option is near the bottom of the Settings⇨Do Not Disturb screen. You can block incoming calls, notifications, and texts while you're driving to prevent distractions and accidents. There are three ways to activate Do Not Disturb While Driving:

» **Manually (default):** You activate the feature through Control Center (see Chapter 3 for more information).

» **When Connected to Car Bluetooth:** The feature activates automatically only when your iPhone connects to your vehicle's Bluetooth.

» **Automatically:** The feature is enabled whenever your iPhone detects that you're in an accelerating vehicle. Yes, it's that smart!

TIP

This could be inconvenient when you're simply a passenger. In this case, simply disable the feature for the duration of the ride.

Phone calls can come through when you're connected to your vehicle's Bluetooth or a hands-free accessory, but not texts or notifications.

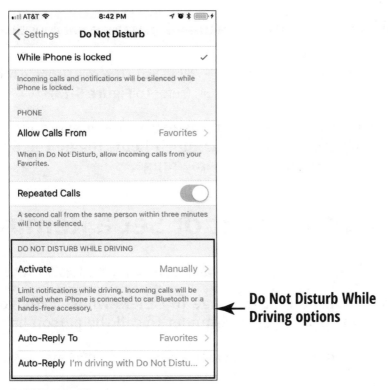

FIGURE 5-13

Do Not Disturb While
Driving options

TIP

You can set up an Auto-Reply feature to send a text to certain people who are texting you (your Favorites are enabled by default). This option is in the Do Not Disturb While Driving section of Settings ➪ Do Not Disturb.

Set Up Exceptions for Do Not Disturb

If there are people whose calls you want to receive even when the Do Not Disturb feature is turned on, you can set up that capability. You can also set up a feature that allows a second call from the same number made within three minutes of the first to ring through. The theory with this feature is that two calls within a few minutes of each other might suggest an emergency situation that you'll want to respond to.

1. With the Do Not Disturb feature turned on (see the previous task), tap Settings.

2. Tap Do Not Disturb, and on the Do Not Disturb screen, toggle the Repeated Calls On/Off switch to On (refer to **Figure 5-13**).

TIP

If you want to schedule Do Not Disturb to be active only during a certain time period, such as your lunch hour, toggle the Scheduled switch to On (green), then set a time range.

Reply to a Call via Text or Set a Reminder to Call Back

You can reply with a text message to callers whose calls you can't answer. You can also set up a reminder to call the person back later.

1. When a call comes in that you want to send a preset message to, tap Message.

2. Tap on a preset reply, or tap Custom, then enter your own message.

3. To set up a reminder, tap Remind Me when the call comes in, then tap In One Hour or When I Leave to be reminded when you leave your current location.

Change Your Ringtone

The music or sound that plays when a call is coming in is called a ringtone. Your phone is set up with a default ringtone, but you can choose among a large number of Apple-provided choices.

1. Tap the Settings icon.

2. Tap Sounds, then tap Ringtone.

3. Scroll down the list of ringtones and tap on one to preview it (see **Figure 5-14**).

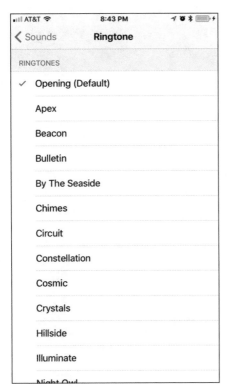

FIGURE 5-14

4. When you have selected the ringtone that you want in the list of ringtones, tap Sounds to return to the Sounds settings with your new ringtone in effect.

TIP

You can also set custom ringtones for contacts using the Contacts app to give that person's calls a unique sound. Open a contact's record, tap Edit, then tap the Ringtone setting to display a list of ringtones. Tap one, then tap Done to save it.

Chapter **6**

Managing Contacts

Contacts is the iPhone equivalent of the dog-eared address book that used to sit by your phone. The Contacts app is simple to set up and use, and it has some powerful features beyond simply storing names, addresses, and phone numbers.

For example, you can pinpoint a contact's address in iPhone's Maps app. You can use your contacts to address email and Facebook messages and Twitter tweets quickly. If you store a contact record that includes a website, you can use a link in Contacts to view that website instantly. In addition, of course, you can easily search for a contact by a variety of criteria, including how people are related to you, such as family or mutual friends, or by groups you create.

In this chapter, you discover the various features of Contacts, including how to save yourself time spent entering contact information by syncing contacts with such services as iCloud.

Add a Contact

1. Tap Phone on the Home screen, then tap the Contacts icon at the bottom of the screen. An alphabetical list of contacts appears, like the one shown in **Figure 6-1.**

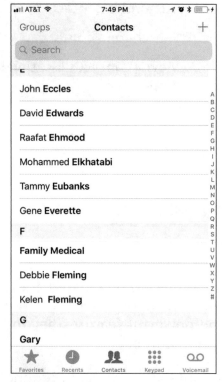

FIGURE 6-1

2. Tap the Add button, the button with the small plus sign (+) on it in the upper-right corner. A blank New Contact page opens (see **Figure 6-2**). Tap in any field and the onscreen keyboard displays.

3. Enter any contact information you want.

TECHNICAL STUFF

   Only one of the First, Last, or Company fields is required.

4. To scroll down the contact's page and see more fields, flick up on the page with your finger.

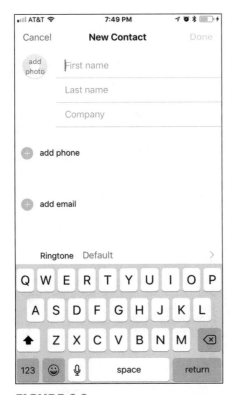

FIGURE 6-2

5. If you want to add information (such as a mailing or street address), you can tap the relevant Add field, which opens additional entry fields.

6. To add an information field, such as Nickname or Job Title, tap Add Field toward the bottom of the page. In the Add Field dialog that appears (see **Figure 6-3**), choose a field to add.

TIP

You have to flick the page up with your finger to view all the fields.

TIP

If your contact has a name that's difficult for you to pronounce, consider adding the Phonetic First Name or Phonetic Last Name field, or both, to that person's record (refer to Step 6).

7. Tap the Done button in the upper-right corner when you finish making entries. The new contact appears in your address book. Tap it to see details (see **Figure 6-4**).

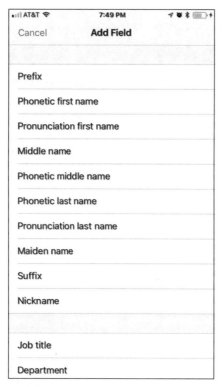

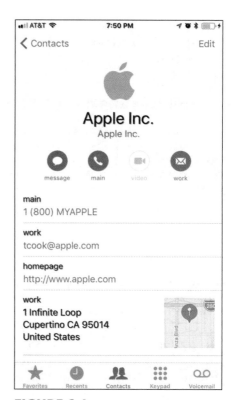

FIGURE 6-3

FIGURE 6-4

TIP

You can choose a distinct ringtone or text tone for a new contact. Just tap the Ringtone or Text Tone field in the New Contact form to see a list of options. When that person calls either on the phone or via FaceTime, or texts you via SMS, MMS, or iMessage, you will recognize him or her from the tone that plays.

Sync Contacts with iCloud

You can use your iCloud account to sync contacts from your iPhone to iCloud to back them up. These also become available to your email account, if you set one up.

TIP

You can also use iTunes to sync contacts among all your Apple devices and even a Windows PC. See Chapter 4 for more about making iTunes settings.

1. On the Home screen, tap Settings, tap the name of your Apple ID account (at the top of the screen), then tap iCloud.

2. In the iCloud settings shown in **Figure 6-5,** make sure that the On/Off switch for Contacts is set to On (green) in order to sync contacts.

3. In the top-left corner of the screen, tap the Apple ID button, then tap the Settings button to return to Settings.

4. To choose which email account to sync with, first tap Accounts & Passwords. In the Accounts section, tap the email account you want to use.

TIP

The email account you sync with is usually listed as iCloud.

5. In the following screen (see **Figure 6-6**), toggle the Contacts switch to On to merge contacts from that account via iCloud.

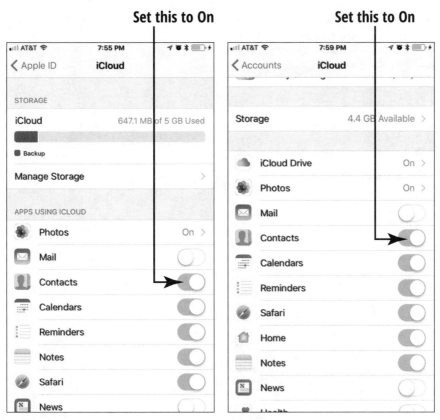

FIGURE 6-5   FIGURE 6-6

TIP

You can use the iTunes Wi-Fi Sync feature in iPhone Settings under General to sync with iTunes wirelessly from a computer connected to the same Wi-Fi network.

Assign a Photo to a Contact

1. With Contacts open, tap a contact to whose record you want to add a photo.

2. Tap the Edit button.

3. On the Info page that appears (see **Figure 6-7**), tap Add Photo.

Tap to add photo

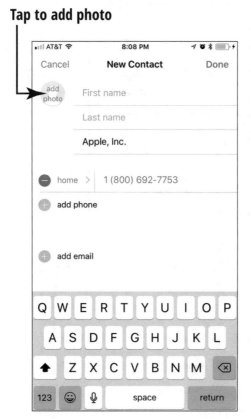

FIGURE 6-7

4. In the popover that appears, tap Choose Photo to choose an existing photo.

TIP

You could also choose Take Photo to take that contact's photo on the spot.

5. In the Photos dialog that appears, choose a source for your photo (such as Favorites, Camera Roll, or other album).

6. In the photo album that appears, tap a photo to select it. The Move and Scale dialog, shown in **Figure 6-8,** appears.

TIP

Center the photo the way you want it by dragging it with your finger.

7. Tap the Choose button to use the photo for this contact.

8. Tap Done to save changes to the contact. The photo appears on the contact's Info page (see **Figure 6-9**).

FIGURE 6-8

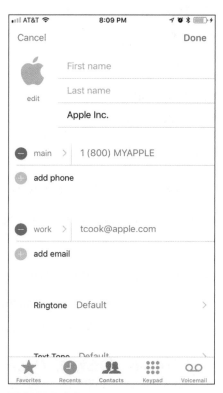

FIGURE 6-9

TIP

While in the Photos dialog, in Step 6, you can modify the photo before saving it to the contact information. You can unpinch your fingers on the iPhone screen to expand the photo and move it around the space to focus on a particular section, then tap the Choose button to use the modified version.

Add Social Media Information

iPhone users can add social media information to their Contacts so that they can quickly tweet (send a short message to) others using Twitter, comment to a contact on Facebook, and more.

You can use any of these social media platforms with Contacts:

» Twitter

» Facebook

» Flickr

» LinkedIn

» Myspace

» Sina Weibo

To add social media information to contacts, follow these steps:

1. Open Contacts within the Phone app and tap a contact.

2. Tap the Edit button in the upper-right corner of the screen.

3. Scroll down and tap Add Social Profile.

You may add multiple social profiles if you like.

TIP

4. Twitter is the default service that pops up, but you can easily change it to a different service by tapping "Twitter" and selecting from the list of services, shown in **Figure 6-10.** Tap Done after you've selected the service you'd like to use.

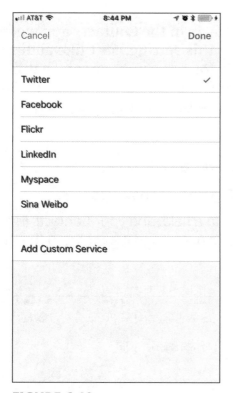

FIGURE 6-10

5. Enter the information for the social profile as needed.

6. Tap Done and the information is saved. The social profile account is now displayed when you select the contact, and you can send tweets, Facebook messages, or what-have-you by simply tapping the user-name, tapping the service you want to use to contact the person, then tapping the appropriate command (such as Facebook posting).

Designate Related People

You can quickly designate relationships in a contact record if those people are saved to Contacts. One great use for this feature is using Siri to simply say, "Call Manager" to call someone who is designated in your contact information as your manager.

TIP

There's a setting for Linked Contacts in the Contacts app when you're editing a contact's record. Using this setting isn't like adding a relation; rather, if you have records for the same person that have been imported into Contacts from different sources, such as Google or Twitter, you can link them to show only a single contact.

1. Tap a contact, then tap Edit.

2. Scroll down the record and tap Add Related Name.

3. The field labeled Mother (see **Figure 6-11**) now appears.

4. Tap the blue Information arrow in a field, and your Contacts list appears. Tap the related person's name, and it appears in the field (see **Figure 6-12**).

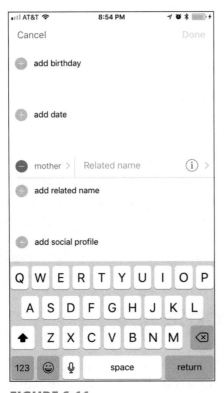

FIGURE 6-11

FIGURE 6-12

5. Tap the Add Related Name and continue to add additional names as needed.

6. Tap Done to complete the edits.

After you add relations to a contact record, when you select the person in the Contacts main screen, all the related people for that contact are listed there.

Set Individual Ringtones and Text Tones

If you want to hear a unique tone when you receive a phone or FaceTime call from a particular contact, you can set up this feature in Contacts. For example, if you want to be sure that you know instantly whether your spouse, sick friend, or boss is calling, you can set a unique tone for that person.

If you set a custom tone for someone, that tone will be used when that person calls or contacts you by FaceTime.

To set up custom tones, follow these steps:

1. Tap to add a new contact or select a contact in the list of contacts and tap Edit.

2. Tap the Ringtone field in a new contact or tap Edit, then the Ringtone field in an existing contact, and a list of tones appears (see **Figure 6-13**).

You can set a custom text tone to be used when the person sends you a text message. Tap Text Tone instead of Ringtone in Step 2, then follow the remaining steps.

3. Scroll up and down to see the full list. Tap a tone, and it previews. When you hear one you like, tap Done.

If your Apple devices are synced via iCloud, setting a unique ringtone for an iPhone contact also sets it for use with FaceTime and Messages on your iPad and Mac. See Chapter 4 for more about iCloud.

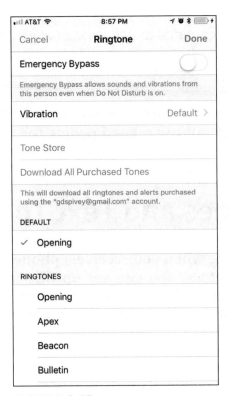

FIGURE 6-13

Search for a Contact

1. With Contacts open, tap in the Search field at the very top of your Contacts list (see **Figure 6-14**). The onscreen keyboard opens.

2. Type the first letters of either the first or last name or company. All matching results appear, as shown in **Figure 6-15.** For example, typing "App" might display Johnny Appleseed and Apple, Inc. in the results, both of which have "App" as the first three letters of the first or last part of the name or address.

You can use the alphabetical listing along the right side of All Contacts and tap a letter to locate a contact. Also, you can tap and drag to scroll down the list of contacts on the All Contacts page.

TIP

3. Tap a contact in the results to display that person's Information page.

Search field

Search results

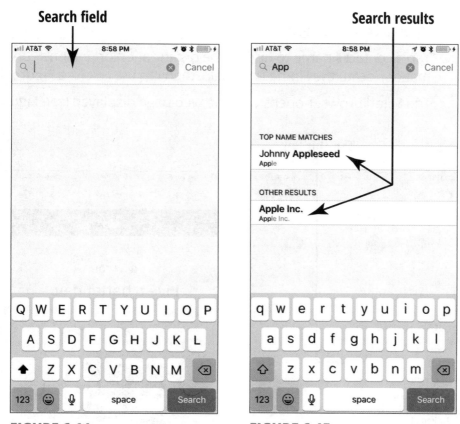

FIGURE 6-14   FIGURE 6-15

TIP

You can search by phone number simply by entering the phone number in the Search field until the list narrows to the person you're looking for. This might be a good way to search for all contacts in your town or company, for example.

Go to a Contact's Website

If you entered website information in the Home Page field, it automatically becomes a link in the contact's record.

1. Open a contact's record.

2. Tap a contact's name to display the organization or person's contact information, locate the Home Page field, then tap the link (see **Figure 6-16**).

3. The Safari browser opens with the web page displayed (see **Figure 6-17**).

Tap this link

FIGURE 6-16

FIGURE 6-17

You can go directly back to Contacts after you follow a link to a website. Simply tap Contacts in the upper–left corner of the screen and you'll be whisked back to the Info page for the contact you last visited.

Address Email Using Contacts

If you entered an email address for a contact, the address automatically becomes a link in the contact's record.

1. Open Contacts.

2. Tap a contact's name to display the person's contact information, then tap the email address link (see **Figure 6-18**).

3. The New Message dialog appears, as shown in **Figure 6-19.** Initially, the title bar of this dialog reads New Message, but as you type a subject, New Message changes to the specific title.

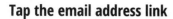

Tap the email address link

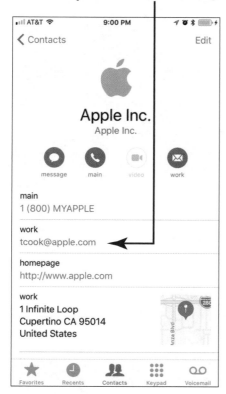

FIGURE 6-18

FIGURE 6-19

4. Tap in a field and use the onscreen keyboard to enter a subject and message.

5. Tap the Send button. The message goes on its way.

Share a Contact

After you've entered contact information, you can share it with others via an email, text message, and other methods.

1. With Contacts open, tap a contact name to display its information.

2. On the Information page, scroll down and tap Share Contact. In the dialog that appears, shown in **Figure 6-20,** tap the method you'd like to use to share the contact.

FIGURE 6-20

To share with an AirDrop-enabled device that is nearby, use the AirDrop button in the screen shown in **Figure 6-20.** Just select a nearby device, and your contact is transmitted to that person's device (such as a smartphone, a Mac with macOS with the AirDrop folder open in Finder, or a tablet).

3. Use the onscreen keyboard to enter a recipient's information if emailing or sharing via text message.

If the person is saved in Contacts, you can just type his or her name here.

4. Tap the Send button if sharing with email or text message. The message goes to your recipient with the contact information attached as a .vcf file. (This vCard format is commonly used to transmit contact information.)

When somebody receives a vCard containing contact information, he or she needs only to click the attached file to open it. At this point, depending on the email or contact management program, the recipient can perform various actions to save the content. Other iPhone, iPod touch, iPad, or iPhone users can easily import .vcf records as new contacts in their own Contacts apps.

View a Contact's Location in Maps

If you've entered a person's address in Contacts, you have a shortcut for viewing that person's location in the Maps application.

1. Open Contacts.

2. Tap the contact you want to view to display that contact's information.

3. Tap Edit, then tap Add Address and enter the address information.

4. Tap Done, then tap the address field. Maps opens and displays a map of the address (see **Figure 6-21**).

FIGURE 6-21

TIP

This task works with more than your friends' addresses. You can save information for your favorite restaurant or movie theater or any other location and use Contacts to jump to the associated website in the Safari browser or to the address in Maps. For more about using Safari, see Chapter 11. For more about the Maps application, see Chapter 21.

Delete a Contact

When it's time to remove a name or two from your Contacts, it's easy to do.

1. With Contacts open, tap the contact you want to delete.

2. On the Information page (refer to **Figure 6-4)**, tap the Edit button.

3. On the Info page that displays, drag your finger upward to scroll down, then tap the Delete Contact button at the bottom (see **Figure 6-22**).

4. The confirming dialog shown in **Figure 6-23** appears; tap the Delete Contact button to confirm the deletion.

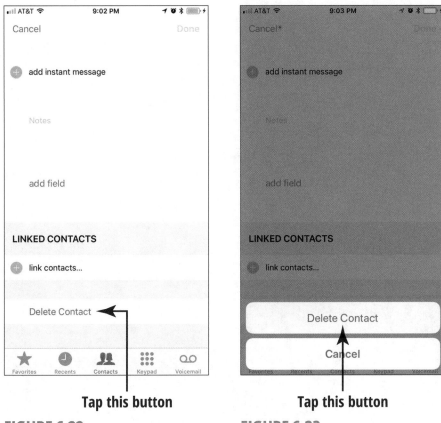

Tap this button   **Tap this button**

FIGURE 6-22   **FIGURE 6-23**

TIP

During this process, if you change your mind before you tap Delete, tap the Cancel button in Step 4. Be careful: After you tap Delete, there's no going back! Your contact is deleted from your iPhone, and also any other device that syncs to your iPhone via iCloud, Google, or other means.

Chapter **7**

Communicating with FaceTime and Messages

aceTime is an excellent video-calling app that lets you call people who have FaceTime on their devices using either a phone number or an email address. You and your friend, colleague, or family member can see each other as you talk, which makes for a much more personal calling experience.

iMessage is a feature available through the preinstalled Messages app for instant messaging (IM). IM involves sending a text message to somebody's iPhone, iPod touch, Mac running macOS 10.8 or later, or iPad (using the person's phone number or email address to carry on an instant conversation). You can even send audio and video via Messages.

In this chapter, I introduce you to FaceTime and the Messages app and review their simple controls. In no time, you'll be socializing with all and sundry.

Understand Who Can Use FaceTime

Here's a quick rundown of the device and information you need for using FaceTime's various features:

» You can use FaceTime to call people over a Wi-Fi connection who have an iPhone 4 or later, an iPad 2 or a third-generation iPad or later, a fourth-generation iPod touch or later, or a Mac (running macOS 10.6.6 or later). If you want to connect over a 3G/4G cellular connection, you're limited to iPhone 4s or later and iPad third generation or later.

» You can use a phone number to connect with anybody with either an iOS device or a Mac and an iCloud account.

» The person you're contacting must have allowed FaceTime to be used in Settings.

Get an Overview of FaceTime

FaceTime works with the iPhone's built-in cameras so that you can call other folks who have a device that supports FaceTime. You can use FaceTime to chat while sharing video images with another person. This preinstalled app is useful for seniors who want to keep up with distant family members and friends and see (as well as hear) the latest-and-greatest news.

You can make and receive calls with FaceTime using a phone number or an email account and make calls to those with an iCloud account. When connected, you can show the person on the other end what's going on around you. Just remember that you can't adjust audio volume from within the app or record a video call. Nevertheless, on the positive side, even though its features are limited, this app is straightforward to use.

You can use your Apple ID and iCloud account to access FaceTime, so it works pretty much right away. See Chapter 4 for more about getting an Apple ID.

TIP

If you're having trouble using FaceTime, make sure that the Face-Time feature is turned on. That's quick to do: Tap Settings on the Home screen, tap FaceTime, then tap the FaceTime On/Off switch to turn it On (green), if it isn't already. On this Settings screen, you can also select the phone number and/or email addresses that others can use to make FaceTime calls to you, as well as which one of those is displayed as your caller ID.

TIP

To view information for recent calls, open the FaceTime app, then tap the Information button on a recent call, and iPhone displays that person's information. You can tap the contact to call the person back.

Make a FaceTime Call with Wi-Fi or 3G/4G (LTE)

If you know that the person you're calling has FaceTime available on his device, adding that person to your iPhone Contacts is a good idea so you can initiate FaceTime calls from within Contacts if you like or from the Contacts list you can access through the FaceTime app.

TIP

When you call somebody using an email address, the person must be signed in to his Apple iCloud account and have verified that the address can be used for FaceTime calls. You can make this setting by tapping Settings, then FaceTime ⇨ Use Your Apple ID for FaceTime; FaceTime for Mac users make this setting by selecting FaceTime ⇨ Preferences.

1. Tap the FaceTime icon to launch the app.

2. Tap to choose a Video or Audio call at the top of the screen. Video includes your voice and image; Audio includes only your voice.

3. If your contact doesn't appear in the Recents list (under a field like Enter Name), tap the Enter Name, Email, or Number field and begin to enter a contact's name; a list of matching contacts appears, or you can tap the plus sign (+) in the upper-right corner to open your complete Contacts list, scroll to locate a contact who has associated a device with FaceTime, tap that contact, then tap the appropriate method to initiate a call (see **Figure 7-1**).

TIP

You'll see a Camera button if that contact's device supports FaceTime video and a Phone button if the contact's device supports FaceTime audio. (If you haven't saved this person in your contacts and you know the phone number to call or email, you can just enter that information in the Enter Name, Email, or Number field.)

4. When the person accepts the call, you see a large screen that displays the recipient's image and a small screen referred to as a Picture in Picture (PiP) containing your image superimposed (see **Figure 7-2**).

FIGURE 7-1

FIGURE 7-2

TIP

If you have iOS 6 or later, you can use FaceTime over both a Wi-Fi network and your iPhone 3G or 4G(LTE) connection. However, if you use FaceTime over a 3G or 4G(LTE) connection, you may incur costly data usage fees. To avoid extra cost, in Settings under Cellular, set the iPhone Cellular Calls switch for FaceTime to Off.

Accept and End a FaceTime Call

If you're on the receiving end of a FaceTime call, accepting the call is about as easy as it gets.

TIP

If you'd rather not be available for calls, you can go to Settings and turn on the Do Not Disturb feature. This stops any incoming calls or notifications other than for the people you've designated as exceptions to Do Not Disturb. After you turn on Do Not Disturb, you can use the feature's settings to schedule when it's active, allow calls from certain people, or allow a second call from the same person in a three-minute interval to go through.

To accept and end a FaceTime call, follow these steps:

TIP

1. When the call comes in, tap the Accept button to take the call (see **Figure 7-3**).

   To reject the call, tap the Decline button.

2. Chat away with your friend, swapping video images. To end the call, tap the End button (see **Figure 7-4**).

TIP

To mute sound during a call, tap the Mute button, which looks like a microphone with a line through it (refer to **Figure 7-4**). Tap the button again to unmute your iPhone.

Tap Decline to refuse a call

FIGURE 7-3

End button

FIGURE 7-4

Switch Views

When you're on a FaceTime call, you might want to use iPhone's built-in, rear-facing camera to show the person you're talking to what's going on around you.

1. Tap the Switch Camera button (refer to **Figure 7-5**) to switch from the front-facing camera that's displaying your image to the back-facing camera that captures whatever you're looking at.

2. Tap the Switch Camera button again to switch back to the front camera displaying your image.

Switch Camera button

FIGURE 7-5

Set Up an iMessage Account

iMessage is a feature available through the preinstalled Messages app that allows you to send and receive instant messages (IMs) to others using an Apple iOS device or suitably configured Macs. iMessage is a way of sending instant messages through a Wi-Fi network, but you can send messages through your cellular connection without having iMessage activated.

TECHNICAL STUFF

Instant messaging differs from email or tweeting in an important way. Whereas you might email somebody and wait for days or weeks before that person responds, or you might post a tweet that could sit there awhile before anybody views it, with instant messaging, communication happens almost immediately. You send an IM, and it appears on somebody's Apple device right away.

Assuming that the person wants to participate in a live conversation, the chat begins immediately, allowing a back-and-forth dialogue in real time.

1. To set up Messages, tap Settings on the Home screen.

2. Tap Messages. The settings shown in **Figure 7-6** appear.

FIGURE 7-6

3. If iMessage isn't set to On (refer to **Figure 7-6**), tap the On/Off switch to turn it on (green).

TIP

Be sure that the phone number and/or email account associated with your iPhone under the Send & Receive setting is correct. (This should be set up automatically based on your iCloud settings.) If it isn't, tap the Send & Receive field, add an email or phone, then tap Messages to return to the previous screen.

4. To allow a notice to be sent to the sender when you've read a message, tap the On/Off switch for Send Read Receipts. You can also choose to show a subject field in your messages.

5. Press the Home button to leave Settings.

TIP

To enable or disable email accounts used by Messages, tap Send & Receive, then tap an email address to either enable (check mark appears to the left) or disable it (no check mark appears to the left).

Use Messages to Address, Create, and Send Messages

Now you're ready to use Messages.

1. From the Home screen, tap the Messages button.

2. Tap the New Message button in the top-right corner to begin a conversation.

3. In the form that appears (see **Figure 7-7**), you can address a message in a few ways:

   - Begin to type a name in the To field, and a list of matching contacts appears.

   - Tap the Dictation key on the onscreen keyboard and speak the address.

   - Tap the plus (+) button on the right side of the address field, and the Contacts list is displayed.

4. Tap a contact on the list you chose from in Step 3. If the contact has both an email address and a phone number stored, the Info dialog appears, allowing you to tap one or the other, which addresses the message.

5. To create a message, simply tap in the message field near the bottom of the screen (see **Figure 7-8**) and type your message.

6. To send the message, tap the Send button (refer to **Figure 7-8**). When your recipient (or recipients) responds, you'll see the conversation displayed on the screen. Tap in the message field again to respond to the last comment.

Message field

FIGURE 7-7

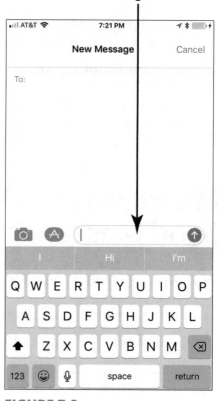

FIGURE 7-8

TIP

You can address a message to more than one person by simply choosing more recipients in Step 2 of the preceding list.

Read Messages

When you receive a message, it's as easy to read as email — easier, to be honest!

1. Tap Messages on the Home screen.

2. When the app opens, you see a list of text conversations you've engaged in.

3. Tap a conversation to see the message string, including all attachments, as shown in **Figure 7-9**.

FIGURE 7-9

4. To view all attachments of a message, tap Details (the encircled 'i' in the upper-right corner) and scroll down.

Clear a Conversation

When you're done chatting, you might want to delete a conversation to remove the clutter before you start a new chat.

1. With Messages open and your conversations displayed, swipe to the left on the message you want to delete.

2. Tap the Delete button next to the conversation you want to get rid of (see **Figure 7-10**).

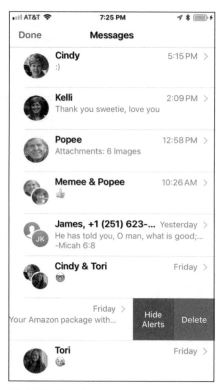

FIGURE 7-10

TIP

Tap the Hide Alerts button to keep from being alerted to new messages in the conversation. To reactivate alerts for the conversation, swipe again, then tap the Show Alerts button.

Send Emojis in Place of Text

Emojis are small pictures that can help convey a feeling or idea. For example, smiley faces and sad faces to show emotions, thumbs up to convey approval, and the like.

1. From within a conversation, tap the Emoji key on the onscreen keyboard. If you can't see the keyboard, tap in the Message field to display it.

2. When the Emojis appear (seen in **Figure 7-11**), swipe left and right to find the right Emoji for the moment and tap to select it. You can add as many as you like to the conversation.

FIGURE 7-11

Utilizing the App Drawer

The App Drawer allows you to add items that spice up your messages with information from other apps that are installed on your iPhone, as well as drawings and other images from the web.

Tap the App Drawer icon (looks like an A) to the left of the iMessage field in your conversation; the App Drawer will display at the bottom of the screen. Tap an item in the App Drawer to see what it offers your messaging.

The App Drawer is populated by

>> **The App Store:** Tap the App Store all the way to the left of the App Drawer to find tons of stickers, games, and apps for your messages.

» **Digital Touch:** Allows you to send special effects in Messages. These can include sending your heartbeat, sketching a quick picture, or sending a kiss.

» **Other apps you have installed:** These may appear if they have the ability to add functions and information to your messages. For example, send the latest scores using ESPN, or let your friend know what the weather's like nearby using icons from the AccuWeather app. Another example could be using Fandango's app to send movie information, as illustrated in **Figure 7-12.**

FIGURE 7-12

Digital Touch is one of the most personal ways to send special effects to others. Here's a close look at it:

1. To send a Digital Touch in a message, open a conversation and tap the Digital Touch button, shown in **Figure 7-13**.

Expansion arrow

Digital Touch button

FIGURE 7-13

2. In the Digital Touch window, tap the gray expansion arrow (seen in **Figure 7-13**) to open the full window. Tap the Information button in the lower-right (a gray circle with a white letter "i") and you'll see a list of the gestures and what they do (see **Figure 7-14**).

3. Perform a gesture in the Digital Touch window and it will go to your recipient, as I've done in **Figure 7-15.**

FIGURE 7-14   FIGURE 7-15

Send and Receive Audio

When you're creating a message, you can also create an audio message.

1. With Messages open, tap the New Message button in the top-right corner.

2. Enter an addressee's name in the To field.

3. Tap and hold the Audio button (the microphone symbol to the right of the screen).

4. Speak your message or record a sound or music near you as you continue to hold down the Audio button.

5. Release the Audio button when you're finished recording.

6. Tap the Send button (an upward-pointing arrow at the top of the recording circle). The message appears as an audio track in the recipient's Messages inbox (see **Figure 7-16**). To play the track, she just holds the phone up to her ear or taps the Play button.

FIGURE 7-16

Send a Photo or Video

When you're creating a message, you can also send a picture or create a short video message.

1. With Messages open, tap the New Message button in the top-right corner.

2. Tap the Camera button. In the tool palette that appears (see **Figure 7-17**), tap the Photo button to take a picture, then return to the message.

Tool palette

FIGURE 7-17

3. If you prefer to capture a video, with the palette in **Figure 7-17** displayed:

   a. Swipe the palette to the right and tap Camera.

   b. When Camera opens, swipe to Video and tap the red Record button.

   c. Tap the red Stop button when you've recorded what you want to record.

   d. Tap Done in the upper-right corner if the video is up to your standards, then tap the Send button. Your video is attached to your message.

Send a Map of Your Location

When responding to a message, you can also send a map showing your current location.

1. Tap a message, then tap the Details button in the upper-right corner.

2. Tap Send My Current Location (see **Figure 7-18**), and a map will be inserted as a message attachment.

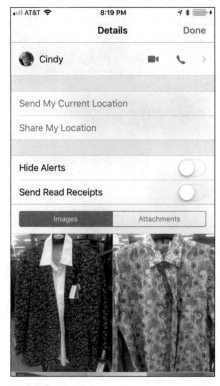

FIGURE 7-18

TIP

You can also share your location in the middle of a conversation rather than send a map attachment with your message. In the screen shown in **Figure 7-18,** tap Share My Location, then tap Share for One Hour, Share Until End of Day, or Share Indefinitely. A map showing your location appears above your conversation until you stop sharing.

Understand Group Messaging

If you want to start a conversation with a group of people, you can use group messaging. Group messaging is great for keeping several people in the conversational loop.

With iOS 8 came a lot of group messaging functionality, including the following features:

» When you participate in a group message, you see all participants in the Details for the message (see **Figure 7-19**). You can drop people whom you don't want to include any longer and leave the conversation yourself when you want to by simply tapping Details, then tapping Leave This Conversation.

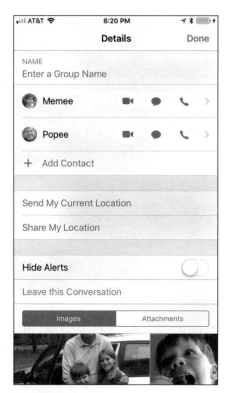

FIGURE 7-19

>> When you turn on Hide Alerts in the Details in a message (see **Figure 7-19**), you won't get notifications of messages from this group, but you can still read the group's messages at a later time (this also works for individuals).

Taking you further into the workings of group messages is beyond the scope of this book, but if you're intrigued, go to `https://support.apple.com/en-us/HT202724` for more information.

Activate the Hide Alerts Feature

If you don't want to get notifications of new messages from an individual or group for a while, you can use the Hide Alerts feature.

1. With a message open, tap Details.

2. Tap the Hide Alerts switch to turn the feature on (refer to **Figure 7-19**).

3. Later, return to Details and tap the Hide Alerts switch again to turn the feature off.

Chapter **8**
Using Handy Utilities

U tilities are simple apps that can be very useful indeed to help with common tasks, such as calculating your meal tip or finding your way on a hike in the woods.

In this chapter, I help you out with using the Calculator app to keep your numbers in line. I also help you explore two other apps: Compass to help you find your way, and Voice Memos so that you can record your best ideas for posterity.

Use the Calculator

This one won't be rocket science. The Calculator app works like just about every calculator app (or actual calculator, for that matter) you've ever used. Follow these steps:

1. Tap the Calculator app icon (shown in **Figure 8-1**) to open it.

Tap this icon

FIGURE 8-1

2. Tap a few numbers (see **Figure 8-2**), then use any of these functions and additional numbers to perform calculations:

- **+, −, ×, and ÷:** These familiar buttons add, subtract, multiply, and divide the number you've entered.

- **+/−:** If the calculator is displaying a negative result, tap this to change it to a positive result, and vice versa.

- **AC/C:** This is the Clear button; its name will change depending on whether you've entered anything. (AC clears all; C clears just the last entry after you've made several entries.)

- **=:** This button produces the result of whatever calculation you've entered.

FIGURE 8-2

If you have a scientific nature, you'll be delighted to see that if you turn your phone to a landscape orientation, you get additional features that turn the basic calculator into a scientific calculator so that you can play with calculations involving such functions as cosines and tangents. You can also use memory functions to work with stored calculations.

Find Your Way with Compass

Compass is a handy tool for figuring out where you are, assuming that you get 3G or 4G/LTE reception wherever you are. To find directions with Compass, follow these steps:

1. Tap the Extras folder on the second Home screen to open it, then tap Compass.

The first time you do this, if you haven't enabled location access, a message appears, asking whether iPhone can use your current location to provide information. Tap OK.

2. If you're using Compass for the first time, you'll be asked to tilt the screen to roll a little red ball around a circle; this helps iPhone to calibrate the Compass app.

When you've completed this exercise, the Compass app appears (see **Figure 8-3**). Move around with your iPhone, and the compass indicates your current orientation in the world.

FIGURE 8-3

3. Tap the bold white line indicating your current location, as shown in **Figure 8-4.** The display changes to True North and indicates with a red wedge how far off True North you are when you move the compass; tap it again to display Magnetic North.

True North refers to the direction you follow from where you are to get to the North Pole; *Magnetic North* is correlated relative to the Earth's magnetic field. True North is the more accurate measurement because of the tilt of the Earth.

4. Swipe to the left to view a compass view with information about how many degrees off of zero a surface is (see **Figure 8-5**). If a surface beneath your phone is flat, the screen turns green. Use this to check to see whether a surface is level.

FIGURE 8-4

FIGURE 8-5

You will know that you have a 4G or LTE connection if you see 4G or LTE in the Status bar. Not every location has LTE capability yet, so this is a good way to check whether you're connected.

Record Voice Memos

Voice Memos is perhaps the most robust of the apps covered in this chapter. The app allows you to record memos, edit memos by trimming them down, share them by email or instant message with Messages, and label recordings so that you find them again.

To record voice memos, follow these steps:

1. On the second Home screen, tap the Extras folder to open it, then tap Voice Memos.

2. In the Voice Memos app (see **Figure 8-6**), tap the red Record button to record a memo.

   This button changes to a red Pause button when you're recording.

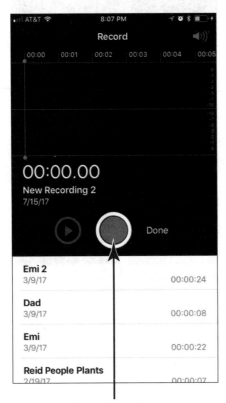

Record button

FIGURE 8-6

A blue line moving from left to right shows that you're in recording mode (see **Figure 8-7**).

While recording, you can tap the red Pause button to pause the recording, then tap Done to stop recording.

When you finish recording, a New Voice Memo dialog appears.

3. Enter a name for the recording, then tap Save. A list of recorded memos appears (see **Figure 8-8**). You can tap a memo to play it back; share it by AirDrop, Messages, Music, or Mail; edit it; save it as note in the Notes app; or delete it.

Pause button

FIGURE 8-7

FIGURE 8-8

TIP

AirDrop allows you to share such items as photos, voice memos, music, and more with another person who has an AirDrop-enabled device and is nearby. You can also share by AirDrop with a Mac using OS X Yosemite or later. (AirDrop requires a fifth-generation iPhone or newer.)

Trim a Voice Memo

Perhaps you repeated yourself at the beginning of your memo. If you want to cut part of a recorded memo, you can trim it. Follow these steps:

1. With the list of recordings displayed (refer to **Figure 8-8**), tap any recording. The recording details appear, as shown in **Figure 8-9.**

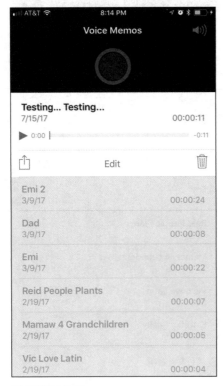

FIGURE 8-9

2. Tap Edit. The Edit screen appears, as shown in **Figure 8-10.**

Trim button

FIGURE 8-10

3. Tap the Trim button (it's a little square with dots coming off of the left and right sides), then drag the red lines on the right or left of the memo bar to trim a portion of the recording.

4. Tap Trim, then select an option to save the versions you want:

- Tap Trim Original to apply the trim and save the recording.

- Save As New Recording to apply the trim and save it as a new version of the recording.

TIP

If you change your mind about trimming the memo, tap the Cancel button.

5. Tap Done.

Rename a Voice Memo

You may occasionally have to rename a voice memo. Follow these steps:

1. With the list of memos displayed (refer to **Figure 8-8**), tap a memo to display its details.

2. Tap the name of the recording. The name becomes available for editing, as shown in **Figure 8-11**.

3. Tap Backspace on your iPhone keyboard to delete the current name.

4. Enter a new name, then tap the Done button at the lower-right corner of the screen. You return to the list of memos, where you see the memo now named with the label you just gave it (see **Figure 8-12**).

FIGURE 8-11

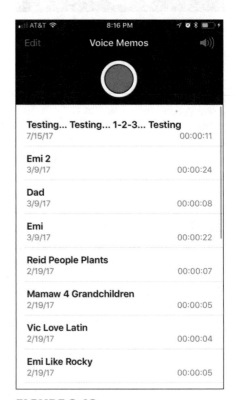

FIGURE 8-12

Share a Voice Memo

To forward a voice memo by email or instant message, follow these steps:

1. Tap a memo in the list of memos (refer to **Figure 8-8**) to select it.
2. Tap the Share button (the box with an arrow pointing out of the top), shown in **Figure 8-13.**

   The menu shown in **Figure 8-14** appears.

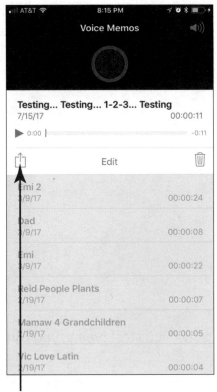

Share button

FIGURE 8-13

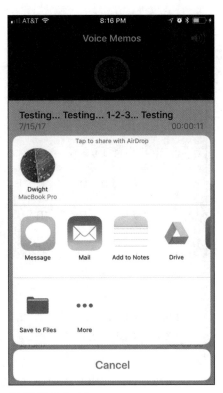

FIGURE 8-14

3. Select the method you'd like to use to share your voice memo:

- Tap Mail to display an email form.

- Tap Message to display a Messages form to send an instant message (see **Figure 8-15**).

FIGURE 8-15

4. Fill in the recipient's information. After you start typing, you can select from your Contacts list.

5. Enter a subject (if you're sending an email) and a message, then tap Send. The voice memo and your message go on their way.

Chapter **9**

Making Your iPhone More Accessible

iPhone users are all different, and some face visual, motor, or hearing challenges. If you're one of these folks, you'll be glad to hear that iPhone offers some handy accessibility features.

To make your screen easier to read, you can adjust the brightness or change wallpaper. You can also set up the VoiceOver feature to read onscreen elements out loud. Then there are a slew of features you can turn on or off, including Zoom, Invert Colors, Speak Selection, Large Type, and more.

If hearing is your challenge, you can do the obvious and adjust the system volume. If you wear hearing aids, you can choose the correct settings for using Bluetooth or another hearing aid mode. The iPhone also has settings for Mono Audio (useful when you're wearing headphones), using an LED flash when an alert sounds, and a Phone Noise Cancellation feature.

Features that help you deal with physical and motor challenges include an AssistiveTouch feature if you have difficulty using the iPhone touchscreen, Switch Control for working with adaptive accessories, and the Home Button and Call Audio Routing settings that allow you to adjust how quickly you have to tap the iPhone screen to work with features and whether you can use a headset or speaker to answer calls.

Finally, the Guided Access feature helps if you have difficulty focusing on one task. It also provides a handy mode for showing presentations of content in settings where you don't want users to flit off to other apps, as in school or a public kiosk.

Set Brightness

Especially when using iPhone as an e-reader, you may find that a slightly less-bright screen reduces strain on your eyes. To adjust screen brightness, follow these steps:

1. Tap the Settings icon on the Home screen.

TIP

If glare from the screen is a problem for you, consider getting a screen protector. This thin film both protects your screen from damage and reduces glare. You can easily find them on Amazon, and just about any cellphone dealer carries them.

2. In Settings, tap Display & Brightness.

3. To control brightness manually, tap the Auto-Brightness On/Off switch (see **Figure 9-1**) to turn off this feature.

4. Tap and drag the Brightness slider (refer to **Figure 9-1**) to the right to make the screen brighter or to the left to make it dimmer.

5. Press the Home button to close Settings.

TIP

In the iBooks e-reader app, you can set a sepia tone for the page. This might be easier on your eyes. See Chapter 16 for more about using iBooks.

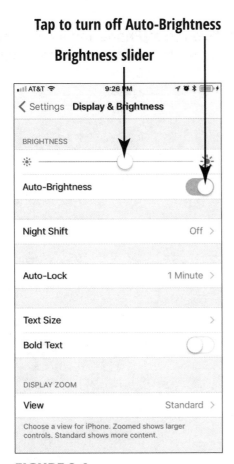

Tap to turn off Auto-Brightness

Brightness slider

FIGURE 9-1

Change the Wallpaper

The default iPhone background image on your iPhone may be pretty, but it may not be the one that works best for you. Choosing differ-ent wallpaper may help you to see all the icons on your Home screen. Follow these steps:

1. Tap the Settings icon on the Home screen.

2. In Settings, tap Wallpaper.

3. In the Wallpaper settings, tap Choose a New Wallpaper.

4. Tap a wallpaper category, as shown in **Figure 9-2,** to view choices. Tap a sample to select it.

If you prefer to use a picture that's on your iPhone, tap an album in the lower part of the Wallpaper screen to locate a picture; tap to use it as your wallpaper.

FIGURE 9-2

5. In the preview that appears (see **Figure 9-3**), tap Set.

Some wallpaper may allow you to select either

- Still (the picture is static)
- Perspective (the picture will seem to move when you move your iPhone)

6. In the following menu, tap your choice of

- Set Lock Screen (the screen that appears when you lock the iPhone by tapping the power button)
- Set Home Screen
- Set Both

Wallpaper Preview

9:29

Saturday, July 15

Still | Perspective

Cancel | Set

FIGURE 9-3

7. Press the Home button.

You return to your Home screen with the new wallpaper set as the background.

Set Up VoiceOver

VoiceOver reads the names of screen elements and settings to you, but it also changes the way you provide input to the iPhone. In Notes, for example, you can have VoiceOver read the name of the Notes buttons to you, and when you enter notes, it reads words or characters that you've entered. It can also tell you whether such features as Auto-Correction are on.

To turn on VoiceOver, follow these steps:

1. Tap the Settings icon on the Home screen.

2. In Settings, tap General, then tap Accessibility.

3. In the Accessibility pane, shown in **Figure 9-4,** tap VoiceOver.

4. In the VoiceOver pane, shown in **Figure 9-5,** tap the VoiceOver On/Off switch to turn on this feature. With VoiceOver on, you must first single-tap to select an item such as a button, which causes VoiceOver to read the name of the button to you. Then you double-tap the button to activate its function.

Tap VoiceOver

Tap to turn on VoiceOver

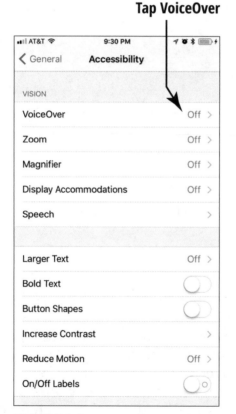

FIGURE 9-4

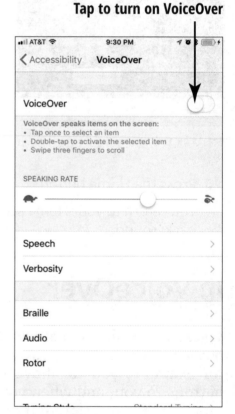

FIGURE 9-5

5. Tap the VoiceOver Practice button to select it, then double-tap the button to open VoiceOver Practice. Practice using gestures (such as pinching or flicking left), and VoiceOver tells you what action each gesture initiates.

6. Tap the Done button, then double-tap the same button to return to the VoiceOver dialog.

7. Tap the Verbosity button once, then double-tap to open its options:

   - Tap the Speak Hints On/Off switch and then double-tap the switch to turn the feature on (or off).

     VoiceOver speaks the name of each tapped item.

   - Tap once, then double-tap the VoiceOver button in the upper-left corner to go back to the VoiceOver screen.

TIP

You can change the language that VoiceOver speaks. In General settings, tap Language & Region, tap iPhone Language, and then select another language. However, this action also changes the language used for labels on Home icons and various settings and fields in iPhone. Be careful with this setting, lest you choose a language you don't understand by accident and have a very difficult time figuring out how to change it back.

8. If you want VoiceOver to read words or characters to you (for example, in the Notes app), scroll down and then tap and double-tap Typing Feedback.

9. In the Typing Feedback dialog, tap and then double-tap to select the option you prefer. The Words option causes VoiceOver to read words to you, but not characters, such as the "dollar sign" ($). The Characters and Words option causes VoiceOver to read both, and so on.

10. Press the Home button to return to the Home screen.

The following section shows how to navigate your iPhone after you've turned on VoiceOver.

TIP

You can use the Accessibility Shortcut setting to help you more quickly turn the VoiceOver, Zoom, Switch Control, AssistiveTouch, Grayscale, or Invert Colors features on and off:

1. In the Accessibility screen, tap Accessibility Shortcut (at the very bottom of the screen).

2. In the screen that appears, choose what you want three presses of the Home button to activate. Now three presses with a single finger on the Home button provide you with the option you selected wherever you go in iPhone.

Use VoiceOver

After VoiceOver is turned on, you need to figure out how to use it. I won't kid you — using it is awkward at first, but you'll get the hang of it!

Here are the main onscreen gestures you should know how to use:

» **Tap an item to select it.** VoiceOver then speaks its name.

» **Double-tap the selected item.** This action activates the item.

» **Flick three fingers.** It takes three fingers to scroll around a page with VoiceOver turned on.

TIP

If tapping with two or three fingers seems difficult for you, try tapping with one finger from one hand and one or two from the other. When double- or triple-tapping, you have to perform these gestures as quickly as you can for them to work.

Table 9-1 provides additional gestures to help you use VoiceOver. If you want to use this feature often, I recommend the VoiceOver section of the iPhone online User Guide, which goes into great detail about using VoiceOver. You'll find the User Guide at https://support.apple.com/manuals/iphone. When there, just click on the model of iPhone or the version of iOS you have to read its manual. You can also get an iBooks version of the manual through that app in the iBooks Store.

TABLE 9-1   VoiceOver Gestures

Gesture	Effect
Flick right or left.	Select the next or preceding item.
Tap with two fingers.	Stop speaking the current item.
Flick two fingers up.	Read everything from the top of the screen.
Flick two fingers down.	Read everything from the current position.
Flick three fingers up or down.	Scroll one page at a time.
Flick three fingers right or left.	Go to the next or preceding page.
Tap three fingers.	Speak the scroll status (for example, line 20 of 100).
Flick four fingers up or down.	Go to the first or last element on a page.
Flick four fingers right or left.	Go to the next or preceding section (as on a web page).

TIP

Check out some of the settings for VoiceOver, including a choice for Braille, Language Rotor for making language choices, the ability to navigate images, and a setting to have iPhone speak notifications.

Several Vision features are simple on/off settings that you can turn on or off after you tap Settings ➪ General ➪ Accessibility:

» **Zoom:** The Zoom feature enlarges the contents displayed on the iPhone screen when you double-tap the screen with three fingers. The Zoom feature works almost everywhere in iPhone: in Photos, on web pages, on your Home screens, in your Mail, in Music, and in Videos — give it a try!

» **Magnifier:** Enable Magnifier to use your iPhone's built-in camera as a magnifying glass. Just triple-click the Home button to activate it (after you've turned the feature on, of course).

» **Display Accommodations:** Includes such features as

  • Color Filters (aids in case of color blindness)

  • Reduce White Point (helps reduce the intensity of bright colors)

- Invert Colors (which reverses colors on your screen so that white backgrounds are black and black text is white)

    The Invert Colors feature works well in some places and not so well in others. For example, in the Photos application, pictures appear almost as photo negatives (which is a really cool trick to try). Your Home screen image will likewise look a bit strange. And don't even think of playing a video with this feature turned on! However, if you need help reading text, White on Black can be useful in several apps.

» **Speech:** Options here include the ability to have your iPhone speak items you've selected or hear the content of an entire screen, highlight content as its spoken, and more.

» **Larger Text:** If having larger text in such apps as Contacts, Mail, and Notes would be helpful to you, you can turn on the Larger Text feature and choose the text size that works best for you.

» **Bold Text:** Turning on this setting restarts your iPhone (after asking you for permission to do so) and then causes text in various apps and in Settings to be bold.

» **Button Shapes:** This setting applies shapes to buttons so they're more easily distinguishable. For an example, check out the General button in the upper-left corner of the screen after you enable Button Shapes by toggling its switch to On. Turn it back off and notice the difference (shown in **Figure 9-6**).

» **Increase Contrast:** Use this setting to set up backgrounds in some areas of iPhone and apps with greater contrast, which should improve visibility.

» **Reduce Motion:** Tap this accessibility feature and then tap the On/Off setting to turn off the parallax effect, which causes the background of your Home screens to appear to float as you move the phone around.

» **On/Off Labels:** If you have trouble making out colors and therefore find it hard to tell when an On/Off setting is On (green) or Off (white), use this setting to add a circle to the right of a setting when it's off and a white vertical line to a setting when it's on.

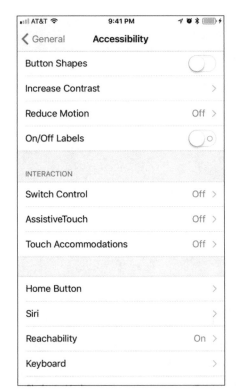
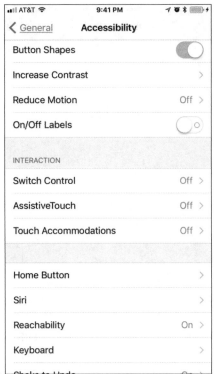

FIGURE 9-6

Use iPhone with Hearing Aids

If you have Bluetooth enabled or use another style of hearing aid, your iPhone may be able to detect it and work with its settings to improve sound on your phone calls. Follow these steps to connect your hearing aid to your iPhone.

1. Tap Settings on the Home screen, then tap General.

2. Tap Accessibility, then scroll down to the Hearing section and tap MFi (Made for iPhone) Hearing Aids. On the following screen, shown in **Figure 9-7,** your iPhone searches for hearing aid devices.

If you have a non-MFi hearing aid, add your hearing aid in Bluetooth settings. To do so, go to Settings ⇨ Bluetooth, make sure the Bluetooth toggle switch is On (green), and select your hearing aid in the list of devices.

TIP

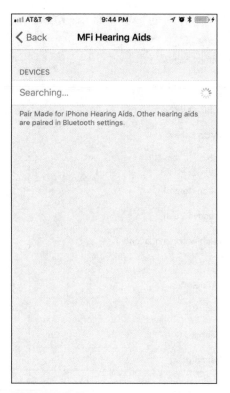

FIGURE 9-7

3. When your device appears, tap it.

4. Tap the Back button in the upper-left corner of the screen, scroll back down to the Hearing section (if you're not returned there), and tap Hearing Aid Compatibility to turn on a feature that could improve audio quality when you're using your hearing aid.

Adjust the Volume

Though individual apps (such as Music and Video) have their own volume settings, you can set your iPhone system volume for your ringer and alerts as well to help you better hear what's going on. Follow these steps:

1. Tap Settings on the Home screen and then tap Sounds.

In the Sounds settings, you can turn on or off the sounds that iPhone makes when certain events occur (such as receiving new Mail or Calendar alerts). These sounds are turned on by default.

2. In the Sounds settings that appear (see **Figure 9-8**), tap and drag the Ringer and Alerts slider to adjust the volume of these audible attention grabbers:

   - Drag to the right to increase the volume.

   - Drag to the left to lower the volume.

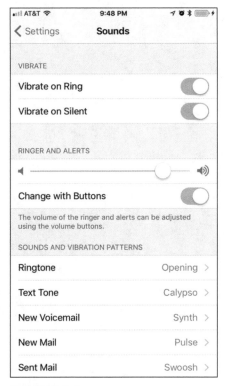

FIGURE 9-8

3. Press the Home button to return to the Home screen.

Even those with perfect hearing sometimes have trouble hearing a phone ring, especially in busy public places. Consider using the Vibrate settings in the Sounds settings to have your phone vibrate when a call is coming in.

Set Up Subtitles and Captioning

Closed captioning and subtitles help folks with hearing challenges enjoy entertainment and educational content. Follow these steps:

1. Tap Settings on the Home screen, tap General, and then tap Accessibility.

2. Scroll down to the Media section and tap Subtitles & Captioning.

3. On the following screen, shown in **Figure 9-9,** tap the On/Off switch to turn on Closed Captions + SDH (Subtitles for the Deaf and Hard of Hearing).

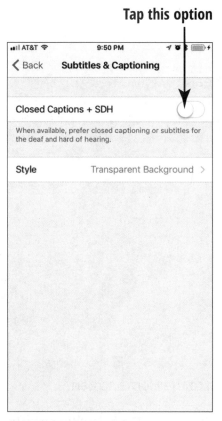

FIGURE 9-9

TIP

You can also tap Style and choose a text style for the captions. A neat video helps show you what your style will look like when the feature is in use.

4. Press the Home button to return to the Home screen.

Manage Other Hearing Settings

Several hearing accessibility settings are simple On/Off settings, including

» **Mono Audio:** Using the stereo effect in headphones or a headset breaks up sounds so that you hear a portion in one ear and a portion in the other ear. The purpose is to simulate the way your ears process sounds. If there is only one channel of sound, that sound is sent to both ears. However, if you're hard of hearing or deaf in one ear, you're hearing only a portion of the sound in your hearing ear, which can be frustrating. If you have such hearing challenges and want to use iPhone with a headset connected, you should turn on Mono Audio. When it's turned on, all sound is combined and distributed to both ears. You can use the slider below Mono Audio to direct more sound to the ear you hear best with.

» **TTY:** TTY is a symbol indicating teletype machine capabilities. The iPhone is compatible with teletype machines via the iPhone TTY Adapter, which can be purchased from Apple. The TTY option allows you to enable either Software TTY, Hardware TTY, or both. TTY is only available for your iPhone if your cell carrier supports it.

» **LED Flash for Alerts:** If you need a visual clue when an alert is spoken, turn this setting on.

» **Phone Noise Cancellation:** If you're annoyed at ambient noise when you make a call in public (or noisy private) settings, with an iPhone 5 or later, turn on the Phone Noise Cancellation feature. When you hold the phone to your ear during a call, this feature reduces background noise to some extent.

Turn On and Work with AssistiveTouch

If you have difficulty using buttons, the AssistiveTouch Control panel aids input using the touchscreen.

1. To turn on AssistiveTouch, tap Settings on the Home screen and then tap General and Accessibility.

2. In the Accessibility pane, scroll down and tap AssistiveTouch. In the pane that appears, tap the On/Off switch for AssistiveTouch to turn it on (see **Figure 9-10**). A gray square (called the AssistiveTouch Control panel) then appears on the right side of the screen; you'll see it on your iPhone's screen, but it doesn't display in screenshots, such as Figure 9-10. This square now appears in the same location in whatever apps you display on your iPhone, though you can move it around with your finger.

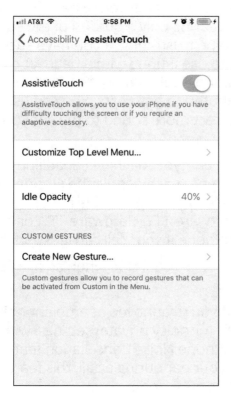

FIGURE 9-10

3. Tap the AssistiveTouch Control panel to display options, as shown in **Figure 9-11**. The panel includes Notifications and Control Center options.

FIGURE 9-11

4. You can tap Custom or Device on the panel to see additional choices, tap Siri to activate the personal assistant feature, tap Notifications or Control Center to display those panels, or press Home to go directly to the Home screen. After you've chosen an option, pressing the Home button takes you back to the Home screen.

Table 9-2 shows the major options available in the AssistiveTouch Control panel and their purpose.

TABLE 9-2   **AssistiveTouch Controls**

Control	Purpose
Siri	Activates the Siri feature, which allows you to speak questions and make requests of your iPhone.
Custom	Displays a set of gestures with only the Pinch gesture preset; you can tap any of the other blank squares to add your own favorite gestures.
Device	You can rotate the screen, lock the screen, turn the volume up or down, mute or unmute sound, or shake iPhone to undo an action using the presets in this option.
Home	Sends you to the Home screen.
Control Center	Open the Control Center common commands.
Notifications	Open Notifications with reminders, Calendar appointments, and so on.

Turn On Additional Physical and Motor Settings

Use these On/Off settings in the Accessibility settings to help you deal with how fast you tap and how you answer phone calls:

» **Home Button:** Sometimes if you have dexterity challenges, it's hard to double-press or triple-press the Home button fast enough to make an effect. Choose the Slow or Slowest option when you tap this setting to allow you a bit more time to make that second or third tap. Also, the Rest Finger to Open feature at the bottom of the screen is helpful by allowing you to simply rest your finger on the Home button to open your iPhone using Touch ID (if enabled), as opposed to needing to press the Home button.

» **Call Audio Routing:** If you prefer to use your speaker phone to receive incoming calls, or you typically use a headset with your phone that allows you to tap a button to receive a call, tap this option and then choose Headset or Speaker. Speakers and headsets can both provide a better hearing experience for many.

TIP

If you have certain adaptive accessories that allow you to control devices with head gestures, you can use them to control your iPhone, highlighting features in sequence and then selecting one. Use the Switch Control feature in the Accessibility settings to turn this mode on and make settings.

Focus Learning with Guided Access

Guided Access is a feature that you can use to limit a user's access to iPhone to a single app, and even limit access in that app to certain features. This feature is useful in several settings, ranging from a classroom, for use by someone with attention deficit disorder, and even to a public setting (such as a kiosk where you don't want users to be able to open other apps).

1. Tap Settings, then tap General.

2. Tap Accessibility, then scroll down and tap Guided Access; then, on the screen that follows (see **Figure 9-12**), tap Guided Access to turn the feature on.

3. Tap Passcode Settings, then tap Set Guided Access Passcode to activate a passcode so that those using an app can't return to the Home screen to access other apps.

4. In the Set Passcode dialog that appears (see **Figure 9-13**), enter a passcode using the numeric pad. Enter the number again when prompted.

5. Press the Home button and tap an app to open it.

6. Rapidly press the Home button three times. You're presented with an Options button along the bottom of the screen; tap the button to display these options:

   • **Sleep/Wake Button:** You can put your iPhone to sleep or wake it up with three presses of the Home button.

   • **Volume Buttons:** You can tap Always On or Always Off. If you don't want users to be able to adjust volume using the volume toggle on the side of the iPhone, for example, use this setting.

FIGURE 9-12

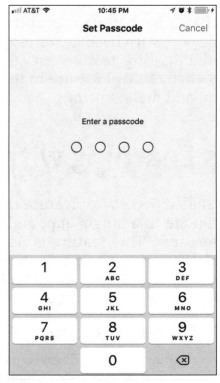

FIGURE 9-13

- **Motion:** Turn this setting off if you don't want users to move the iPhone around — for example, to play a race car driving game.

- **Keyboards:** Use this setting to prohibit people using this app from entering text using the keyboard.

- **Touch:** If you don't want users to be able to use the touchscreen, turn this off.

- **Time Limit:** Tap this and use settings that are displayed to set a time limit for the use of the app.

7. Tap Done to hide the options.

TIP

At this point, you can also use your finger to circle areas of the screen that you want to disable, such as a Store button in the Music app.

8. Press the Start button and then press the Home button three times. Enter your passcode, if you set one, and tap End.

9. Tap the Home button again to return to the Home screen.

One-Handed Keyboard

iOS 11 introduces a much-needed feature to make typing on the onscreen keyboard that much easier: the one-handed keyboard. For those with dexterity issues, or simply for those of us with smaller hands using the larger iPhones, this option allows the onscreen keyboard to "slide over" to one side or the other to better facilitate typing.

1. Open any app that uses the onscreen keyboard. I'm using Notes for this example.

2. With the onscreen keyboard displayed, tap-and-hold the Emoji (smiley face) or International (globe) icon to display the Keyboard Settings menu, seen in **Figure 9-14**.

Tap-and-hold here

FIGURE 9-14

3. At the bottom of the Keyboard Settings menu, tap either the left-sided keyboard icon or the right-sided keyboard icon to shift the keyboards keys in the desired direction.

4. Your keyboard will now appear either shifted to the left or right, as shown in **Figure 9-15**.

5. To quickly return to the standard keyboard, tap the white arrow to the left or right side of your shifted keyboard (its position depends on which side you shifted your keyboard).

 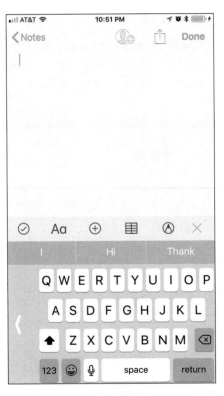

FIGURE 9-15

Chapter **10**

Conversing with Siri

O ne of the hottest features on iPhone is Siri, a personal assistant feature that responds to the commands you speak to your iPhone 4s or later. With Siri, you can ask for nearby restaurants, and a list appears. You can dictate your email messages rather than type them. You can open apps with a voice command or open the App Store. Calling your mother is as simple as saying, "Call Mom." Want to know the capital of Rhode Island? Just ask. Siri checks several online sources to answer questions ranging from the result of a mathematical equation to the next scheduled flight to Rome (Italy or Georgia). You can have Siri search photos and videos and locate what you need by date, location, or album name. Ask Siri to remind you about an app you're working in, such as Safari, Mail, or Notes at a later time so you can pick up where you left off.

You can also have Siri perform tasks, such as returning calls and controlling Music. Finally, you can even play music or have Siri identify tagged songs (songs that contain embedded information that identifies them by categories such as artist or genre of music) for you.

Siri has gained some other improvements with its newest incarnation. For example, you can hail a ride with Uber or Lyft, watch live TV just by saying "Watch ESPN" (or say another app you might use, such as CBS), find tagged photos, make payments with some third-party apps, and more.

Activate Siri

When you first go through the process of registering your phone, you'll see a screen similar to **Figure 10-1;** tap Get Started to begin making settings for your location, using iCloud, and so on, and at one point you will see the option to activate Siri. As you begin to use your phone, iPhone reminds you about using Siri by displaying a message.

TIP

Siri is available only on iPhone 4s and later with Internet access, and cellular data charges could apply when Siri checks online sources. In addition, Apple warns that available features may vary by area.

If you didn't activate Siri during the registration process, you can use Settings to turn Siri on by following these steps:

1. Tap the Settings icon on the Home screen.

2. Tap Siri (see **Figure 10-2**).

3. In the dialog in **Figure 10-3,** toggle the On/Off switch to On (green) to activate any or all of the following features:

- If you want to be able to activate Siri for hands-free use, toggle the Listen for "Hey Siri" switch to turn on the feature.

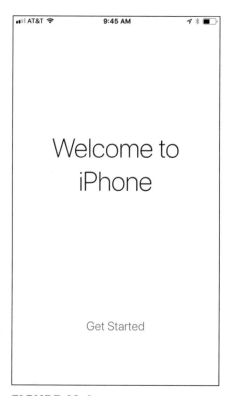

FIGURE 10-1

Tap here

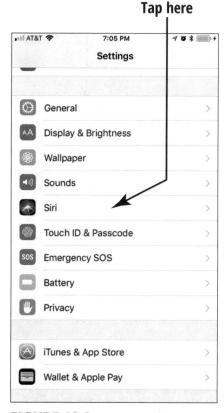

FIGURE 10-2

With this feature enabled, just say "Hey, Siri" and Siri opens up, ready for a command. In addition, with streaming voice recognition, Siri displays in text what it's hearing as you speak, so you can verify that it has understood you correctly. This streaming feature makes the process of interacting with Siri faster.

REMEMBER

iPhone models older than the 6s and 6s Plus must be plugged into an outlet, car, or computer to use the "Hey Siri" feature.

- Press Home for Siri requires you to press the Home button to activate Siri.

- Allow Siri When Locked allows you to use Siri even when the iPhone is locked.

4. If you want to change the language Siri uses, tap Language and choose a different language in the list that appears.

Toggle these options

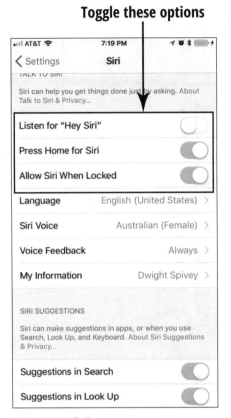

FIGURE 10-3

5. To change the nationality or gender of Siri's voice from American to British or Australian (for example), or from female to male, tap Siri Voice and make your selections.

6. Let Siri know about your contact information by tapping My Information and selecting yourself from your Contacts.

TIP

If you want Siri to verbally respond to your requests only when the iPhone isn't in your hands, tap Voice Feedback and choose Hands-Free Only. Here's how this setting works and why you might want to use it: In general, if you're holding your iPhone, you can read responses on the screen, so you might choose not to have your phone talk to you out loud. But if you're cooking dinner while helping your spouse make travel plans and want to speak requests for destinations and hear the answers rather than have to read them, Hands-Free is a useful setting.

Understand All That Siri Can Do

Siri allows you to interact by voice with many apps on your iPhone.

No matter what kind of action you want to perform, first press and hold the Home button until Siri opens.

You can pose questions or ask to do something like make a call or add an appointment to your calendar, for example. Siri can also search the Internet or use an informational service called Wolfram|Alpha to provide information on just about any topic.

Siri also checks with Wikipedia, Bing, and Twitter to get you the information you ask for. In addition, you can use Siri to tell iPhone to return a call, play your voice mail, open and search the App Store, or control Music playback.

Siri knows what app you're using, though you don't have to have that app open to make a request involving it. However, if you are in the Messages app, you can make a statement like "Tell Susan I'll be late," and Siri knows that you want to send a message. You can also ask Siri to remind you about what you're working on and Siri notes what you're working on, in which app, and reminds you about it at a later time you specify.

If you want to dictate text in an app like Notes, use the Dictation key on the onscreen keyboard to do so. See the task "Use Dictation," later in this chapter, for more about this feature.

Siri requires no preset structure for your questions; you can phrase things in several ways. For example, you might say, "Where am I?" to see a map of your current location, or you could say, "What is my current location?" or "What address is this?" and get the same results.

If you ask a question about, say, the weather, Siri responds to you both verbally and with text information (see **Figure 10-4**) or by opening a form, as with email, or by providing a graphic display for some items, such as maps. When a result appears, you can tap it to make a choice or open a related app.

Siri works with Phone, the App Store, Music, Messages, Reminders, Calendar, Maps, Mail, Weather, Stocks, Clock, Contacts, Notes, social media apps (such as Twitter), and Safari (see **Figure 10-5**). In the following tasks, I provide a quick guide to some of the most useful ways you can use Siri.

FIGURE 10-4

FIGURE 10-5

TIP

Siri now supports many different languages, so you can finally show off those language lessons you took in high school. Some languages supported include Chinese, Dutch, English, French, German, Italian, Spanish, Arabic, Danish, Finnish, Hebrew, Japanese, Korean, and more!

Get Suggestions

Siri anticipates your needs by making suggestions when you swipe from left to right on the initial Home screen and tap within the Search field at the top of the screen. Siri will list contacts you've communicated with recently, apps you've used, and nearby businesses, such as restaurants, gas stations, or coffee spots. If you tap on an app in the suggestions, it will open displaying the last viewed or listened to item.

Additionally, Siri lists news stories that may be of interest to you based on items you've viewed before.

Call Contacts

First, make sure that the person you want to call is entered in your Contacts app and include that person's phone number in his or her record. If you want to call somebody by stating your relationship to her, such as "Call sister," be sure to enter that relationship in the Add Related Name field in her contact record. Also make sure that the settings for Siri (refer to **Figure 10-3**) include your own contact name in the My Information field. (See Chapter 6 for more about creating contact records.) Follow these steps:

1. Press and hold the Home button (or say "Hey Siri," if you're using that feature) until Siri appears.

2. Speak a command, such as "Call Harold Smith," "Return Joe's call," or "Call Mom." If you want to make a FaceTime call, you can say "FaceTime Mom."

3. If you have two contacts who might match a spoken name, Siri responds with a list of possible matches (see **Figure 10-6**). Tap one in the list or state the correct contact's name to proceed.

4. The call is placed. To end the call before it completes, press the Home button, then tap End.

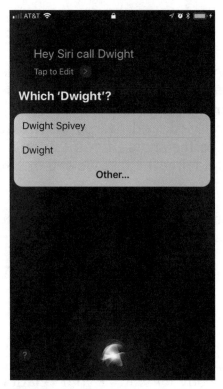

FIGURE 10-6

TIP

To cancel any spoken request, you have three options: Say "Cancel," tap the Siri button on the Siri screen (looks like swirling bands of light), or press the Home button. If you're using a headset or Blue-tooth device, tap the End button on the device.

You can also access your voice mail using Siri. Just press and hold the Home button until Siri activates, then say something like "Check voice mail." Siri responds by telling you whether you have a new voice mail message and displays a list of any new messages. Press one, then tap the Play button to play it back. If you want to get rid of it, tap Delete. It's that simple.

Create Reminders and Alerts

You can also use Siri with the Reminders app.

1. To create a reminder or alert, press and hold the Home button, then speak a command, such as "Remind me to call Dad on Thursday at 10 a.m." or "Wake me up tomorrow at 6:15 a.m."

2. A preview of the reminder or alert is displayed (see **Figure 10-7**). Tell Siri to Cancel or Remove if you change your mind.

FIGURE 10-7

3. If you want a reminder ahead of the event that you created, activate Siri and speak a command, such as "Remind me tonight about the play on Thursday at 8 p.m." A second reminder is created, which you can confirm or cancel if you change your mind.

Add Tasks to Your Calendar

You can also set up events on your Calendar using Siri.

1. Press and hold the Home button, then speak a phrase, such as "Set up meeting at 3 p.m. tomorrow."

2. Siri sets up the appointment (see **Figure 10-8**) and asks whether you want to schedule the new appointment. You can say, "Confirm" or "Cancel" at that point, or tap the Confirm or Cancel button.

FIGURE 10-8

Play Music

You can use Siri to play music from the Music app.

1. Press and hold the Home button until Siri appears.

2. To play music, speak a command, such as "Play music" or "Play Jazz radio station" to play a specific song, album, or radio station, as seen in **Figure 10-9.**

FIGURE 10-9

You can use the integration of Siri with Shazam, a music identifier app, to identify tagged music.

1. First, when you're near an audio source playing music, press and hold the Home button to activate Siri.

2. Ask Siri a question, such as "What music is playing?" or "What's this song?"

3. Siri listens for a bit and if Siri recognizes the song, it shows you the song name, artist, any other available information, and the ability to purchase the music in the iTunes Store.

TIP

If you're listening to music or a podcast with earphones plugged in, and stop midstream, the next time you plug in earphones, Siri recognizes that you might want to continue with the same item.

Get Directions

You can use the Maps app and Siri to find your current location, get directions, find nearby businesses (such as restaurants or a bank), or get a map of another location. Be sure to turn on Location Services to allow Siri to know your current location (go to Settings and tap Privacy⇨Location Services; make sure Location Services is on and that Siri & Dictation is turned on further down in these settings).

Here are some of the commands that you can try to get directions or a list of nearby businesses:

» **"Where am I?":** Displays a map of your current location.

» **"Where is Auburn, Alabama?":** Displays a map of that city, as shown in **Figure 10-10**.

FIGURE 10-10

- » **"Find pizza restaurants.":** Displays a list of restaurants near your current location; tap one to display a map of its location.

- » **"Find Bank of America.":** Displays a map with the location of the indicated business (or in some cases, several nearby locations, such as a bank branch and all ATMs).

- » **"Get directions to the Empire State Building.":** Loads a map with a route drawn and provides a narration of directions to the site from your current location.

After a location is displayed on a map, tap the Information button on the location's label to view its address, phone number, and website address, if available.

Ask for Facts

Wolfram|Alpha is a self-professed online computational knowledge engine. That means that it's more than a search engine because it provides specific information about a search term rather than multiple search results. If you want facts without having to spend time browsing websites to find those facts, Wolfram|Alpha is a very good resource.

Siri uses Wolfram|Alpha and such sources as Wikipedia and Bing to look up facts in response to questions, such as "What is the capital of Kansas?", "What is the square root of 2,300?", or "How large is Mars?" Just press and hold the Home button and ask your question; Siri consults its resources and returns a set of relevant facts.

You can also get information about other things, such as the weather, stocks, or the time. Just say a phrase like one of these to get what you need:

- » **"What is the weather?":** This shows the weather report for your current location. If you want weather in another location, just specify the location in your question.

>> **"What is the price of Apple stock?":** Siri tells you the current price of the stock or the price of the stock when the stock market last closed.

>> **"How hot is the sun?":** Siri tells you the temperature of the sun, and even breaks it down into various unit conversions (see **Figure 10-11**).

FIGURE 10-11

Search the Web

Although Siri can use its resources to respond to specific requests such as "Who is the Queen of England?", more general requests for information will cause Siri to search further on the web. Siri can also search Twitter for comments related to your search.

For example, if you speak a phrase, such as "Find a website about birds" or "Find information about the World Series," Siri can respond in a couple of ways. The app can simply display a list of search results by using the default search engine specified in your settings for Safari or by suggesting, "If you like, I can search the web for such and such." In the first instance, just tap a result to go to that website. In the second instance, you can confirm that you want to search the web or cancel.

Send Email, Messages, or Tweets

You can create an email or an instant message using Siri and existing contacts. For example, if you say, "Email John Michael Bassett," a form opens that is already addressed to that stored contact. Siri asks for a subject, then a message. Speak your message contents, then say, "Send" to speed your message on its way.

Siri also works with messaging apps, such as Messages. If you have the Messages app open and you say, "Tell Tori I'll call soon," Siri creates a message for you to approve and send.

TIP

Siri can also tweet, connect with Flickr and Vimeo, and post to Facebook. Go to Settings and turn on Flickr, Vimeo, Twitter, or Facebook support and provide your account information. Now you can say such things to Siri as "Post Tweet" or "Post to Facebook." Siri asks what you want to say, lets you review it, and posts it.

Use Dictation

Text entry isn't Siri's strong point. Instead, you can use the Dictation key that appears with a microphone symbol on the onscreen keyboard (see **Figure 10-12**) to speak text rather than type it. This feature is called Dictation.

1. Go to any app where you enter text, such as Notes or Mail, and tap in the document or form. The onscreen keyboard appears.

2. Tap the Dictation key on the keyboard and speak your text.

Dictation Key

FIGURE 10-12

3. To end the dictation, tap Done.

TIP

When you finish speaking text, you can use the keyboard to make edits to the text Siri entered, although as voice recognition programs go, Dictation is pretty darn accurate. If a word sports a blue under-line, which means there may be an error, you can tap to select and make edits to it.

Translate Words and Phrases

One of Siri's best new features in iOS 11 is the ability to translate English into Mandarin, French, German, Italian, or Spanish. That's great if you're on a road trip and don't speak the local language.

Apple plans to expand this feature. Its potential is exciting.

To translate text between languages, follow these steps:

1. Activate Siri.

2. Say "translate," followed by your phrase and the language of your choice, as shown in **Figure 10-13**.

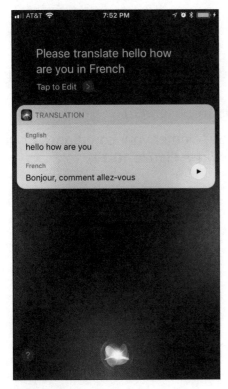

FIGURE 10-13

Siri displays the translation on your screen and speaks it.

Tap the Play button to the left of the translation to hear Siri speak it again.

Type Your Commands or Questions

Type to Siri is another great addition to Siri that comes with iOS 11. This feature allows you to type commands or inquiries instead of speaking.

TIP

This is great if you have difficulty speaking, or when you're in a situation where you can't speak.

To enable Type to Siri, follow these steps:

1. Go to General ⇨ Accessibility.

2. Tap Siri.

3. Toggle the switch for Type to Siri to On (green).

Now, a keyboard appears for you to enter your commands or questions when you activate Siri (shown in **Figure 10-14**).

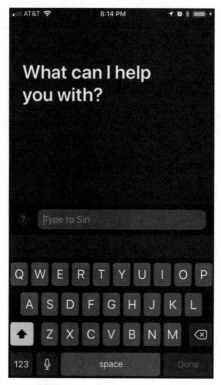

FIGURE 10-14

TIP

Tap the Play button to the left of the translation to hear Siri speak it again.

Get Helpful Tips

I know you're going to have a wonderful time learning the ins and outs of Siri, but before I close this chapter, here are some tips to get you going:

» **If Siri doesn't understand you:** Siri has vastly improved at recognizing voices, but it isn't perfect. When you speak a command and Siri displays what it thought you said, if it misses the mark, you have a few options. To correct a request you've made, you can tap Tap to Edit under the command Siri heard and edit the question by typing or tapping the Dictation key on the onscreen keyboard and dictating the correct information. If a word is underlined in blue, it's a possible error. Tap the word, then tap an alternative that Siri suggests. You can also simply speak to Siri and say something like "I meant Sri Lanka" or "No, send it to Sally." If even corrections aren't working, you may need to restart your phone to reset the Siri software.

» **Headsets and earphones:** If you're using iPhone earphones or a Bluetooth headset to activate Siri, instead of pressing the Home button, press and hold the center button (the little button on the headset that starts and stops a call).

» **Using Find My Friends:** There is a free app you can download from the App Store called Find My Friends that, in addition to allowing you to use it with keyboard input, allows you to ask Siri to locate your friends geographically.

» **Getting help:** To get help with Siri features, just press and hold the Home button and ask Siri, "What can you do?"

» **Joking around:** If you need a good laugh, ask Siri to tell you a joke. It has quite the sense of humor.

3

Exploring the Internet

Chapter **11**

Browsing with Safari

Getting on the Internet with your iPhone is easy, by using its Wi-Fi or 3G/4G (LTE) capabilities. After you're online, the built-in browser (software that helps you navigate the Internet's contents), Safari, is your ticket to a wide world of information, entertainment, education, and more. Safari will look familiar to you if you've used it on a PC or Mac computer, though the way you move around by using the iPhone touchscreen may be new to you. If you've never used Safari, this chapter takes you by the hand and shows you all the basics of making Safari work for you.

In this chapter, you see how to go online with your iPhone. You see how to navigate among web pages and use iCloud tabs to share your browsing experience between devices. Along the way, you see how to place a bookmark for a favorite site or place a web clip on your Home screen. You can also view your browsing history, save online images to your Photo Library, post photos to sites from within Safari, or email or tweet a link to a friend. You also explore Safari's Reader and Reading List features and learn how to keep yourself safer while online by using private browsing. Finally, you review the simple steps involved in printing what you find online.

Connect to the Internet

How you connect to the Internet depends on which connections are available:

>> You can connect to the Internet via a Wi-Fi network. You can set up this type of network in your own home using your computer and some equipment from your Internet provider. You can also connect over public Wi-Fi networks, referred to as *hotspots*.

You'll probably be surprised to discover how many hotspots your town or city has. Look for Internet cafés, coffee shops, hotels, libraries, and transportation centers (such as airports or bus stations). Many of these businesses display signs alerting you to their free Wi-Fi.

>> You can use the paid data network provided by AT&T, Sprint, T-Mobile, Verizon, or most any other cellular provider, to connect by using 3G or 4G (LTE) from just about anywhere you can get cellphone coverage through a cellular network.

To enable 3G/4G (LTE) data, tap Settings, then Cellular. Toggle the switch (just tap it) to turn on the Cellular Data setting.

WARNING

Browsing the Internet using a 3G/4G (LTE) connection can eat up your data plan allotment quickly if your plan doesn't include unlimited data access. If you think you'll often use the Internet with your iPhone away from a Wi-Fi connection, double-check your data allotment with your cellular provider.

To connect to a Wi-Fi network, you have to complete a few steps:

1. Tap Settings on the Home screen, then tap Wi-Fi.

2. Be sure that Wi-Fi is set to On (green), then choose a network to connect to by tapping it.

Network names should appear automatically when you're in range of them. When you're in range of a public hotspot, if access to several nearby networks is available, you may see a message asking you to tap a network name to select it. After you select one (or if only one network is available), you may see a message asking for your password. Ask the owner of the hotspot (for example, a hotel desk clerk or business owner) for this password, or enter your own network password if you're connecting to your home network.

TIP

Free public Wi-Fi networks usually don't require passwords, or the password is posted prominently for all to see. (If you can't find the password, don't be shy to ask someone.)

3. Tap the Join button when prompted. Once done, you're connected! Your iPhone will now recognize the network and connect without repeatedly entering the password.

WARNING

After you connect to public Wi–Fi, someone else can track your online activities because these are unsecured networks. Avoid accessing financial accounts, or sending emails with sensitive information in them, when connected to a public hotspot.

Explore Safari

1. After you're connected to a network, tap Safari on the Dock at the bottom of the Home screen. Safari opens, probably displaying the Apple iPhone Home page the first time you go online (see **Figure 11-1**).

2. Put two fingers together on the screen and spread them apart to expand the view (also known as zooming in). Double-tap the screen with a single finger to restore the default view size.

TIP

Using your fingers on the screen to enlarge or reduce the size of a web page allows you to view what's displayed at various sizes, giving you more flexibility than the double-tap method.

Address/Search field

Status bar

Next button

Previous button

Share button

Show/Hide Tabs button

Bookmarks button

FIGURE 11-1

3. Put your finger on the screen and flick upward to scroll down on the page.

4. To return to the top of the web page, put your finger on the screen and drag downward or tap the Status bar at the very top of the screen twice.

TIP

When you zoom in, you have more control by using two fingers to drag from left to right or from top to bottom on the screen. When you zoom out, one finger works fine for making these gestures.

Navigate among Web Pages

1. Tap in the Address field just under the Status bar. The onscreen keyboard appears (see **Figure 11-2**).

← Delete key

Go key

FIGURE 11-2

2. Enter a web address; for example, you can go to www.dummies.com.

TIP

By default, AutoFill is turned on in iPhone, causing entries you make in fields, such as the Address field and password fields, to automatically display possible matching entries.

TIP

You can turn off AutoFill by using iPhone Settings for Safari.

3. Tap the Go key on the keyboard (refer to **Figure 11-2**). The website appears.

- If a page doesn't display properly, tap the Reload button at the right end of the Address field.

- If Safari is loading a web page and you change your mind about viewing the page, you can stop loading the page. Tap Cancel (looks like an X), which appears at the right end of the Address field during this process, to stop loading the page.

4. Tap the Previous button (looks like <) to go to the last page you displayed.

5. Tap the Next button (looks like >) to go forward to the page you just backed up from.

6. To follow a link to another web page (links are typically indicated by colored text or graphics), tap the link with your finger.

TIP

To view the destination web address of the link before you tap it, just touch and hold the link; a menu appears that displays the address at the top, as shown in **Figure 11-3**.

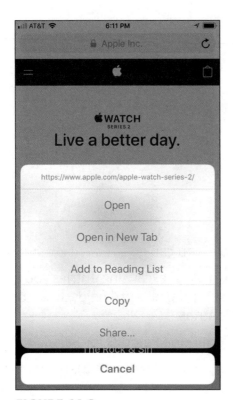

FIGURE 11-3

Apple QuickType supports predictive text in the onscreen keyboard. This feature adds the capability for iPhone to spot what you probably intend to type from text you've already entered and suggests it to save you time typing.

TIP

Use Tabbed Browsing

Tabbed browsing is a feature that allows you to have several websites open at one time so that you can move easily among those sites.

1. With Safari open and a web page already displaying, tap the Show/Hide Tabs button in the bottom-right corner (refer to **Figure 11-1**). The new Tab view appears.

2. To add a new page (meaning that you're opening a new website), tap the New Page button (shaped like a plus [+] symbol) in the lower middle of the screen (see **Figure 11-4**). A page with your favorite sites and an address bar appears.

You can get to the same new page by simply tapping in the address bar from any site.

TIP

3. Tap in the Address field and use the onscreen keyboard to enter the web address for the website you want to open. Tap the Go key. The website opens on the page.

Repeat Steps 1 to 3 to open as many new web pages as you'd like.

TIP

4. You can now switch among open sites by tapping outside the keyboard to close it and tapping the Show/Hide Tabs button and scrolling among recent sites. Find the one you want, then tap it.

You can easily rearrange sites in the tabs window. Just touch-and-hold the tab you want to move, then drag it up or down the list until it's in the spot you'd like it to be (the other sites in the window politely move to make room). To drop it in the new location, simply remove your finger from the screen.

TIP

5. To delete a tab, tap the Show/Hide Tabs button, scroll to locate the tab, then tap the Close button in the upper-left corner of the tab (looks like an X; it may be difficult to see on some sites, but trust me, it's there).

New Page button

FIGURE 11-4

View Browsing History

As you move around the web, your browser keeps a record of your browsing history. This record can be handy when you want to visit a site that you viewed previously but whose address you've now forgotten.

1. With Safari open, tap the Bookmarks button.

TIP

After you master the use of the Bookmarks button options, you might prefer a shortcut to view your History list. Tap and hold the Previous button at the bottom left on any screen, and your browsing history for the current session appears. You can also tap and hold the Next button to look at sites you backtracked from.

2. On the menu shown in **Figure 11-5,** tap the History tab (looks like a clock).

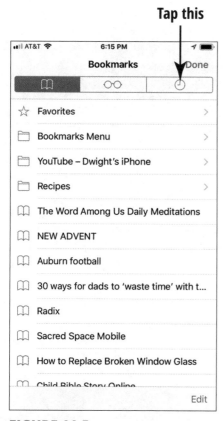

FIGURE 11-5

3. In the History list that appears (see **Figure 11-6**), tap a site to navigate to it. Tap Done to leave History and return to browsing.

TIP

To clear the history, tap the Clear button (refer to **Figure 11-6**) and on the screen that appears, tap an option: The Last Hour, Today, Today and yesterday, or All time. This button is useful when you don't want your spouse or grandchildren to see where you've been browsing for anniversary, birthday, or holiday presents!

Clear button

FIGURE 11-6

Search the Web

If you don't know the address of the site that you want to visit (or you want to research a topic or find other information online), get acquainted with Safari's Search feature on iPhone. By default, Safari uses the Google search engine.

1. With Safari open, tap in the Address field (refer to **Figure 11-1**). The onscreen keyboard appears.

TIP

To change your default search engine from Google to Yahoo!, Bing, or DuckDuckGo, from the Home screen, tap Settings, tap Safari, then tap Search Engine. Tap Yahoo!, Bing, or DuckDuckGo, and your default search engine changes.

2. Enter a search term. With recent versions of Safari, the search term can be a topic or a web address because of what's called the Unified smart search field. You can tap one of the suggested sites or complete your entry and tap the Go key (see **Figure 11-7**) on your keyboard.

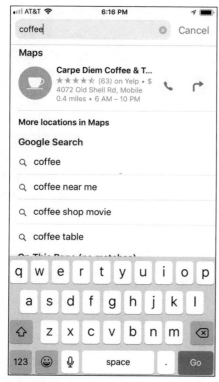

FIGURE 11-7

3. In the search results that are displayed, tap a link to visit that site.

Add and Use Bookmarks

Bookmarks are a way to save favorite sites so that you can easily visit them again.

TIP

1. With a site open that you want to bookmark, tap the Share button.

   If you want to sync your bookmarks on your iPhone browser, go to Settings on iPhone and make sure that iCloud is set to sync with Safari.

2. On the menu that appears (see **Figure 11-8**), tap Add Bookmark.

FIGURE 11-8

3. In the Add Bookmark dialog, shown in **Figure 11-9,** edit the name of the bookmark if you want. Tap the name of the site and use the onscreen keyboard to edit its name.

4. Tap the Save button in the upper-right corner. The item is saved to your Favorites by default.

5. To go to the bookmark, tap the Bookmarks button.

6. On the Bookmarks menu that appears (see **Figure 11-10**), if you saved a site to a folder, tap to open the folder, then tap the book-marked site that you want to visit.

FIGURE 11-9

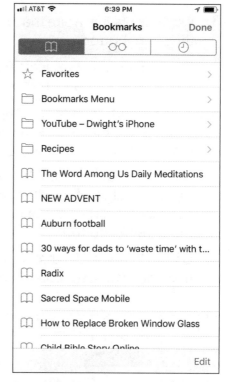

FIGURE 11-10

TIP

When you tap the Bookmarks button, you can tap Edit in the lower-right corner, then use the New Folder option (in the lower-left corner) to create folders to organize your bookmarks or folders. When you next add a bookmark, you can then choose, from the dialog that appears, any folder to which you want to add the new bookmark.

Save Links and Web Pages to Safari Reading List

The Safari Reading List provides a way to save content that you want to read at a later time so that you can easily call up that content again. You essentially save the content rather than a web page address, which allows you to read the content even when you're offline. You can scroll from one item to the next easily.

1. While displaying a site that you want to add to your Reading List, tap the Share button.

2. On the menu that appears (refer to **Figure 11-8**), tap the Add to Reading List button. The site is added to your Reading List.

3. To view your Reading List, tap the Bookmarks button, then tap the Reading List tab (the middle tab with the eyeglasses icon near the top of the page).

TIP

   If you want to see both the Reading List material you've read and the material you haven't read, tap the Show Unread button in the bottom-left corner of the Reading List. To see all reading material, tap the Show All button.

4. On the Reading List that appears (see **Figure 11-11**), tap the content that you want to revisit and resume reading.

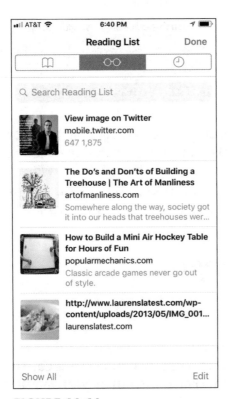

FIGURE 11-11

TIP

To delete an item, with the Reading List displaying, swipe right to left on an item; a Delete button appears. Tap this button to delete the item from the Reading List. To save an item for offline (when you aren't connected to the Internet) reading, tap the Save Offline button when you swipe.

Enjoy Reading More with Safari Reader

The Safari Reader feature gives you an e-reader type of experience right within your browser, removing other stories and links as well as those distracting advertisements.

When you're on a site where you're reading content (such as an article), Safari displays a Reader button on the left side of the Address field for sites that support this feature (see **Figure 11-12**).

1. Tap the Reader button. The content appears in a reader format (see **Figure 11-13**).

2. Scroll down the page. The entire content is contained in this one long page.

3. When you finish reading the material, just tap the Reader button again to leave that view.

TIP

Tap the small/large letter A button at the top right of the Address field to adjust the background color, font, and font size for the article.

Reader button

FIGURE 11-12

FIGURE 11-13

Add Web Clips to the Home Screen

The Web Clips feature allows you to save a website as an icon on your Home screen so that you can go to the site at any time with one tap.

1. With Safari open and displaying the site you want to add, tap the Share button.

2. On the menu that appears (refer to **Figure 11-8**), tap Add to Home Screen (you may have to swipe the menu from right to left to find the button).

3. In the Add to Home dialog that appears (see **Figure 11-14**), you can edit the name of the site to be more descriptive, if you like. To do so, tap the name of the site and use the onscreen keyboard to edit its name.

FIGURE 11-14

4. Tap the Add button in the upper right. The site is added to your Home screen.

TIP

You can have from 11 to 15 Home screens on your iPhone (depending on the model) to accommodate all the web clips you create and apps you download. (There is a limit to how many items will fit on these screens; however, you can place up to 135 apps in folders on Home screens, and up to 24 folders per Home screen.)

Save an Image to Your Photo Library

1. Display a web page that contains an image you want to copy.

2. Tap and hold the image.

   The menu shown in **Figure 11-15** appears.

Some websites are set up to prevent you from copying images on them, or they display a pop-up stating that the contents on the site are copyrighted and shouldn't be copied.

3. Tap the Save Image option (refer to **Figure 11-15**). The image is saved to your Camera Roll.

Tap this

FIGURE 11-15

Be careful about copying images from the Internet and using them for business or promotional activities. Most images are copyrighted, and you may violate the copyright even if you simply use an image in (say) a brochure for your association or a flyer for your community group. Note that some search engines' advanced search settings offer the option of browsing only for images that aren't copyrighted.

Send a Link

If you find a great site that you want to share, you can easily send a link in a variety of ways (via Messages, Mail, Twitter, Facebook, or even saving a link to Reminders or Notes).

1. With Safari open and the site that you want to share displaying, tap the Share button.

2. On the menu that appears (refer to **Figure 11-8**), tap the method you want to use for sharing the link (I use Messages for this example).

3. On the message form that appears (see **Figure 11-16**), enter a recipient in the To field.

FIGURE 11-16

4. Tap the Send button; the message is sent.

Make Privacy Settings

Apple has provided some privacy settings for Safari that you should consider using.

Private Browsing automatically stops Safari from using AutoFill to save information used to complete certain entries as you type, and erases some browsing history information. This feature can keep your online activities more private. To enable Private Browsing, tap the Show/Hide Tabs button (refer to **Figure 11-1**), then tap Private in the lower-left corner; you're now in Private Browsing Mode (as illustrated in **Figure 11-17**). Tap the Private button in the lower-left corner again to disable Private Browsing.

FIGURE 11-17

Cookies are small files that document your browsing history so that you can be recognized by a site the next time you go to or move within that site. Cross-site tracking is a technique used by some sites to collect your data with cookies, whether you've directly visited that site or not. Safari in iOS 11 provides a new feature called Prevent Cross-Site Tracking to stop just this sort of activity. Go to Settings from the Home screen; in Safari, toggle the Prevent Cross-Site Tracking switch to On (green). A cousin setting is the Block All Cookies option; it can be found directly under the Prevent Cross-Site Tracking option.

WARNING Blocking all cookies keep some websites from functioning properly. If you can't use a website the way it's intended, trying disabling the Block All Cookies option (if it's enabled).

Toggle the Ask Websites Not To Track Me switch in Safari settings to turn on the Do Not Track feature (see **Figure 11-18**). This setting stops some sites from tracking your online activities, but no privacy setting in a browser completely hides all of your Internet activities.

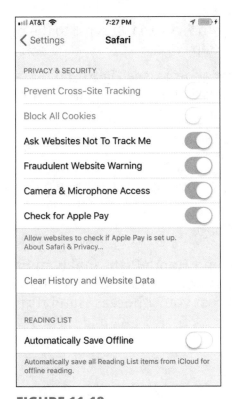

FIGURE 11-18

TIP

You can also tap the Clear History and Website Data option (refer to **Figure 11-18**) to manually clear your browsing history, saved cookies, and other data.

Print a Web Page

If you have a wireless printer that supports Apple's AirPrint technology, you can print web content using a wireless connection.

1. With Safari open and the site that you want to print displaying, tap the Share button.

TIP

If you don't have an AirPrint-compatible wireless printer or don't want to use an app to help you print wirelessly, just email a link to the web page to yourself, open the link on your computer, and print from there.

2. On the menu that appears (refer to **Figure 11-8**), scroll to the right in the bottom row of buttons, then tap Print.

3. In the Printer Options dialog that appears (see **Figure 11-19**), tap Select Printer. In the list of printers that appears, tap the name of your wireless printer.

4. Tap either the plus or minus button in the Copy field to adjust the number of copies to print.

If your printer supports two-sided printing, you'll also see a Double-Sided On/Off switch.

5. Tap Print to print the displayed page.

TIP

The Mac applications Printopia and HandyPrint make any shared or network printer on your home network visible to your iPhone. Printopia has more features, but will cost you, whereas HandyPrint is free.

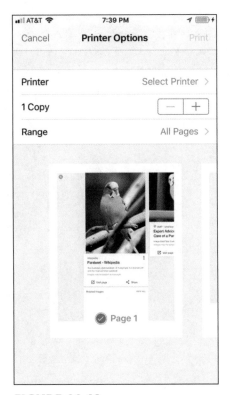

FIGURE 11-19

Understand iCloud Tabs

The iCloud Tabs feature allows you to access all browsing history among your different devices from any device. If you begin to research a project on your iPad before you leave home, you can then pick up where you left off as you sit in a waiting room with your iPhone.

1. Tap Settings, then tap your Apple ID (at the top of the screen); swipe down, then check to make sure that the iPhone is using the same iCloud account as your other devices.

2. Open Safari on another device and tap the Show/Hide Tabs button. Scroll down to see a list of every device using your iCloud account.

   All items in your iPhone's browsing history are displayed on the other devices.

- » Read, reply to, or forward email
- » Create, format, and send emails
- » Search email
- » Mark or flag email
- » Create events with email contents
- » Delete and organize email
- » Create a VIP list

Chapter **12**

Working with Email in Mail

Staying in touch with others by using email is a great way to use your iPhone. You can access an existing account using the handy Mail app supplied with your iPhone or sign in to your email account using the Safari browser. In this chapter, you take a look at using Mail, which involves adding an existing email account by way of Settings. Then you can use Mail to write, format, retrieve, and forward messages from that account.

Mail offers the capability to mark the messages you've read, delete messages, and organize your messages in a small set of folders, as well as use a handy search feature. You can create a VIP list so that you're notified when that special person sends you an email.

In this chapter, you read all about Mail and its various features.

Add an Email Account

You can add one or more email accounts, including the email account associated with your iCloud account, using iPhone Settings. If you have an iCloud, Microsoft Exchange (often used for business accounts), Gmail, Yahoo!, AOL, or Outlook.com (this includes Microsoft accounts from Live, Hotmail, and so on) account, iPhone pretty much automates the setup.

1. To set up iPhone to retrieve messages from your email account at one of these popular providers, first tap the Settings icon on the Home screen.

2. In Settings, tap Accounts & Passwords. The screen shown in **Figure 12-1** appears.

3. Tap Add Accounts, found under the Accounts section. The options shown in **Figure 12-2** appear.

Tap here

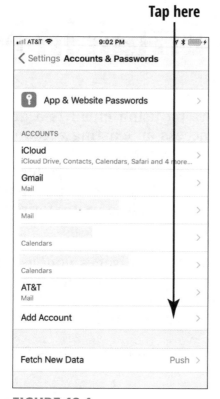

FIGURE 12-1   **FIGURE 12-2**

4. Tap iCloud, Google, Yahoo!, AOL, Exchange, or Outlook.com. Enter your account information in the form that appears and tap Sign In, or, for AOL and Outlook accounts, tap Next.

5. After iPhone takes a moment to verify your account information, on the next screen (shown in **Figure 12-3**), you can tap any On/Off switch to have services from that account synced with iPhone.

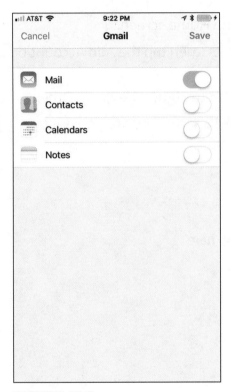

FIGURE 12-3

6. When you're done, tap Save. The account is saved, and you can now open it using Mail.

Manually Set Up an Email Account

You can also set up most popular email accounts, such as those available through Earthlink or a cable provider's service, by obtaining the host name from the provider. To set up an existing account with a provider other than iCloud, Gmail (Google), Yahoo!, AOL, Exchange, or Outlook.com, you enter the account settings yourself.

1. First, tap the Settings icon on the Home screen.

2. In Settings, tap Mail, tap Accounts, then tap the Add Account button (refer to **Figure 12-1**).

3. On the screen that appears (refer to **Figure 12-2**), tap Other.

4. On the screen shown in **Figure 12-4**, tap Add Mail Account.

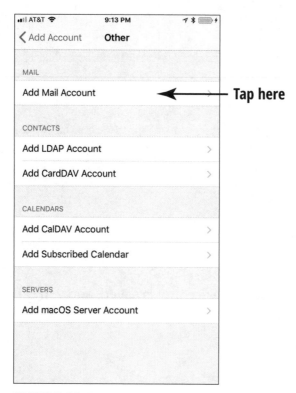

FIGURE 12-4

5. In the form that appears, enter your name and an account email address, password, and description, then tap Next. iPhone takes a moment to verify your account, then returns you to the Mail, Contacts, Calendars page, with your new account displayed.

iPhone will probably add the outgoing mail server (SMTP) information for you. If it doesn't, you may have to enter it yourself. If you have a less mainstream email service, you may have to enter the mail server protocol (POP3 or IMAP — ask your provider for this information) and your password.

6. To make sure that the Account field is set to On for receiving email, tap the account name. In the dialog that appears, toggle the On/Off switch for the Mail field to On (green), then tap the Accounts button to return to Mail settings. You can now access the account through iPhone's Mail app.

If you turn on Calendars in the Mail account settings, any information that you've put into your calendar in that email account is brought over into the Calendar app on your iPhone (discussed in more detail in Chapter 23).

Open Mail and Read Messages

1. Tap the Mail app icon located on the Home screen (see **Figure 12-5**). A red circle on the icon, called a badge, indicates the number of unread emails in your Inbox.

2. In the Mail app (see **Figure 12-6**), tap the Inbox whose contents you want to display.

3. Tap a message to read it. It opens (see **Figure 12-7**).

The 3D Touch feature allows you to preview an email before you open it. Simply press lightly to select the message, press with medium pressure to preview it, and press a bit harder to open the message.

4. If you need to scroll to see the entire message, just place your finger on the screen and flick upward to scroll down. You can swipe right while reading a message to open the Inbox's list of messages, then swipe right again to return to your list of mailboxes.

Tap the Mail app

FIGURE 12-5

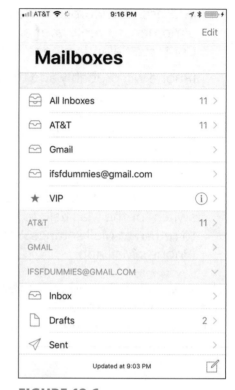

FIGURE 12-6

TIP

You can tap the Next or Previous buttons (top-right corner of the message) to move to the next or previous message in the Inbox or tap All Inboxes in the top-left corner to return to your Inbox.

Email messages that you haven't read are marked with a blue circle in your Inbox. After you read a message, the blue circle disappears. You can mark a read message as unread to help remind you to read it again later. With the inbox displayed, swipe to the right (starting your swipe just a little in from the edge of the screen) on a message, then tap Unread. If you swipe quickly to the right you don't need to tap, it will just mark as unread automatically.

If you have a Plus iPhone model (iPhone 8 Plus, for example) and you hold it horizontally, you will view both the Inbox and currently selected message. This is because the larger screen can accommodate more content, and such apps as Mail and Weather take advantage of this.

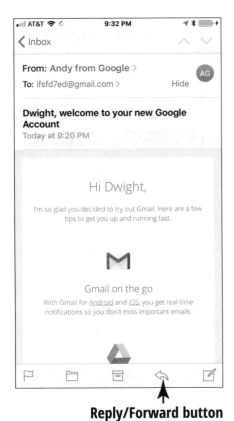

Reply/Forward button

FIGURE 12-7

TIP

To escape your email now (or to avoid having messages retrieved while you're at a public Wi-Fi hotspot), you can stop retrieval of data including email by tapping Settings, Cellular, then the On/Off switch on the Cellular Data option. Now you'll get data on your device only if you're logged in to a Wi-Fi network.

Reply To or Forward Email

1. With an email message open, tap the Reply/Forward button, which looks like a left-facing arrow (refer to **Figure 12-7**). Then tap Reply, Reply All (available if there are multiple recipients), or Forward in the menu that appears (see **Figure 12-8**).

2. In the new email message that appears (see **Figure 12-9**), tap in the To field and enter another addressee if you like (you have to do this if you're forwarding); next, tap in the message body and enter a message (see **Figure 12-10**).

FIGURE 12-8

FIGURE 12-9

Tap here to enter a recipient

TIP

If you want to move an email address from the To field to the Cc or Bcc field, tap and hold the address and drag it to the other field.

3. Tap the Send button in the upper-right corner. The email goes on its way.

TIP

If you tap Forward to send the message to somebody else and the original message had an attachment, you're offered the option of including or omitting the attachment.

Tap in the
message body to
enter a message

FIGURE 12-10

Create and Send a New Message

1. With Mail open, tap the New Message button in the bottom-right corner (this looks like a page with a pencil on it). A blank email appears (see **Figure 12-11**).

2. Enter a recipient's address in the To field. If you have addresses in Contacts, tap the plus sign (+) in the Address field to choose an addressee from the Contacts list that appears.

3. If you want to send a copy of the message to other people, tap the Cc/Bcc field. When the Cc and Bcc fields open, enter addresses in either or both. Use the Bcc field to specify recipients of blind carbon copies, which means that no other recipients are aware that that person received this reply.

4. Enter the subject of the message in the Subject field.

FIGURE 12-11

5. Tap in the message body and type your message.

6. If you want to check a fact or copy and paste some part of another message into your draft message, swipe down near the top of the email to display your Inbox and other folders. Locate the message, and when you're ready to return to your draft, tap the Subject of the email, which is displayed near the bottom of the screen.

7. When you've finished creating your message, tap Send.

Format Email

You can apply some basic formatting to email text. You can use bold, underline, and italic formats, and indent text using the Quote Level feature.

1. Press and hold the text in a message you're creating and choose Select or Select All to select a single word or all the words in the email (see **Figure 12-12**).

TIP

   When you make a selection, handles appear that you can drag to add adjacent words to your selection. If the menu disappears after you select the text, just tap one of the selection handles and it will reappear.

2. To see more tools, tap the arrow on the toolbar that appears; to apply bold, italic, or underline formatting, tap the BIU button.

3. In the toolbar that appears (see **Figure 12-13**), tap Bold, Italic, or Underline to apply formatting.

FIGURE 12-12

FIGURE 12-13

4. To change the indent level, tap and hold at the beginning of a line, then tap Quote Level.

5. Tap Increase to indent the text or Decrease to move indented text farther toward the left margin.

TIP

To use the Quote Level feature, make sure that it's on. From the Home screen, tap Settings, tap Mail, tap Increase Quote Level, then toggle (tap) the Increase Quote Level On/Off switch to turn it On (green).

Search Email

What do you do if you want to find all messages from a certain person or containing a certain word in the Subject field? You can use Mail's handy Search feature to find these emails (though you can't search message contents).

1. With Mail open, tap an account to display its Inbox.

2. In the Inbox, tap and drag down near the top email to display the Search field. Tap in the Search field, and the onscreen keyboard appears.

TIP

You can also use the Search feature covered in Chapter 2 to search for terms in the To, From, or Subject lines of mail messages.

3. Enter a search term or name, as shown in **Figure 12-14**. Matching emails are listed in the results (refer to **Figure 12-14**).

4. Tap the All Mailboxes tab to view messages that contain the search term in one of those fields in any mailbox, or tap the Current Mailbox tab to see only matches within the current mailbox (refer to **Figure 12-14**). (These options may vary slightly, depending on which email service you use.)

TIP

To start a new search or go back to the full Inbox, either tap the Delete icon (the circled X) on the far-right end of the Search field to delete the term or tap the Cancel button.

Enter a search term here

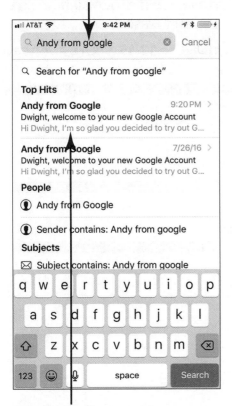

Search results appear here

FIGURE 12-14

Mark Email as Unread or Flag for Follow-Up

You can use a simple swipe to access tools that either mark an email as unread after you've read it (placing a blue dot before the message) or flag an email (which places an orange circle before it). If the email is both marked as unread and is flagged, a blue dot in an orange circle will appear in front of the message. These methods help you to remember to reread an email that you've already read or to follow up on a message at a later time.

1. With Mail open and an Inbox displayed, swipe to the left on an email to display three options: More, Flag, and Trash.

2. Tap More. On the menu shown in **Figure 12-15**, you're given several options, including Mark. Tapping Mark accesses both the Mark As Read/Unread and Flag commands. Tapping either command applies it and returns you to your Inbox.

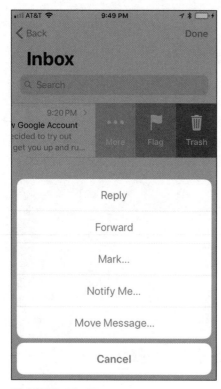

FIGURE 12-15

TIP

You can also get to this command by swiping to the right on a message displayed in your Inbox.

3. There's another way to get to the Flag command. Swipe to the left on another email, then tap Flag. An orange circle appears before the email.

TIP

On the menu shown in **Figure 12-15,** you can also select Notify Me. This option causes Mail to notify you whenever somebody replies to this email thread.

Create an Event from Email Contents

A neat feature in Mail is the ability to create a Calendar event from within an email.

1. To test this out, create an email to yourself mentioning a reservation on a specific airline on a specific date and time; you can also mention another type of reservation, such as for dinner, or mention a phone number.

2. Send the message to yourself, then open Mail.

3. In your Inbox, open the email. (The pertinent information is displayed in underlined blue text.)

4. Tap the underlined text, and in the menu shown in **Figure 12-16**, tap Create Event. A New Event form from Calendar appears. Enter additional information about the event, then tap Done.

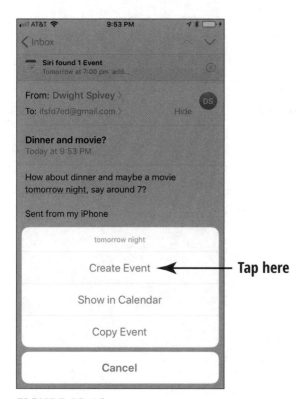

FIGURE 12-16

Delete Email

When you no longer want an email cluttering your Inbox, you can delete it.

1. With the Inbox displayed, tap the Edit button. Circular check boxes are displayed to the left of each message (see **Figure 12-17**).

2. Tap the circle next to the message that you want to delete. A message marked for deletion shows a check mark in the circular check button (refer to **Figure 12-17**).

TIP

You can tap multiple items if you have several emails to delete.

Tap to select a message

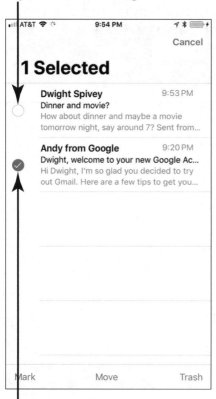

Selected message

FIGURE 12-17

3. Tap the Trash or Archive button at the bottom-left of the Inbox dialog. The message is moved to the Trash or Archive folder.

Some email services default to Trash; others default to Archive. The difference is that email sent to a Trash folder typically is deleted forever after a certain amount of time (usually 30 days); email sent to an Archive folder is removed from the Inbox but kept indefinitely for future use.

You can also delete an open email by tapping the Trash or Archive icon on the toolbar that runs across the bottom of the screen, or swiping left on a message displayed in an Inbox and tapping the Trash or Archive button that appears.

Organize Email

You can move messages into any of several predefined folders in Mail (these will vary depending on your email provider and the folders you've created on your provider's server).

1. After displaying the folder containing the message that you want to move (for example, Inbox), tap the Edit button. Circular check boxes are displayed to the left of each message (refer to **Figure 12-17**).

2. Tap the circle next to the message you want to move.

3. Tap the Move button.

4. In the Mailboxes list that appears (see **Figure 12-18**), tap the folder where you want to store the message. The message is moved.

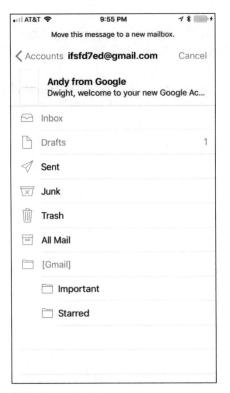

FIGURE 12-18

Create a VIP List

A VIP list is a way to create a list of senders you deem to be more important than others. When any of these senders sends you an email, you'll be notified of it through the Notifications feature of iPhone.

1. In the list of all Mailboxes, tap the Info button (circle with lower-case "i") in the VIP option (see **Figure 12-19**).

2. Tap Add VIP (see **Figure 12-20**), and your Contacts list appears.

3. Tap a contact to make that person a VIP.

4. To make settings for whether VIP mail is flagged on the Cover Sheet (the screen where notifications appear on your iPhone), press the Home button, then tap Settings.

Tap here

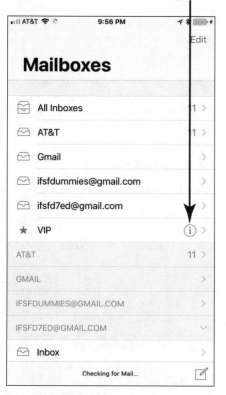

FIGURE 12-19

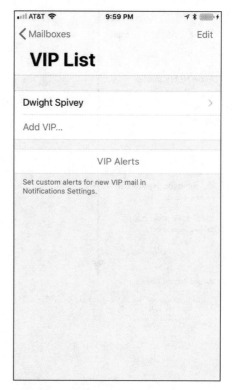

FIGURE 12-20

5. Tap Notifications, then tap Mail. In the settings that appear, shown in **Figure 12-21,** tap VIP.

6. Tap the Show on Cover Sheet On/Off switch to turn on notifications for VIP mail.

7. Tap an alert style and choose what sound should play or what badge icon should appear (see **Figure 12-22**).

8. Press the Home button to close Settings. New mail from your VIPs should now appear on the Cover Sheet when you swipe down from the top of the screen, and, depending on the settings you chose, may cause a sound to play or a badge icon to appear on your Lock screen, and a blue star icon to appear to the left of these messages in the Inbox in Mail.

Tap here

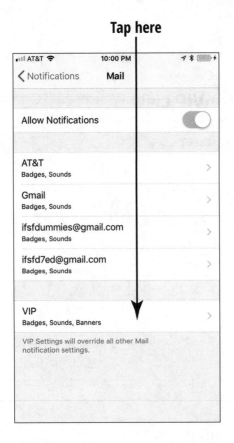

FIGURE 12-21

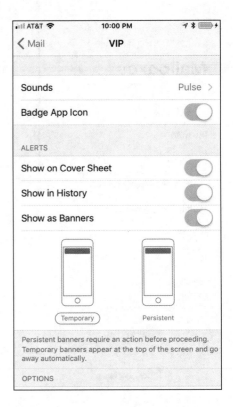

FIGURE 12-22

Chapter 13

Expanding Your iPhone Horizons with Apps

Some apps (short for applications) come preinstalled on your iPhone, such as Contacts and TV. But you can choose from a world of other apps out there for your iPhone, some for free (such as Facebook) and some for a price (typically, ranging from 99 cents to about $10, though some can top out at much steeper prices).

Apps range from games to financial tools (such as loan calculators) to apps that help you when you're planning or taking a trip. There are still more apps that are developed for use by private entities, such as hospitals and government agencies.

In this chapter, I suggest some apps that you might want to check out and explain how to use the App Store feature of your iPhone to find, purchase, and download apps.

Explore Senior-Recommended Apps

As I write this book, new iPhone apps are in development, so even more apps that could fit your needs are available seemingly every day. Still, to get you exploring what's possible, I provide a quick list of apps that might whet your appetite.

Access the App Store (completely redesigned in iOS 11) by tapping the App Store icon on the Home screen. You can start by exploring either the Today tab (which features special apps and articles), by Categories, or by the Top Charts (see the buttons along the bottom of the screen). Or you can tap Search and find apps on your own. Tap an app to see more information about it.

Here are some interesting apps to explore:

» **Sudoku (free)**: If you like this mental logic puzzle in print, try it out on your iPhone. It has three lessons and several levels ranging from easiest to nightmare, making it a great way to make time fly by in a doctor's or dentist's waiting room.

» **StockWatch Portfolio Tracking and Stock Market Quotes ($2.99)**: Even though Apple offers a Stocks app for the iPhone, this app will help you keep track of your investments in a portfolio format. You can use the app to create a watch list and record your stock performance.

» **Goodreads (free)**: If you're a reader, this is an app you won't want to be without (see **Figure 13-1**). This app will keep you up-to-date on the latest releases, and you can browse reading lists from thousands of other users.

» **Paint Studio ($3.99)**: Get creative! You can use this powerful app to draw, add color, and even create special effects.

» **Virtuoso Piano Free 4 (free)**: If you love to make music, you'll love this app, which gives you a virtual piano keyboard to play and compose on the fly.

» **Travelzoo (free)**: Get great deals on hotels, airfare, rental cars, entertainment, and more. This app also offers tips from travel experts.

» **Blood Pressure Monitor (free):** This app helps you keep track of your blood pressure and maintain records over extended periods of time in one convenient place: your iPhone. Use the accompanying reports to give your doctor a good overview of your blood pressure.

» **Skype (free):** Make Internet calls to your friends and family for free. While your iPhone comes with FaceTime, some members of your circle may not have iPhones, so Skype would be the best way to communicate.

» **Nike+ Training Club (free):** Use this handy utility to help design personalized workouts, see step-by-step instructions to help you learn new exercises, and watch video demonstrations. The reward system in this app may just keep you going toward your workout goals.

FIGURE 13-1

TIP

Note that you can work on documents using apps in the cloud. Use Keynote, Numbers, Pages, and more apps to get your work done from any device. See Chapter 4 for more about using iCloud Drive.

Search the App Store

1. Tap the App Store icon on the Home screen; by default, the first time you use App Store it will open to the Today tab, as seen in **Figure 13-2.**

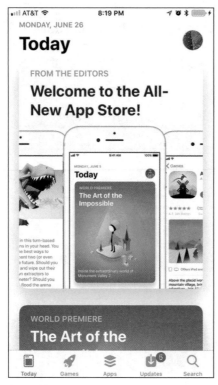

FIGURE 13-2

2. At this point, you have several options for finding apps:

- Scroll downward to view featured apps and articles, such as The Daily List and Our Favorites.

  Swipe sideways to see more apps in a category.

- Tap the Apps tab at the bottom of the screen to browse by the type of app you're looking for, or search by categories such as Education or Entertainment, as shown in **Figure 13-3.**

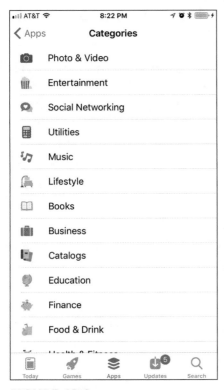

FIGURE 13-3

- Tap the Games tab at the bottom of the screen to see the newest releases and bestselling games. Explore by either Paid apps or free apps, by categories, and by special subjects, such as The Most Beautiful Games.

- Tap the Search button at the bottom of the screen, then tap in the Search field, enter a search term, and tap the result you want to view.

Get Applications from the App Store

Buying or getting free apps requires that you have an iTunes account, which I cover in Chapter 4. After you have an account, you can use the saved payment information there to buy apps or download free apps with a few simple steps.

1. With the App Store open, tap the Apps tab, then tap the See All button in the Top Free section, as shown in **Figure 13-4.**

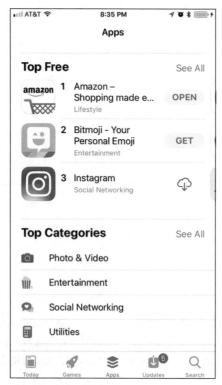

FIGURE 13-4

2. Tap the Get button for an app that appeals to you, or simply tap the app's icon if you want more information. A sheet opens on the screen, listing the app and the iTunes account being used to get/purchase the app.

To get a paid app, you tap the same button, which is then labeled with a price.

If you've opened an iCloud account, you can set it up so that anything you purchase on your iPhone is automatically pushed to other Apple iOS devices and your iTunes library, and vice versa. See Chapter 4 for more about iCloud.

3. To complete the download/purchase of the app, tap Enter Password at the bottom of the sheet, tap the Password field, then enter the password. The Get button changes to the Installing button, which looks like a circle; the thick blue line on the circle represents the progress of the installation.

4. The app downloads and can be found on one of the Home screens. If you purchase an app that isn't free, your credit card or gift card balance is charged at this point for the purchase price.

Out of the box, only preinstalled apps are located on the first iPhone Home screen, with a few (such as Voice Memos and Podcasts) located on the second Home screen. Apps that you download are placed on available Home screens, and you have to scroll to view and use them; this procedure is covered later in this chapter. See the next task for help in finding your newly downloaded apps using multiple Home screens.

Organize Your Applications on Home Screens

iPhone can display up to 11 to 15 Home screens, depending on your iPhone model. By default, the first Home screen contains preinstalled apps, and the second contains a few more preinstalled apps. Other screens are created to contain any apps you download or sync to your iPhone. At the bottom of any iPhone Home screen (just above the Dock), dots indicate the number of Home screens you've filled with apps; a solid dot specifies which Home screen you're on now, as shown in **Figure 13-5**.

1. Press the Home button to open the last displayed Home screen.

2. Flick your finger from right to left to move to the next Home screen. To move back, flick from left to right.

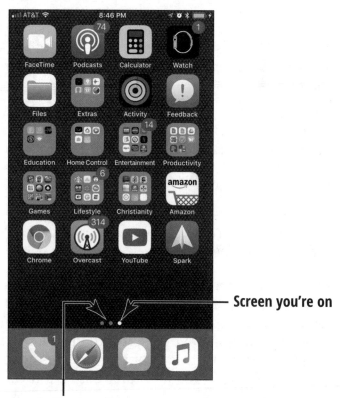

Screen you're on

Dots indicating the number of home screens

FIGURE 13-5

3. To reorganize apps on a Home screen, press and hold any app on that page. The app icons begin to jiggle (see **Figure 13-6**), and many (not all) apps will sport a Delete button (a gray circle with a black X on it).

4. Press, hold, and drag an app icon to another location on the screen to move it.

TIP

To move an app from one page to another, while the apps are jiggling, you can press, hold, and drag an app to the left or right to move it to the next Home screen. You can also manage which app resides on which Home screen and change the order of the Home screens from iTunes when you've connected iPhone to iTunes via a cable or wireless sync.

5. Press the Home button to stop all those icons from jiggling!

A delete button

FIGURE 13-6

TIP

You can use the multitasking feature for switching between apps easily. Press the Home button twice and you get a preview of open apps. Swipe right or left to scroll among the apps and tap the one you want to go to. You can also swipe an app upward from this preview list to close it.

Organize Apps in Folders

iPhone lets you organize apps in folders so that you can find them more easily. The process is simple:

1. Tap and hold an app until all apps start jiggling.

2. Drag one app on top of another app.

The two apps appear in a box with a placeholder name in a box above them (see **Figure 13-7**).

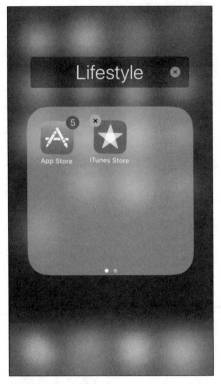

FIGURE 13-7

3. To change the name, tap in the field at the end of the placeholder name, and the keyboard appears.

4. Tap the Delete key to delete the placeholder name and type one of your own.

5. Tap Done, then tap anywhere outside the box to close it.

6. Press the Home button to stop the icons from dancing around. You'll see your folder on the Home screen where you began this process.

TIP

iOS 11 introduces the neat trick of allowing you to move multiple apps together at the same time. Follow these steps:

1. Tap and hold the first app you'd like to move. When the apps are jiggling, you're ready for the next step.

2. Move the app just a bit so that it's no longer in its original place.

3. With your free hand, tap the other app(s) you'd like to move along with the first app. As you tap additional apps, their icons "move under" or "attach themselves" to the first app.

4. When you've selected all your apps, drag them to their new location. They'll all move together in a caravan!

Delete Apps You No Longer Need

When you no longer need an app you've installed, it's time to get rid of it. You can also remove most of the preinstalled apps that are native to iOS 11. If you use iCloud to push content across all Apple iOS devices, deleting an app on your iPhone won't affect that app on other devices.

1. Display the Home screen that contains the app you want to delete.

TIP

If you remove a native iOS 11 app, it's hidden, not deleted. If you need it later you can go to the App Store, find the name of the app there, and reinstall it (or technically, just unhide it).

2. Press and hold the app until all apps begin to jiggle.

3. Tap the Delete button for the app you want to delete (refer to **Figure 13-6**). A confirmation like the one shown in **Figure 13-8** appears.

4. Tap Delete (or Remove if the app is preinstalled by iOS 11) to proceed with the deletion.

TIP

Don't worry about wiping out several apps at one time by deleting a folder. When you delete a folder, the apps that were contained within the folder are placed back on a Home screen if space is available, and you can still find the apps using the Search feature.

FIGURE 13-8

Offload Apps to Keep Data

When you delete an app from your iPhone, usually you're simultaneously deleting its data and documents. In iOS 11, you can also delete an app without removing its data and documents. This feature is called Offloading. If you find later that you'd like to revisit the app, simply download it again from the App Store and its data and settings will be retained.

To offload apps, follow these steps:

TECHNICAL STUFF

1. Open Settings and go to General ⇨ iPhone Storage.

   You may need to wait a few seconds for content to load.

2. You can allow your iPhone to automatically offload unused apps as storage gets low, or you can offload individual apps manually:

- To automatically offload unused apps, scroll down the screen to the Offload Unused Apps option and tap the Enable button, shown in **Figure 13-9.**

  To disable the feature, go to Settings ⇨ iTunes & App Store, scroll to the bottom of the page, then toggle the Offload Unused Apps switch to Off (white).

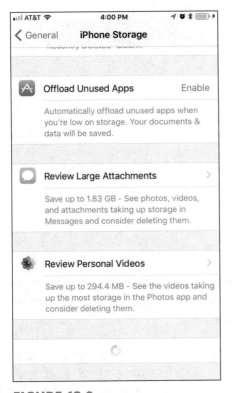

FIGURE 13-9

- To offload an individual app, scroll down to find the app and tap it, then tap the Offload App option, seen in **Figure 13-10**; tap Offload App again to confirm. The offloaded app's icon is grayed out on your iPhone's Home screen, indicating that the app is not loaded but its data still is.

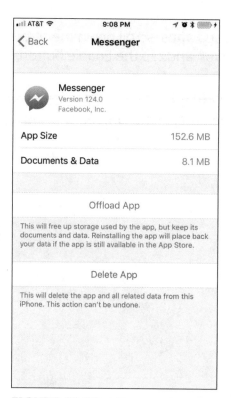

FIGURE 13-10

3. You can restore an app by either tapping its grayed-out icon (when the app is ready to use the icon will no longer be grayed out) or by reinstalling it from the App Store.

TIP

Often, most of your iPhone's memory is taken by the data used in apps, not by the apps themselves. Offloading apps is a great idea if the app itself is of a significant size, but otherwise may not be very handy unless you're just super-strapped for space.

Update Apps

App developers update their apps all the time, so you might want to check for those updates. The App Store icon on the Home screen displays the number of available updates in a red circle. To update apps, follow these steps:

1. Tap the App Store icon on the Home screen.

2. Tap the Updates button to access the Updates screen, then tap the Update button for any item you want to update. Note that if you have Family Sharing turned on, there will be a folder titled Family Purchases that you can tap to display apps that are shared across your family's devices. To update all, tap the Update All button.

You can download multiple apps at one time. If you choose more than one app to update instead of downloading apps sequentially, several items will download simultaneously.

3. You may be asked to confirm that you want to update, or to enter your Apple ID; after you do, tap OK to proceed. You may also be asked to confirm that you are over a certain age or agree to terms and conditions; if so, scroll down the terms dialog and, at the bottom, tap Agree. The download progress is displayed.

If you have an iCloud account that you have activated on several devices and update an app on your iPhone, any other Apple iOS devices are also updated automatically and vice versa.

iOS 11 performs what Apple calls "intelligently scheduled updates," meaning that updates to apps and the iOS happen at times when your iPhone isn't using much power — for example, when you're connecting to the Internet via Wi-Fi. And speaking of updating, iOS 11 studies your habits and can update apps that require updated content, such as Facebook or Stocks, around the time you usually check them so that you have instant access to current information.

Customize Individual App Settings

Some apps allow you to customize their settings via the Settings app. This is typically to let you tell an app how you'd like to interact with it, as opposed to it telling you what to do all the time.

1. To see a list of apps that you can customize settings for, tap the Settings app on your Home screen.

2. Swipe down the screen until you see the names of apps you've installed.

3. Tap the name of an app to see the features that you can customize, as illustrated in **Figure 13-11.**

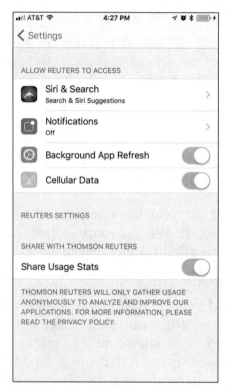

FIGURE 13-11

Chapter **14**

Socializing with Facebook and Twitter

S ocial media apps keep us in close digital contact with friends and family, and have become as important a digital staple as email, if not more so for some folks. Facebook and Twitter are two of the most popular social media apps, and therefore I focus on obtaining and setting up these apps for use with your iPhone in this chapter.

Facebook is a platform for sharing posts about your life, with or without photos and video, and allows you to be as detailed as you please in your posts. Twitter, on the other hand, is meant to share information in quick bursts, allowing users on 140 characters in which to alert you to their latest comings and goings.

Finding and Installing Facebook and Twitter

To begin using Facebook and Twitter, you first need to find and install them on your iPhone.

TECHNICAL STUFF

If this isn't your first experience with iPhone and iOS, you might think that there's more than one way to install these apps. Once upon a time, you could install Facebook, Twitter, and a couple of other social media apps from within the Settings app. However, that isn't an option in iOS 11.

To install the apps using the App Store, follow these steps:

1. Open the App Store.

2. Tap the Search tab at the bottom of the screen.

3. Tap the Search field and enter either Facebook or Twitter.

4. Tap the Install button, and enter your Apple ID and password when asked for them.

TECHNICAL STUFF

If you've had the app installed before, but have since deleted it, you will instead see a cloud with a downward-pointing arrow (as seen in **Figure 14-1**); tap that to begin the download.

The app will download and install on one of your Home screens.

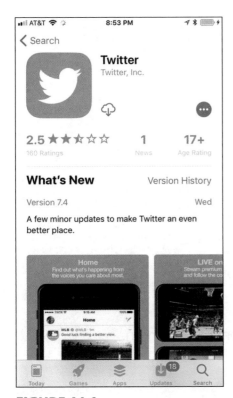

FIGURE 14-1

Creating a Facebook Account

You can create a Facebook account from within the app.

TIP

If you already have a Facebook account, you can simply use that account information to log in.

To create an account in the Facebook app, follow these steps:

1. Launch the newly downloaded Facebook app.

2. Tap the Sign Up for Facebook option near the bottom of the screen, as seen in **Figure 14-2** (you almost need binoculars to see it).

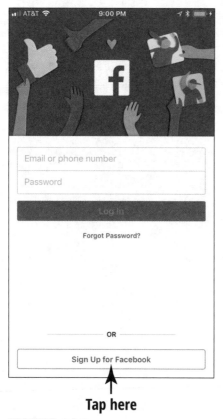

Tap here

FIGURE 14-2

3. Tap Get Started and walk through the steps to complete the registration of your account.

4. When finished, you'll be logged into your account in the Facebook app.

You may also create a Facebook account by visiting its website at www.facebook.com.

TIP

Customize Facebook Settings for Your iPhone

Facebook has a few settings that you'll want to configure when entering your account information into the Settings app.

1. Open the Settings app.

2. Tap Facebook.

3. Toggle the switches, seen in **Figure 14-3,** On (green) or Off for the following options:

   - **Background App Refresh:** This allows Facebook to refresh its content in the background, or put another way, when you aren't actually using it.

   - **Cellular Data:** Turning this On allows Facebook to refresh itself and allows you to post updates when you aren't connected to a Wi-Fi network.

   - **Upload HD:** If you record HD video on your iPhone, this setting allows you to upload that high-quality video to Facebook. Keep in mind that HD video files are very large files and will therefore consume vast quantities of your cellular data allotment, as well as take much longer to upload.

4. Tap the remaining items in the Allow Facebook to Access section (Location, Photos, Siri, and Notifications) to customize how Facebook can interact with these iOS 11 features. For example, tap Photos and allow or deny Facebook access to the Photos app, as illustrated in **Figure 14-4**.

WARNING

If you're a frequent Facebook user and you tend to upload quite a bit of photos and videos, consider toggling the Cellular Data switch to Off. If you have an account with a cellular provider that provides a limited amount of data, you could be in danger of exceeding your data allotment if you're a heavy Facebook user.

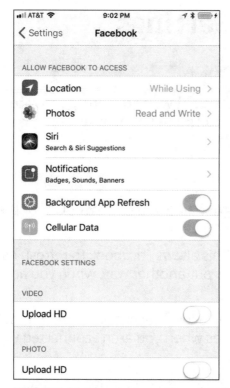

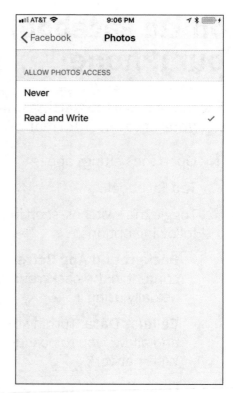

FIGURE 14-3　　　　　　　　　　　**FIGURE 14-4**

Creating a Twitter Account

To create an account in the Twitter app, follow these steps:

1. Open the Twitter app by tapping its icon.

2. Tap the Get Started button in the middle of the screen, as illustrated in **Figure 14-5.**

TIP

If you already have a Twitter account, tap the tiny blue Log In button at the very bottom of the screen to log in.

3. The app will ask you a series of friendly questions to help you create your account.

4. When you're done, the app will log you into your new account.

See what's happening in the world right now.

Get started ◄—————— **Tap here**

Have an account already? Log in

FIGURE 14-5

Just like Facebook, you can create an account on the Twitter website at www.twitter.com.

TIP

Customize Twitter Settings for Your iPhone

Like Facebook, Twitter also has a handful of options that you need to consider when installing it. Follow these steps:

1. Open the Settings app.

2. Tap Twitter.

3. Tap Siri and toggle the Search & Siri Suggestions switch On (green) or Off. This option, if enabled, allows Siri to learn how you use the Twitter app and offer suggestions to you based on that information.

4. Toggle the switches, seen in **Figure 14-6,** On (green) or Off for the following options:

FIGURE 14-6

- **Background App Refresh:** This allows Twitter to refresh its content in the background, when you aren't using the app.

- **Cellular Data:** Turning this On allows Twitter to refresh itself and allows you to post updates when you aren't connected to a Wi-Fi network.

4

Enjoying Media

IN THIS PART . . .

Navigating iTunes

Reading e-books

Listening to audio

Taking and sharing photos

Mastering videos

Enjoying games

Getting directions

» Preview music, videos, and audiobooks

» Find and buy selections

» Rent movies

» Shop anywhere else

» Use Apple Pay and Wallet

» Auto-download your purchases

» Set up Family Sharing

Chapter **15**

Shopping the iTunes Store

The iTunes Store app that comes preinstalled in iPhone lets you easily shop for music, movies, and TV shows. As Chapter 16 explains, you can also get electronic and audio books via the iBooks app.

In this chapter, you discover how to find content in the iTunes Store. You can download the content directly to your iPhone or to another device, then sync it to your iPhone. With the Family Sharing feature, which I cover in this chapter, as many as six people in a family can share purchases using the same credit card. Finally, I cover a few options for buying content from other online stores and using Apple Pay to make real-world purchases using a stored payment method.

TIP I cover opening an iTunes account and downloading iTunes software to your computer in Chapter 4. If you need to, read Chapter 4 to see how to handle these two tasks before digging into this chapter.

Explore the iTunes Store

Visiting the iTunes Store from your iPhone is easy with the built-in iTunes Store app.

TIP If you're in search of other kinds of content, the Podcasts app and iTunes U app allow you to find, then download podcasts and online courses to your phone.

To check out the iTunes Store, follow these steps:

1. If you aren't already signed in to iTunes, tap Settings and go to iTunes & App Stores. Tap Sign In and enter your Apple ID and Password in their respective fields, as shown in **Figure 15-1,** then tap Sign In.

2. Go to your Home screen and tap the iTunes Store icon.

3. Tap the Music button (if it isn't already selected) in the row of buttons at the bottom of the screen. Swipe up and down the screen and you'll find several categories of selections, such as New Music, Hot Tracks, and Recent Releases (these category names change from time to time).

4. Flick your finger up to scroll through the featured selections or tap the See All button to see more selections in any category, as shown in **Figure 15-2.**

TIP The navigation techniques in these steps work essentially the same in any of the content categories (the buttons at the bottom of the screen), which include Music, Movies, and TV Shows.

FIGURE 15-1

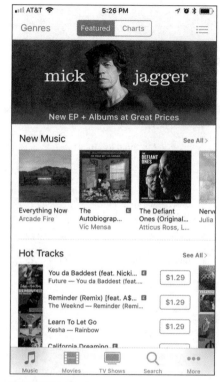

FIGURE 15-2

5. Tap the Charts tab at the top of the screen. This displays lists of best-selling songs, albums, and music videos in the iTunes Store.

6. Tap any listed item to see more detail about it, as shown in **Figure 15-3**, and hear a brief preview when you tap the number to the left of a song.

TIP

If you want to use the Genius playlist feature, which recommends additional purchases based on the contents of your library in the iTunes app on your iPhone, tap the More button at the bottom of the screen, then tap Genius. If you've made enough purchases in iTunes, song and album recommendations appear based on those purchases as well as the content in your iTunes Match library (a fee-based service), if you have one.

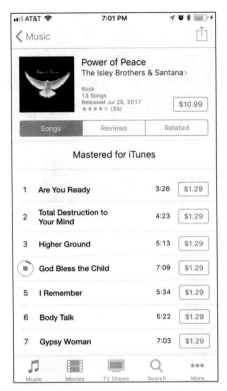

FIGURE 15-3

Find a Selection

You can look for a selection in the iTunes Store in several ways. You can use the Search feature, search by genre or category, or view artists' pages. Here's how these work:

» Tap the Search button at the bottom of the screen and the Search field shown in **Figure 15-4** appears. Tap in the field and enter a search term using the onscreen keyboard. Tap the Search button on the keyboard or, if a suggestion in the list of search results appeals to you, just tap that suggestion.

» Tap an item at the bottom of the screen (such as Music), then tap the Genres button at the top of the screen.

A list of genres like the one shown in **Figure 15-5** appears.

Enter search term here

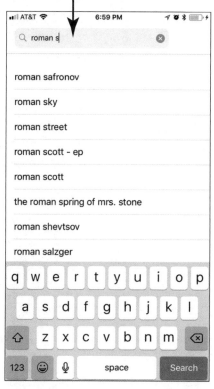

FIGURE 15-4

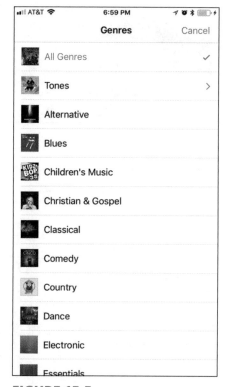

FIGURE 15-5

TIP

» On a description page that appears when you tap a selection, you can find more offerings by the people involved with that particular work. For example, for a music selection, tap to display details about it, then tap the Reviews tab at the middle of the page to see all reviews of the album (see **Figure 15-6**). For a movie (tap Movies at the bottom of the iTunes Store Home page), tap to open details, then tap Reviews, or tap the Related tab to see more movies starring any of the lead actors.

If you find a selection that you like, tap the Share button in the top right of its description page to share your discovery with a friend via AirDrop, Mail, Message, Twitter, or Facebook. A message form appears with a link that your friend can tap to view information about the selection. You must have set up an associated account (such as Twitter) before you can use this feature. Tap Settings from the Home screen to set up an account.

FIGURE 15-6

Preview Music, a Video, or an Audiobook

Because you've already set up an iTunes account (if you haven't done so yet, refer to Chapter 4), when you choose to buy an item, it's automatically charged either to the credit or debit card you have on file, to your PayPal account, or against any allowance you have outstanding from an iTunes gift card. You might want to preview an item before you buy it. If you like it, buying and downloading are easy and quick.

TIP

If you don't want to allow purchases from within apps (for example, Music or TV) but rather want to allow purchases only through the iTunes Store, you can go to the Settings app, tap General, tap Restrictions, then tap Enable Restrictions and enter a passcode. After you've set a passcode, you can tap individual apps to turn on restrictions for them, as well as for such actions as installing apps, deleting apps, or using Siri.

To preview items in the iTunes Store, follow these steps:

1. Open the iTunes Store app and use any method outlined in earlier tasks to locate a selection that you might want to buy.

2. Tap the item to see detailed information about it, as shown in **Figure 15-7.**

Tap an episode for more info

FIGURE 15-7

3. For a TV show, tap an episode to get further information (refer to **Figure 15-7**). If you're looking at a music selection, tap the track number or name of a selection to play a preview. For a movie or audiobook selection, tap the Trailers Play button (movies) shown in **Figure 15-8.**

TIP

Note the Redeem button on some iTunes screens. Tap this button to redeem any iTunes gift certificates that you might get from your generous friends, or from yourself.

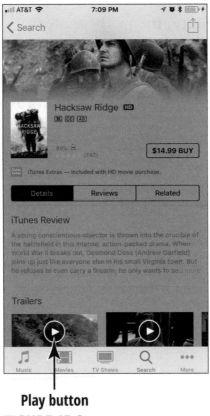

Play button

FIGURE 15-8

Buy a Selection

1. When you find an item that you want to buy, tap the button that shows either the price (if it's a selection available for purchase; see **Figure 15-9**) or the button with the word Get on it (if it's a selection available for free). The button label changes to Buy X, where X is the type of content, such as a song or album, that you're buying. If the item is free, the label changes to Get Song (or whatever item you're purchasing).

TIP

If you want to buy music, you can open the description page for an album and tap the album price, or buy individual songs rather than the entire album. Tap the price for a song, then proceed to purchase it.

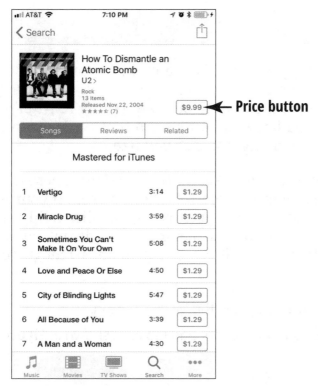

←— Price button

FIGURE 15-9

2. Tap the Buy X button. The iTunes Password dialog appears (refer to **Figure 15-1**).

3. Enter your password and tap OK. The item begins downloading, and the cost, if any, is automatically charged against your account. When the download finishes, tap OK in the Purchase Complete message and you can then view the content using the Music or Video app, depending on the type of content.

TIP

You can allow content to be downloaded over your 3G/4G cellular network if you aren't near a Wi-Fi hotspot. If you aren't near a Wi-Fi hotspot, downloading over your cellular network might be your only option. Tap Settings, tap iTunes & App Store, scroll down, and set the Use Cellular Data setting switch to On (green).

WARNING

You could incur hefty data charges with your provider if you run over your allotted data.

Rent Movies

In the case of movies, you can either rent or buy content. If you rent, which is less expensive but only a one-time deal, you have 30 days from the time you rent the item to begin watching it. After you have begun to watch it, you have 24 hours from that time left to watch it on the same device, as many times as you like.

TIP

Some movies are offered in high-definition versions. These HD movies look pretty good on that crisp, colorful iPhone screen. If your selection is available in SD it won't have quite as high quality (still very good, mind you), but it will take up less bandwidth to download or stream it to your phone. SD is also a bit cheaper than an HD movie to rent or purchase.

1. With the iTunes Store open, tap the Movies button.

2. Locate the movie you want to rent and tap it, as shown in **Figure 15-10**.

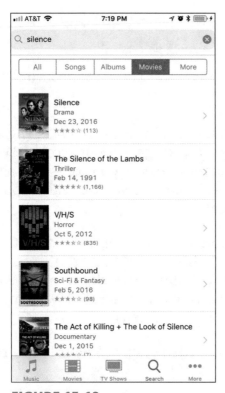

FIGURE 15-10

3. In the detailed description of the movie that appears, tap the Rent button (if it's available for rental); see **Figure 15-11**.

Rent button

FIGURE 15-11

4. The Rent button changes to a green Rent Movie button; tap it to confirm the rental. The movie begins to download to your iPhone immediately, and your account is charged the rental fee.

5. After the download is complete, you can use the TV app to watch it. (See Chapter 19 to read about how this app works.)

TIP

You can also download content to your computer and sync it to your iPhone. Refer to Chapter 4 for more about this process.

Shop Anywhere Else

One feature that's missing from the iPhone is support for Adobe Flash, a format of video playback that many online video-on-demand services and interactive games use (although development for Flash has stopped and services are moving away from it). However, most (if not all) online stores that sell such content such as movies and music have added iPhone-friendly videos to their collections, so you have alternatives to iTunes for your choice of movies and TV shows. You can also shop for music from sources other than iTunes, such as Amazon.com.

You can open accounts at one of these stores by using your computer or your iPhone's Safari browser, then following the store's instructions for purchasing and downloading content.

TIP

For non–iPhone friendly formats, you can download the content on your computer and stream it to your iPhone using Air Video (for $2.99) on the iPhone and Air Video Server (for free) using your Mac or Windows computer. For more information, go to www.inmethod.com/air-video/index.html.

Use Apple Pay and Wallet

Apple is the creator of a relatively new, and increasingly popular, method of paying for items by using your iPhone (or other Apple devices). It's called Apple Pay. Fancied as a mobile wallet, this service uses the Touch ID feature in your iPhone's Home button to identify you and any credit cards you've stored at the iTunes Store to make payments via a feature called Wallet.

Your credit card information isn't stored on your phone, and Apple doesn't know a thing about your purchases. In addition, Apple considers Apple Pay safer because the store cashier doesn't even have to know your name.

There are millions of merchant locations that are set up to use Apple Pay. Originally supported by Amex, Visa, MasterCard, and six of the largest banks in the United States, you'll find that even more credit cards (such as Discover) and store cards (such as Kohls or JCPenney) work with Apple Pay.

To set up Apple Pay, go to Settings and tap Wallet & Apple Pay. Add information about a credit card, then double-tap the Home button when the lock screen is displayed to initiate a purchase. You can also make settings from within the Wallet app itself.

Enable Auto-Downloads of Purchases from Other Devices

With iCloud, you can make a purchase or download free content on any of your Apple devices, and iCloud automatically shares those purchases with all your Apple devices.

To use iCloud, first set up an iCloud account. See Chapter 4 for detailed coverage of iCloud, including setting up your account.

1. To enable this auto-download feature on iPhone, start by tapping Settings on the Home screen.

2. Tap iTunes & App Store.

3. In the options that appear, scroll down, then set the switch to On for any category of purchases you want to auto-download to your iPhone from other Apple devices: Music, Apps, or Books (see **Figure 15-12**).

At this point, Apple doesn't offer an option of auto-downloading video content using these settings, probably because video is such a memory and bandwidth hog.

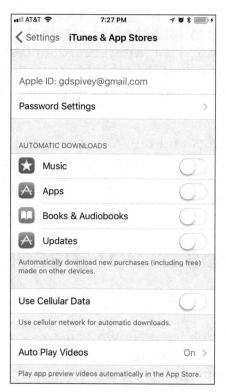

FIGURE 15-12

Set Up Family Sharing

Family Sharing is a feature that allows as many as six people in your family to share whatever anybody in the group has purchased from the iTunes, iBooks, and App Stores even though you don't share Apple IDs. Your family must all use the same credit card to purchase items (tied to whichever Apple ID is managing the family), but you can approve purchases by children under 13 years of age (this age can vary depending on your country or region). You can also share calendars, photos, and a family calendar (see Chapter 22 for information about Family Sharing and Calendar and Chapter 18 for information on sharing photos in a family album). Start by turning on Family Sharing.

1. Tap Settings, then tap the Apple ID at the top of the screen.

2. Tap Set Up Family Sharing.

3. Tap Get Started. On the next screen, you can add a photo for your family. Tap Continue.

4. On the Share Purchases screen, tap Share Purchases from a different account to use another Apple account.

5. Tap Continue and check the payment method that you want to use. Tap Continue.

6. On the next screen, tap Add Family Member. Enter the person's name (assuming that this person is listed in your contacts) or email address. An invitation is sent to the person's email. When the invitation is accepted, the person is added to your family (see **Figure 15-13**).

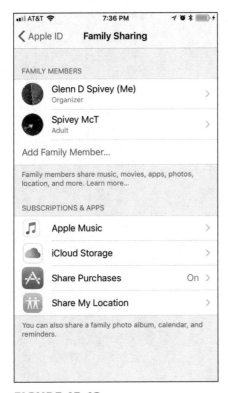

FIGURE 15-13

The payment method for this family is displayed under Shared Payment Method in this screen. All those involved in a family have to use a single payment method for family purchases.

There's also a link called Create a Child Account. When you click this link and enter information to create the ID, the child's account is automatically added to your Family and retains the child status until he or she turns 13. If a child accesses iTunes to buy something, he or she gets a prompt to ask permission. You get an Ask to Buy notification on your phone as well as via email. You can then accept or decline the purchase, giving you control over family spending in the iTunes Store.

Chapter **16**

Reading Books

A traditional e-reader is a device that's used primarily to read the electronic version of books, magazines, and newspapers. If you're happy reading on your smaller iPhone screen, your phone can be a great e-reader, although it isn't a traditional e-reader device like the Kindle because it gets its functionality from an e-reader app.

Apple's free app that turns your iPhone into an e-reader is iBooks, which also enables you to buy and download books (and audiobooks) from Apple's iBooks Store (offering more than 2 million books and growing). You can also use one of several other free e-reader apps — for example, Kindle or Nook. Then you can download books to your iPhone from a variety of online sources, such as Amazon and Google, so that you can read to your heart's content.

In this chapter, you discover the options available for reading material and how to buy books. You also learn how to navigate a book or periodical and adjust the brightness and type, as well as how to search books and organize your iBooks libraries.

Discover E-Reading

An e-reader is any electronic device that enables you to download and read books, magazines, PDF files, or newspapers. Many e-readers use E Ink technology to create a paper-like reading experience. These devices are typically portable and dedicated only to reading the electronic version of published materials.

The iPhone is a bit different from an e-reader. It isn't only for reading books, and you have to use iBooks or download another e-reader app to enable it as an e-reader (though the apps are usually free). Also, the iPhone doesn't offer the paper-like reading experience — you read from a phone screen (though you can adjust the brightness and background color of the screen).

When you buy a book online (or get one of many free publications), it downloads to your iPhone in a few seconds (or minutes, depending on your Internet connection speed and the size of the files) using a Wi-Fi or 3G/4G connection. The iPhone offers several navigation tools to move around an electronic book, which you will explore in this chapter.

Find Books with iBooks

1. To shop using iBooks, tap the iBooks application icon to open it. (It's on your first Home screen.)

2. In the iBooks library that opens (see **Figure 16-1**), you see a bookshelf; yours probably has only one free book already downloaded to it. (If you don't see the bookshelf, tap the My Books button in the lower-left corner to go there.) Tap the Featured button at the bottom of the screen and you're taken to the iBooks Store with featured titles displayed.

3. In the iBooks Store, shown in **Figure 16-2,** featured titles are shown. You can do any of the following to find a book:

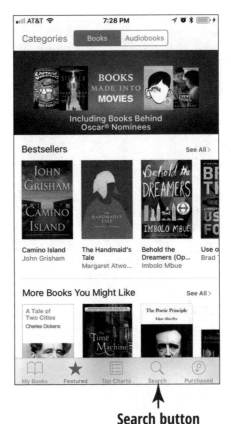

Featured button

FIGURE 16-1

Search button

FIGURE 16-2

- Tap the Search button at the bottom of the screen, then tap in the Search field that appears and type a search word or phrase, using the onscreen keyboard.

- Tap the Featured button, then tap the Categories button in the upper-left corner of the screen and scroll down to see links to popular categories of books, as shown in **Figure 16-3.** Tap a category to view those selections.

- Swipe up and down the screen to scroll to more suggested titles on a page.

- Tap the Top Charts button at the bottom of the screen to view both Paid and Free books listed on top bestseller lists.

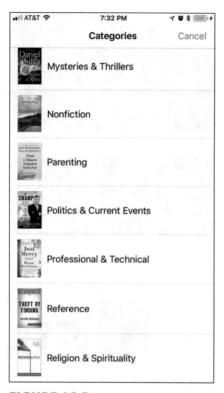

FIGURE 16-3

- Tap Purchased in the lower-right corner of the screen to see only titles that you've already purchased on any Apple device connected via iCloud.

- Tap a suggested selection or featured book to read more information about it.

TIP

Many books let you download free samples before you buy. You get to read several pages of the book to see whether it appeals to you, and it doesn't cost you a dime! Look for the Sample button when you view book details. (The button usually is below the price of the book.)

Explore Other E-Book Sources

Beyond using iBooks, the iPhone is capable of using other e-reader apps to read book content from other bookstores. You first have to download another e-reader application, such as Kindle from Amazon or the Barnes & Noble Nook reader from the App Store (see Chapter 13 for how to download apps). You can also download a non-vendor-specific app such as Bluefire Reader, which handles ePub and PDF formats, as well as the format that most public libraries use (protected PDF). Then use the app's features to search for, purchase, and download content.

The Kindle e-reader application is shown in **Figure 16-4.** After downloading the free app from the App Store, you just open the app and enter the email address and password associated with your Amazon account. Any content you've already bought from the Amazon.com Kindle Store from your computer or Kindle Fire tablet is archived online and can be placed on your Kindle Home page on the iPhone for you to read anytime you like. Tap the Device tab to see titles stored on iPhone rather than in Amazon's Cloud library. To enhance your reading experience, use such features as changing the background to a sepia tone or changing font. To delete a book from this reader, press-and-hold the title with your finger, and the Remove from Device button appears; simply tap the button to remove the book from your iPhone.

TIP

E-books are everywhere! You can get content from a variety of other sources, such as Project Gutenberg, Google Play, and some publishers like Baen. Download the content using your computer, if you like, then just add the items to Books in iTunes and sync them to your iPhone. You can also open items from a web link or email, and they're copied to iBooks for you. You can also make settings to iCloud so that books are pushed across your Apple devices or you can place them in an online storage service (such as Dropbox or Google Drive) and access them from there.

TECHNICAL
STUFF

E-books come in different formats, and iBooks won't work with formats other than ePub or PDF (for example, it can't use such formats as the Kindle's Mobi and AZW).

FIGURE 16-4

Buy Books

If you've set up an account with iTunes, you can buy books at the iBooks Store using the iBooks app. (See Chapter 4 for more about iTunes.)

1. Open iBooks, tap Featured, and begin looking for a book.

2. When you find a book in the iBooks Store, either in Featured titles or by searching, you can buy it by tapping it, then tapping the Price button or the Get button (if it's free), as shown in **Figure 16-5**.

3. A confirmation dialog sheet appears at the bottom of the screen, as shown in **Figure 16-6**. Tap either the Purchase or Get button, depending on the cost of the book.

Price button

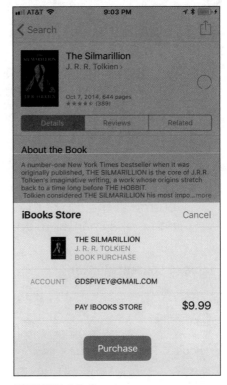

FIGURE 16-5   **FIGURE 16-6**

TIP

If you have signed in, your purchase is accepted immediately.

4. Tap Enter Password, enter your password in the Password field, then tap Done.

5. The book appears on your bookshelf, and the cost is charged to whichever credit card you specified when you opened your iTunes account. Tap the Read button that appears and read your tome.

TIP

Books that you've downloaded to your computer can be accessed from any Apple device through iCloud. Content can also be synced with your iPhone by using the Lightning to USB Cable and your iTunes account, or by using the wireless iTunes Wi-Fi Sync setting on the General Settings menu. See Chapter 4 for more about syncing.

Navigate a Book

Getting around in iBooks is half the fun!

1. Open iBooks and, if your Library (the bookshelf) isn't already displayed, tap the My Books button.

2. Tap a book to open it. The book opens to its title page or the last spot you read on any compatible device, as shown in **Figure 16-7.**

3. Take any of these actions to navigate the book:

   - To go to the book's Table of Contents: Tap the Table of Contents button at the top of the page (refer to **Figure 16-7**), then tap the name of a chapter to go to it (see **Figure 16-8**).

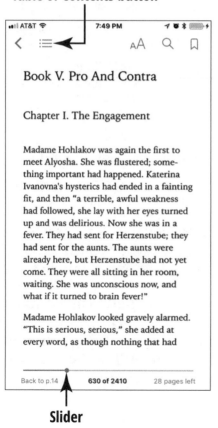

FIGURE 16-7

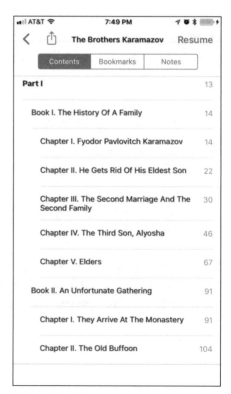

FIGURE 16-8

- To turn to the next page: Place your finger anywhere along the right edge of the page and tap or flick to the left.

- To turn to the preceding page: Place your finger anywhere on the left edge of a page and tap or flick to the right.

- To move to another page in the book: Tap and drag the slider at the bottom of the page (refer to **Figure 16-7**) to the right or left.

TIP

To return to the Library to view another book at any time, tap the Library button, which looks like a left-pointing arrow and is found in the upper-left corner of the screen. If the button isn't visible, tap anywhere on the page, and the button and other tools appear.

Adjust Brightness in iBooks

iBooks offers an adjustable brightness setting that you can use to make your book pages more comfortable to read.

1. With a book open, tap the Fonts button (looks like ᴀA), shown in **Figure 16-9.**

2. On the Brightness setting that appears at the top (refer to **Figure 16-9**), tap and drag the slider to the right to make the screen brighter, or to the left to dim it.

3. Tap anywhere on the page to close the Fonts dialog.

TIP

Experiment with the brightness level that works for you, or try out the Sepia setting, which you find by tapping the sepia-colored circle in the Fonts dialog. Bright-white screens are commonly thought to be hard on the eyes, so setting the brightness halfway relative to its default setting or less is probably a good idea (and saves on battery life).

Slider to adjust screen brightness

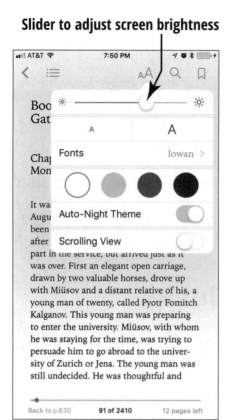

FIGURE 16-9

Change the Font Size and Type

If the type on your screen is a bit small for you to make out, you can change to a larger font size or choose a different font for readability.

1. With a book open, tap the Fonts button, shown in **Figure 16-10**.

2. In the Fonts dialog that appears (refer to **Figure 16-10**), tap the button with a smaller A, on the left, to use smaller text, or the button with the larger A, on the right, to use larger text.

3. Tap the Fonts button. The list of fonts shown in **Figure 16-11** appears.

4. Tap a font name to select it. The font changes on the book page.

Fonts button

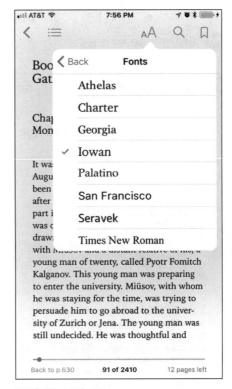

FIGURE 16-10

FIGURE 16-11

5. If you want a sepia tint on the pages, which can be easier on the eye, tap the Back button in the upper-left of the Fonts list to redisplay the Fonts dialog, then tap one of the screen color options (the colored circles) to activate it.

6. Tap outside the Fonts dialog to return to your book.

TIP

Some fonts appear a bit larger on your screen than others because of their design. If you want the largest font, use Iowan.

Search in Your Book

You may want to find certain sentences or references in your book. iBooks has a built-in Search feature that makes it simple.

1. With a book displayed, tap the Search button shown in **Figure 16-12**. The onscreen keyboard appears.

2. Enter a search term, then tap the Search key on the keyboard. iBooks searches for any matching entries.

3. Use your finger to scroll down the entries (see **Figure 16-13**).

Search button

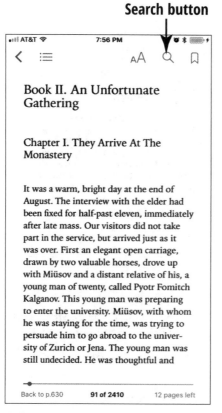

FIGURE 16-12

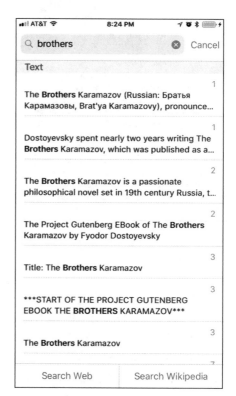

FIGURE 16-13

4. Flick your finger to scroll down the search results, then use either the Search Web or Search Wikipedia button at the bottom of the Search dialog if you want to search for information about the search term online. Tap a result and you're taken to the page containing that result with a highlight applied to it.

TIP

You can also search for other instances of a particular word while in the book pages by pressing your finger on the word for just a moment, then releasing; a toolbar will appear. Tap the right-facing arrow, then tap Search.

Use Bookmarks and Highlights

Bookmarks and highlights in your e-books operate like favorite sites that you save in your web browser: They enable you to revisit a favorite passage or refresh your memory about a character or plot point.

1. To bookmark a page, display that page and tap the Bookmark button in the top-right corner (see **Figure 16-14**).

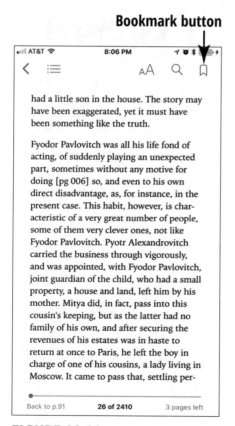

FIGURE 16-14

2. To highlight a word or phrase, press-and-release a word and the toolbar shown in **Figure 16-15** appears.

3. Tap the Highlight button. A colored highlight is placed on the word, and the toolbar shown in **Figure 16-16** appears.

Tap Highlight

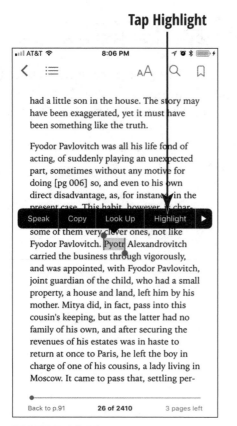

FIGURE 16-15

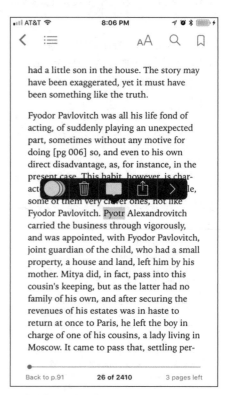

FIGURE 16-16

4. Tap one of these four buttons (from left to right):

   - Colors: Displays a menu of colors that you can tap to change the highlight color as well as an underline option.

   - Remove Highlight (looks like a trashcan): Removes the highlight.

   - Note: Lets you add a note to the item.

- Share: Allows you to share the highlighted text with others via AirDrop, Messages, Mail, Notes, Twitter, or Facebook, or to copy the text.

5. You can also tap the arrow button at the right side of the toolbar to access Copy, Define, Highlight, and Note tools. Tap outside the high-lighted text to close the toolbar.

6. To go to a list of bookmarks and notes (including highlighted text), tap the Table of Contents button in the upper left of the screen.

7. In the Table of Contents, tap the Bookmarks tab shown in **Figure 16-17**; all bookmarks are displayed. If you want to see highlighted text and associated notes, you display the Notes tab.

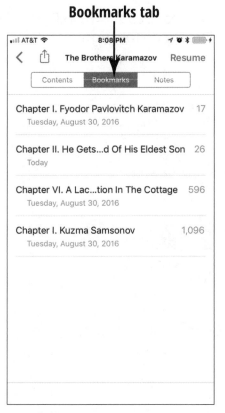

Bookmarks tab

FIGURE 16-17

8. Tap a bookmark in the bookmark list to go to that location in the book.

TIP

iPhone automatically bookmarks where you left off reading in a book so that you don't have to mark your place manually. If you use any other device registered to your iTunes or iCloud account, you also pick up where you left off reading.

Check Words in the Dictionary

As you read a book, you may come across unfamiliar words. Don't skip over them — take the opportunity to learn a new word!

1. With a book open, press-and-release your finger on a word and the toolbar shown in **Figure 16-18** appears.

2. Tap the Look Up button. A dialog appears, as shown in **Figure 16-19**, which offers several options for looking up the term.

Tap Look Up

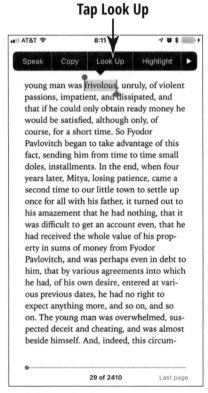

FIGURE 16-18

FIGURE 16-19

To see the definition, tap the Dictionary option and scroll down to view more.

When you finish reviewing the definition, tap Done in the upper-right corner, and the definition disappears.

Organize Books in Collections

iBooks lets you create and name collections of books to help you organize them by your own logic, such as Tear Jerkers, Work-Related, and Great Recipes. You can place a book in only one collection, however.

1. To create a collection from the Library bookshelf, tap Select in the upper-right corner.

2. On the screen that appears, tap a book, then tap Move in the upper-left corner, as seen in **Figure 16-20**.

3. In the Collections screen shown in **Figure 16-21**, tap New Collection. On the blank line that appears, type a name.

4. Tap Done on the keyboard, which returns you to the Collections screen.

5. Tap the collection you want to add your book; this takes you to the bookshelf for the collection you just created, and your book is contained there.

6. To add another book to the collection, follow these steps:

   a. Tap the Collections drop-down menu (the title that appears is the name of the collection you're currently viewing) in the upper-center of the screen and choose All Books.

   b. Tap Select in the upper-right corner, tap the book (or books) you want to move to the collection, then tap the Move button that appears in the top of the screen.

Tap Move

FIGURE 16-20

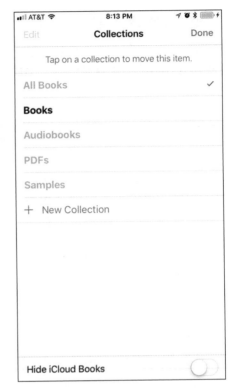

FIGURE 16-21

c. In the dialog that appears, tap the collection to which you'd like to move the book, and the book now appears on the bookshelf in that collection (see **Figure 16-22**).

7. To delete a book from a collection with the collection displayed, tap Select, tap the book, then tap Delete.

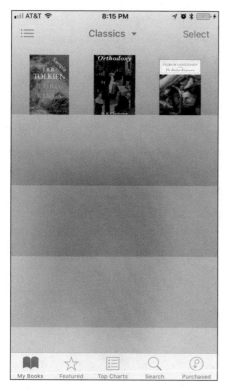

FIGURE 16-22

TIP

To delete a collection with the Collections dialog displayed, select the collection that you want to delete, then tap Edit. Tap the Delete button (looks like a minus sign) to the left of the collection, then tap Delete to get rid of it. A message appears, asking you to tap Delete Collection and Content (to remove the contents of the collection from your iPhone) or Delete Collection Only.

TECHNICAL
STUFF

If you choose Delete Collection Only, all titles within a deleted collection are returned to their original collections in your library; the default collection is All Books.

Chapter **17**

Enjoying Music and Podcasts

iPhone includes an iPod-like app called Music that allows you to take advantage of its amazing little sound system to play your favorite music.

In this chapter, you get acquainted with the Music app and its features that allow you to sort and find music and control playback. You also get an overview of AirPlay for accessing and playing your music over a home network or over any connected device (this also works with videos and photos). Finally, I introduce you to Podcasts for your listening pleasure.

View the Library Contents

The Library in Music contains the music or other audio files that you've placed on your iPhone, either by purchasing them through the iTunes Store or copying them from your computer. Let's see how to work with those files on your iPhone.

1. Tap the Music app, located in the Dock on the Home screen. The Music library appears, as shown **Figure 17-1.**

2. Swipe down the screen to scroll through the Recently Added section of the Music app's Library.

3. Tap a category (see **Figure 17-2**) to view music by Playlists, Artists, Albums, Songs, or Downloaded Music. Tap Library in the upper-left corner to return to the main Library screen.

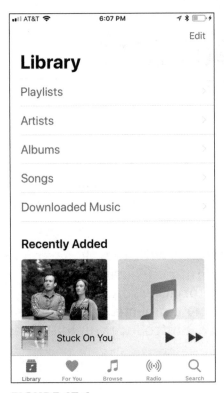

FIGURE 17-1

FIGURE 17-2

TIP

iTunes has several free items that you can download and use to play around with the features in Music. You can also sync content (such as iTunes Smart Playlists stored on your computer or other Apple devices) to your iPhone, and play it using the Music app. (See Chapter 4 for more about syncing and Chapter 15 for more about getting content from iTunes.)

4. Tap Edit in the upper-right corner to edit the list of categories, as seen in **Figure 17-3.** Tap the check box to the left of categories that you'd like to sort your Music Library by; uncheck those you don't want to use.

5. Tap Done when you're finished.

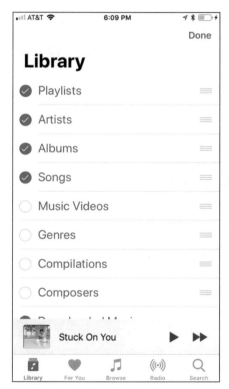

FIGURE 17-3

TIP

Apple offers a service called iTunes Match (visit https://support.apple.com/en-us/HT204146 for more information). You pay $24.99 per year for the capability to match the music you've bought from other providers (and stored in the iTunes Library on your computer) to what's in the iTunes Library. If there's a match (and there usually is), that content is added to your iTunes Library on iCloud. Then, using iCloud, you can sync the content among all your Apple devices. Is this service worth $24.99 a year? That's entirely up to you, my friend.

Create Playlists

You can create your own playlists to put tracks from various sources into collections of your choosing.

1. Tap the Playlists category at the top of the Library screen.

2. Tap New Playlist. In the dialog that appears (see **Figure 17-4**), tap Playlist Name and enter a title for the playlist.

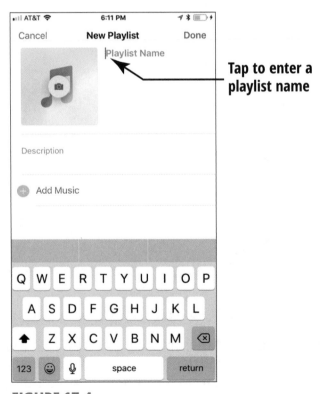

FIGURE 17-4

3. Tap Add Music, then tap a category, such as Songs or Artists, to display songs.

4. In the list of selections that appears (see **Figure 17-5**), tap the plus sign next to each item you want to include.

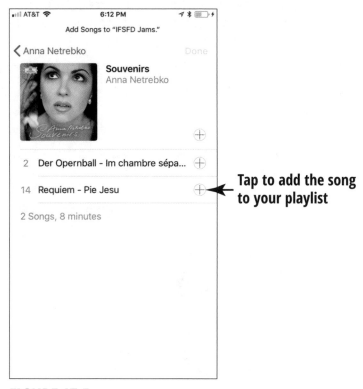

Tap to add the song
to your playlist

FIGURE 17-5

5. Tap the Done button, then tap Done on the next screen to return to the Playlists screen.

6. Your playlist appears in the list, and you can now play it by tapping the list name, then tapping a track to play it.

TIP

To search for a song in your music libraries, use the Search feature. From your first Home screen, you can swipe down from the screen outside the Dock and enter the name of the song. A list of search results appears.

Search for Music

You can search for an item in your Music library by using the Search feature.

1. With Music open, tap the Search button (see **Figure 17-6**). The Search screen appears showing Recent Searches and Trending Searches, along with a Search field at the top of the screen.

2. Enter a search term in the Search field. Results are displayed, narrowing as you type, as shown in **Figure 17-7**.

3. Tap an item to play it.

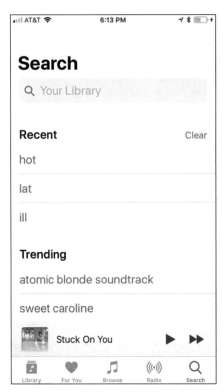

FIGURE 17-6

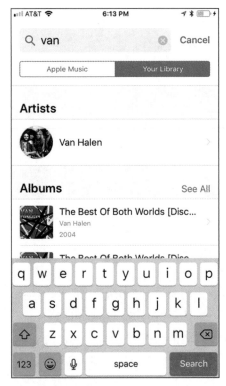

FIGURE 17-7

You can enter an artist's name, a lyricist's or a composer's name, or a word from the item's title in the Search field to find what you're looking for.

Play Music

Now that you know how to find your music, let's have some real fun by playing it!

TIP

You can use Siri to play music hands free. Just press and hold the Home button, and when Siri appears, say something like "Play 'L.A. Woman'" or "Play 'Fields of Gold.'"

To play music on your iPhone, follow these steps:

1. Locate the music that you want by using the methods described in previous tasks in this chapter.

2. Tap the item you want to play. If you're displaying the Songs category, you don't have to tap an album to open a song; you need only tap a song to play it. If you're using any other categories, you have to tap items such as albums (or multiple songs from one artist) to find the song you want to hear.

TIP

Home Sharing is a feature of iTunes that you can use to share music among up to five devices that have Home Sharing turned on. After Home Sharing is set up via iTunes, any of your devices can stream music and videos to other devices, and you can even click and drag content between devices using iTunes. For more about Home Sharing, visit this site: www.apple.com/support/homesharing.

3. Tap the item you want to play from the list that appears; it begins to play (see **Figure 17-8**).

4. Tap the currently playing song title near the bottom of the screen to open it displaying playback controls. Use the Previous and Next buttons at the bottom of the screen shown in **Figure 17-9** to navigate the audio file that's playing:

- The Previous button takes you back to the beginning of the item that's playing if you tap it, or rewinds the song if you press-and-hold it.

- The Next button takes you to the next item if you tap it, or fast-forwards the song if you press-and-hold it.

Use the Volume slider on the bottom of the screen (or the Volume buttons on the side of your iPhone) to increase or decrease the volume.

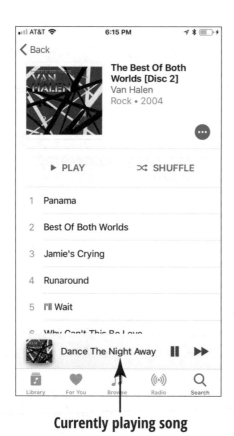

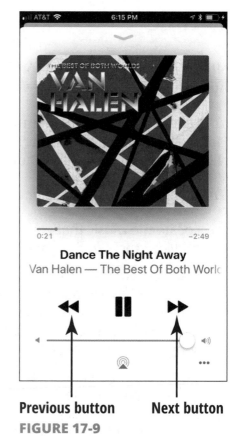

Currently playing song

FIGURE 17-8

Previous button   **Next button**

FIGURE 17-9

5. Tap the Pause button to pause playback. Tap the button again to resume playing.

TIP

You can also use music controls for music that's playing from the lock screen.

6. Tap and drag the red line (it appears gray until you touch it) near the middle of the screen (underneath the album art) that indicates the current playback location. Drag the line to the left or right to "scrub" to another location in the song.

7. If you don't like what's playing, here's how to make another selection: Tap the downward-pointing arrow at the top of the playback controls to view other selections in the album that's playing.

Family Sharing allows up to six members of your family to share purchased content even if they don't share the same iTunes account. You can set up Family Sharing under iCloud in Settings. See Chapter 15 for more about Family Sharing.

Shuffle Music

If you want to play a random selection of the music in an album on your iPhone, you can use the Shuffle feature.

1. Tap the name of the currently playing song at the bottom of the screen.

2. Swipe up on the screen until you see Up Next.

3. Tap the Shuffle button, located just above Up Next, which looks like two lines crossing to form an X (see **Figure 17-10**). Your content plays in random order.

4. Tap the Repeat button (refer to **Figure 17-10**) to play the songs over again continuously.

If you're playing music and have set the Volume slider as high as it goes and you're still having trouble hearing, consider using the earbuds that came with your iPhone. These cut out extraneous noises and improve the sound quality of what you're listening to, as well as add stereo to iPhone's mono speaker. For iPhone models older than the iPhone 7 and 7 Plus, use 3.5 mm stereo earbuds; insert them in the headphone jack at the bottom of your iPhone. If you have an iPhone 7, 7 Plus, or a newer model, you'll need earbuds that use a Lightning connector, or you can use the Lightning-to-3.5mm adaptor that also came with your iPhone with standard 3.5mm headphones. You might also look into purchasing Bluetooth earbuds, which allow you to listen wirelessly. For a top-of-the-line wireless experience, try out Apple's AirPods (go to https://www.apple.com/airpods/ for more info); they're getting rave reviews, and for good reason.

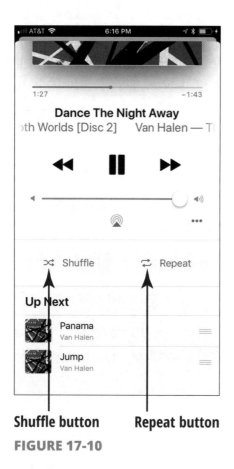

Shuffle button   Repeat button

FIGURE 17-10

Use AirPlay

The AirPlay streaming technology is built into the iPhone, iPod touch, Macs and PCs running iTunes, and iPad. Streaming technology allows you to send media files from one device that supports AirPlay to be played on another. You can send (for example) a movie that you've purchased on your iPhone or a slideshow of your photos to be played on your Apple TV, then control the TV playback from your iPhone. You can also send music to be played over compatible speakers. Check out the Apple Remote app, which you can use to control your Apple TV.

You can use the AirPlay button in Control Center, which you display by swiping up from the bottom edge of your iPhone screen, to take advantage of AirPlay in a few ways:

>> Purchase Apple TV and stream video, photos, and music to the TV.

>> Purchase AirPort Express and attach it to your speakers to play music.

>> If you buy AirPort Express, you can stream audio directly to your speakers.

If you're interested in using AirPlay, visit an Apple Store and find out which hardware combination will work best for you.

>> Get AirPlay-compatible speakers. With these, you don't need AirPort Express at all because you can AirPlay to the speakers directly. Apple's new HomePod (www.apple.com/homepod) is yet another of its new musically-oriented products, and may be exactly what you're looking for in a home audio system that does much more than simply play music.

To use AirPlay with another AirPlay-enabled device on your network or in close proximity, swipe up from the bottom of your screen and tap the AirPlay button in the Control Center; then select the AirPlay device to stream the content to, or choose your iPhone to move the playback back to it.

If you get a bit antsy watching a long movie, one of the beauties of AirPlay is that you can still use your iPhone to check email, browse photos or the Internet, or check your calendar while the media file is playing on the other device.

Play Music with Radio

You can access Radio by tapping the Radio button at the bottom of the Music screen, as seen in **Figure 17-11**.

Swipe from left to right and you'll find lots of music categories to listen to, or tap View All Stations to see the entire gamut of Radio's offerings (see **Figure 17-12**).

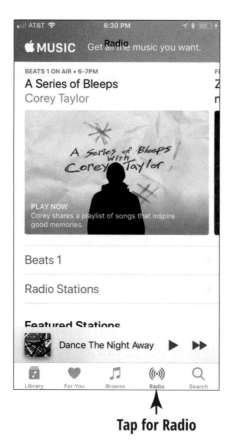

Tap for Radio

FIGURE 17-11

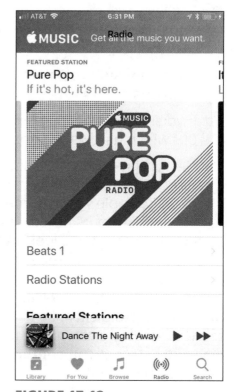

FIGURE 17-12

TECHNICAL STUFF

At one time the Radio feature was free in the Music app, but now it's tied into Apple's Music service, which is subscription-based. So, if you want to listen to stations in Radio, you'll have to become a member of Apple Music, or you can listen to Apple's flagship radio station, Beats 1, for free. To learn more about Apple Music (which is a great service), visit www.apple.com/music.

Find and Subscribe to Podcasts

First, what the heck is a podcast? A podcast is sort of like a radio show that you can listen to at any time. You'll find podcasts covering just about any subject imaginable, including:

- » News of the day
- » Sports
- » Gardening
- » Cooking
- » Education
- » Comedy
- » Religion

The Podcasts app is the vehicle by which you'll find and listen to podcasts on your iPhone.

To search Apple's library of podcasts and subscribe to them (which is free, by the way):

1. Tap the Podcasts icon to open it.

2. There are three ways to discover podcasts:
   - Tap Browse at the bottom of the screen, then tap Featured. There you'll find podcasts that are featured by the good folks at Apple, as shown in **Figure 17-13.**
   - Tap Browse at the bottom of the screen, then tap Top Charts; you'll be greeted with lists of the most popular podcasts. Tap the All Categories button in the upper-right corner to sift through the podcasts based on the category (such as Arts, Health, or Music).
   - Tap Search, then tap the Search field at the top of the screen. When the keyboard appears, type the name or subject of a podcast to see a list of results.

3. When you find a podcast that intrigues you, tap its name to see its information page, which will be similar to the one in **Figure 17-14.**

4. Tap the Subscribe button (refer to **Figure 17-14**). The podcast will appear in the Library section of the app, and the newest episode will be downloaded to your iPhone.

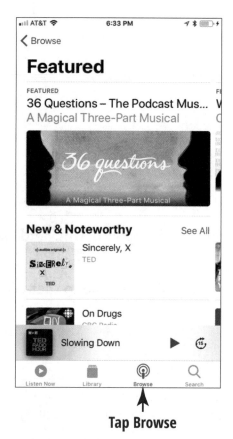

Subscribe button

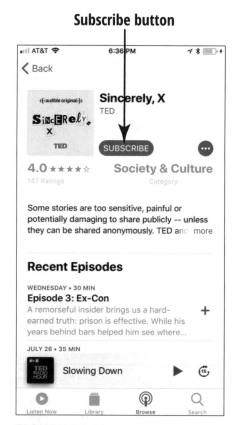

Tap Browse

FIGURE 17-13

FIGURE 17-14

5. Tap Library in the toolbar at the bottom of the screen, then tap the name of the podcast you subscribed to and view its information screen.

6. Tap the More button (looks like a circle containing three dots), then tap the Settings icon (looks like a gear) to see the settings for the podcast. From here (see **Figure 17-15**) you can customize how the podcast downloads and organizes episodes.

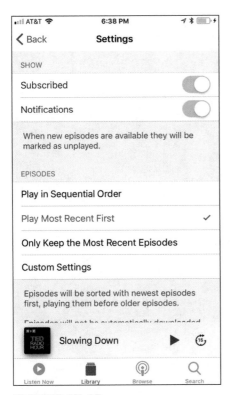

FIGURE 17-15

Play Podcasts

Playing podcasts is a breeze, and works very much like playing audio files in the Music app.

1. Open the Podcasts app and tap My Podcasts at the bottom of the screen.

2. Tap the name of the podcast you'd like to listen to.

3. Tap the episode you want to play. The episode begins playing; you can see the currently playing episode near the bottom of the screen, just above the toolbar.

4. Tap the currently playing episode to open the playback controls, shown in **Figure 17-16.**

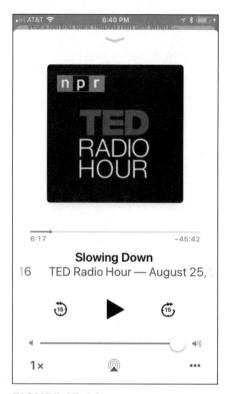

FIGURE 17-16

5. Drag the line in the middle of the screen to scrub to a different part of the episode, or tap the Rewind or Fast Forward buttons to the left and right of the Pause/Play button, respectively.

6. Adjust the playback speed by tapping the 1x icon in the lower-left of the Play controls. Each tap increases or decreases playback speed.

7. Adjust the volume by dragging the Volume slider near the bottom of the screen, or using the Volume buttons on the side of your iPhone.

Tap the Listen Now button in the toolbar at the bottom of the app's screen to see a list of the newest episodes that have been automatically downloaded to your iPhone.

- » Save photos from the web

- » View albums and single photos

- » Edit and organize photos

- » View photos by time and place

- » Share and delete photos

- » Print photos and run slideshows

- » Create time-lapse videos from photos

Chapter **18**

Taking and Sharing Photos

With its gorgeous screen, the iPhone is a natural for taking and viewing photos. It supports most common photo formats, such as JPEG, TIFF, and PNG. You can shoot your photos by using the built-in cameras in iPhone with built-in square or panorama modes. With recent iPhone models, you can edit your images using smart adjustment filters. You can also sync photos from your computer, save images that you find online to your iPhone, or receive them by email, MMS, or iMessage.

The Photo Sharing feature lets you share groups of photos with people using iCloud on an iOS device or on a Mac or Windows computer with iCloud access. Your iCloud Photo Library makes all this storage and sharing easy.

When you have taken or downloaded photos to play with, the Photos app lets you organize photos and view photos in albums, one by one, or in a slideshow. You can also view photos by the years in which they were taken, with images divided into collections by the location or time you took them. You can also AirDrop (iPhone 5 and later), email, message, or tweet a photo to a friend, print it, share it via AirPlay, or post it to Facebook. Finally, you can create time-lapse videos with the Camera app, allowing you to record a sequence in time, such as a flower opening as the sun warms it or your grandchild stirring from sleep. You can read about all these features in this chapter.

Take Pictures with the iPhone Cameras

The cameras in the iPhone are just begging to be used, so no matter which phone model you have, get started!

TIP

To go to the camera with the lock screen displayed, swipe up from the bottom of the screen and tap the Camera app icon in Control Center to go directly to the Camera app. You can also swipe down from the top of the screen to open Cover Sheet, then swipe from right to left to access Camera.

1. Tap the Camera app icon on the Home screen to open the app.

2. If the camera type at the bottom of the screen (see **Figure 18-1**) is set to Video, slide to the left to choose Photo (the still camera).

TIP

iPhone's front- and rear-facing cameras allow you to capture photos and video (see Chapter 19 for more about the video features) and share them with family and friends. Newer models offer up to a 12MP iSight camera with such features as

- Autofocus with Focus Pixels
- Automatic image stabilization to avoid fuzzy moving targets
- True Tone Flash, a sensor that tells iPhone when a flash is needed

Slide to Photo

FIGURE 18-1

The following are options for taking pictures after you've opened the Camera app:

» You can set the Pano (for panorama) and Square options using the slider control above the Capture button. These controls let you create square images like those you see on the popular Instagram site. With Pano selected, tap to begin to take a picture and pan across a view, then tap Done to capture a panoramic display.

» Tap the Flash button in the top-left corner of the screen when using the rear camera, then select a flash option:

- On, if your lighting is dim enough to require a flash

- Off, if you don't want iPhone to use a flash

- Auto, if you want to let iPhone decide for you

» To use the High Dynamic Range or HDR feature, tap the HDR setting at the top of the screen and tap to turn it on. This feature uses several images, some underexposed and some overexposed, and combines the best ones into one image, sometimes providing a more finely detailed picture.

HDR pictures can be very large in file size, meaning they'll take up more of your iPhone's memory than standard pictures.

» If you want a time delay before the camera snaps the picture, tap the Time Delay button at the top of the screen, then tap either 3s or 10s for a 3- or 10-second delay, respectively.

» Move the camera around until you find a pleasing image. You can do a couple of things at this point to help you take your photo:

- Tap the area of the grid where you want the camera to autofocus.

- Place two fingers apart from each other on the screen, then pinch them together (still touching the screen) to display a digital zoom control. Drag the circle in the zoom bar to the right or left to zoom in or out on the image.

» Tap the Capture button at the bottom center of the screen (the big, white button). You've just taken a picture, and it's stored in the Photos app gallery automatically.

You can also use a Volume button (located on the left side of your iPhone) to capture a picture or start or stop video camera recording.

» Tap the Switch Camera button in the lower-right corner to switch between the front camera and rear camera. You can then take selfies (pictures of yourself), so go ahead and tap the Capture button to take another picture.

» To view the last photo taken, tap the thumbnail of the latest image in the bottom-left corner of the screen; the Photos app opens and displays the photo.

» Tap the Share button (it's the box with an arrow coming out of it, located in the bottom-left corner of the screen) to display a menu that allows you to AirDrop, email, or instant message the photo, assign it to a contact, use it as iPhone wallpaper, tweet it, post it to Facebook, share via iCloud Photo Sharing or Flickr, or print it (see **Figure 18-2**).

FIGURE 18-2

» You can tap images to select more than one.

» To delete the image, have it displayed and tap the Trash button in the bottom-right corner of the screen. Tap Delete Photo in the confirming menu that appears.

You can use the iCloud Photo Sharing feature to automatically sync your photos across various devices. Turn on iCloud Photo Sharing by tapping Settings on the Home screen, then tapping Photos.

TIP

Save Photos from the Web

The web offers a wealth of images that you can download to your Photo Library.

TIP A number of sites protect their photos from being copied by applying an invisible overlay. This blank overlay image ensures that you don't actually get the image you're tapping. Even if a site doesn't take these precautions, be sure that you don't save images from the web and use them in ways that violate the rights of the person or entity that owns them.

To save an image from the web, follow these steps:

1. Open Safari and navigate to the web page containing the image you want.

TIP For more about how to use Safari to navigate to or search for web content, see Chapter 11.

2. Press and hold the image. A menu appears at the bottom of the screen, as shown in **Figure 18-3.**

3. Tap Save Image. The image is saved to your Camera Roll album in the Photos app, as shown in **Figure 18-4.**

TIP If you want to capture your iPhone screen as a photo, the process is simple. Press the Sleep/Wake button and Home button simultaneously; the screen flashes white, and the screen capture is complete. The capture is saved in PNG format to your Recently Added album.

TIP To save a picture sent as an email attachment in Mail, tap the attachment icon and the picture opens. Press the screen until a menu appears, then tap Save.

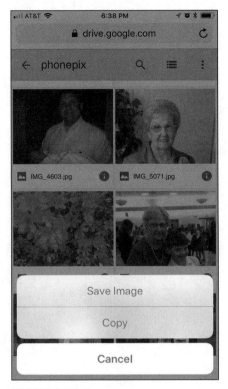

FIGURE 18-3

FIGURE 18-4

View an Album

The Photos app organizes your pictures into albums, using such criteria as the folder or album on your computer from which you synced the photos or photos captured using the iPhone camera (saved in the Camera Roll album). You may also have albums for images that you synced from other devices through iTunes or shared via Photos.

1. To view your albums, start by tapping the Photos app icon on the Home screen.

2. Tap the Albums button at the bottom of the screen to display your albums, as shown in **Figure 18-5.**

3. Tap an album. The photos in it are displayed.

Tap Albums

FIGURE 18-5

TIP

You can associate photos with faces and events. When you do, additional tabs appear at the bottom of the screen when you display an album containing that type of photo.

View Individual Photos

You can view photos individually by opening them from within an album.

TIP

With the 3D Touch feature, you can preview a photo before you open it. Tap lightly to select the photo. Tap with a medium press to display a preview, then press harder to open the photo.

1. Tap the Photos app icon on the Home screen.

2. Tap Albums (refer to **Figure 18-5**).

3. Tap an album to open it; then, to view a photo, tap it. The picture expands, as shown in **Figure 18-6.**

FIGURE 18-6

4. Flick your finger to the left or right to scroll through the album to look at the individual photos in it.

5. You can tap the Back button in the upper-left corner (looks like a left-pointing arrow), then the Albums button to return to the Album view.

You can place a photo on a person's information record in Contacts. For more about how to do this, see Chapter 6.

TIP

Edit Photos

iPhone Photos isn't Photoshop, but it does provide some tools for editing photos.

1. Tap the Photos app on the Home screen to open it.

2. Using methods previously described in this chapter, locate and display a photo you want to edit.

3. Tap the Edit button at the bottom of the screen (looks like three parallel lines with circles on each); the Edit Photo screen shown in **Figure 18-7** appears.

Crop   Adjustments

Filters

FIGURE 18-7

4. At this point, you can take three possible actions with these tools:

- **Crop:** To crop the photo to a portion of its original area, tap the Crop button. You can then tap any corner of the image and drag inward or outward to remove areas of the photo. Tap Crop, then Save to apply your changes.

- **Filters:** Apply any of nine filters (such as Vivid, Mono, or Noir) to change the look of your image. These effects adjust the brightness of your image or apply a black-and-white tone to your color photos. Tap the Filters button in the middle of the tools at the bottom of the screen and scroll to view available filters. Tap one, then tap Apply to apply the effect to your image.

- **Adjustments:** Tap Light, Color, or B&W to access a slew of tools that you can use to tweak contrast, color intensity, shadows, and more.

5. If you're pleased with your edits, tap the Done button. A copy of the edited photo is saved.

TIP

Each of the editing features has a Cancel button. If you don't like the changes you made, tap this button to stop making changes before you save the image.

Organize Photos

You'll probably want to organize your photos to make it simpler to find what you're looking for.

1. If you want to create your own album, open the Camera Roll album.

2. Tap the Select button in the top-right corner, then tap individual photos to select them. Small check marks appear on the selected photos (see **Figure 18-8**).

3. Tap the Add To button at the bottom of the screen, then tap New Album.

TIP

If you've already created albums, you can choose to add the photo to an existing album at this point.

Checkmarks show selected items

FIGURE 18-8

4. Enter a name for a new album, then tap Save. If you create a new album, it appears in the Photos main screen with the other albums that are displayed.

TIP

You can also choose the Share or Delete buttons when you've selected photos in Step 2 of this task. This allows you to share or delete multiple photos at a time.

View Photos by Years and Location

You can view your photos in logical categories, such as by date or a location where they were taken. These so-called smart groupings let you, for example, view all photos taken this year or all the photos from your summer vacation.

1. Tap Photos on the Home screen to open the Photos app.

2. Tap Photos at the bottom of the screen on the left. The display of photos by date appears (see **Figure 18-9**).

3. Tap a year or years on the left; you see collections of photos by location and date (see **Figure 18-10**).

FIGURE 18-9

FIGURE 18-10

4. Tap a collection and you can view the individual "moments" in that collection by category, such as Groups & People, Places, Related, and more.

TIP

To go back to larger groupings, such as from a moment in a collection to the larger collection to the entire last year, just keep tapping the Back button at the top left of the screen.

Share Photos with Mail, Twitter, or Facebook

You can easily share photos stored on your iPhone by sending them as email attachments, as a text message, by posting them to Facebook, sharing them via iCloud Photo Sharing or Flickr, or as tweets on Twitter. (You have to go to Chapter 14 to learn how to set up accounts for Facebook or Twitter before you can use this feature.)

1. Tap the Photos app icon on the Home screen.

2. Tap the Photos or Albums button and locate the photo you want to share.

3. Tap the photo to select it, then tap the Share button. (It looks like a box with an arrow jumping out of it.) The menu shown in **Figure 18-11** appears. Tap to select additional photos, if you want them.

4. Tap the Mail, Message, Twitter, iCloud Photo Sharing, Facebook, Flickr, or any other option you'd like to use.

5. In the message form that appears, make any modifications that apply in the To, Cc/Bcc, or Subject fields, then type a message for email, or enter your Facebook posting or Twitter tweet.

6. Tap the Send or Post button, and the message and photo are sent or posted.

TIP

You can also copy and paste a photo into documents, such as those created in the Pages word-processor app. To do this, tap a photo in Photos and tap Share. Tap the Copy command. In the destination app, press and hold the screen and tap Paste.

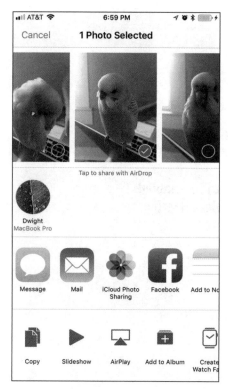

FIGURE 18-11

Share a Photo Using AirDrop

AirDrop, available to users of iPhone 5 and later, provides a way to share content, such as photos with others who are nearby and who have an AirDrop-enabled device (more recent Macs that can run macOS 10.10 or later).

Follow the steps in the previous task to locate a photo you want to share.

1. Tap the Share button.

2. If an AirDrop-enabled device is in your immediate vicinity (such as within 30 feet or so), you see the device listed (see **Figure 18-12**). Tap the device name and your photo is sent to the other device.

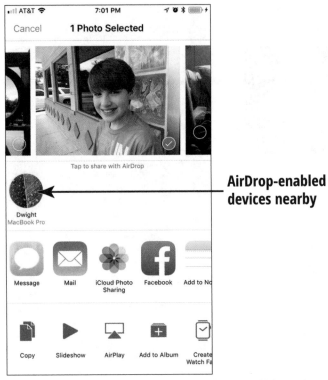

AirDrop-enabled
devices nearby

FIGURE 18-12

TIP

Other iOS devices (iPhones or iPads) must have AirDrop enabled to use this feature. To enable AirDrop, open Control Center (swipe up from the bottom of any screen) and tap AirDrop. If you don't see Air-Drop as an option, 3D-Touch (press-and-hold) the Communications area in Control Center. The Communications area houses Wi-Fi and other options; the options will expand and you'll see AirDrop there, as illustrated in **Figure 18-13**. Choose Contacts Only or Everyone to specify whom you can use AirDrop with.

Tap AirDrop

FIGURE 18-13

Share Photos Using iCloud Photo Sharing

iCloud Photo Sharing allows you to automatically share photos using your iCloud account.

1. Tap the Share button to the right of a moment, then choose to share either the whole moment or selected photos.

2. In the Share screen that opens, tap to select the photos you want to share, then tap iCloud Photo Sharing.

3. Enter a comment if you like (see **Figure 18-14**), then tap Post. The photos or moment are posted to your iCloud Photo Library.

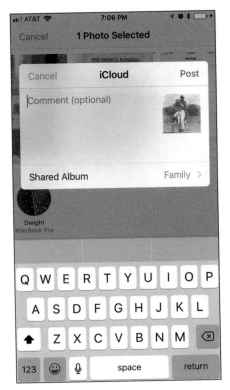

FIGURE 18-14

Work in iCloud Photo Library

iCloud Photo Library automatically backs up all your photos and videos to the cloud.

1. Open the Settings app, then tap Photos.

2. Toggle the iCloud Photo Library switch to On (green) to post all your photos to this library in the cloud.

TIP

If you want to automatically make photos available to your other devices from iCloud, also toggle the My Photo Stream switch to On.

3. Press the Home button on your iPhone, then tap the Safari app icon to open it.

4. Go to iCloud.com using your browser, sign in, and click Photos to view all photos and videos stored in the iCloud Library.

Print Photos

If you have a printer that's compatible with Apple's AirPrint technology, you can print photos from your iPhone.

1. With Photos open, locate the photo you want to print and tap it to maximize it.

2. Tap the Share button, and on the menu that appears (refer to **Figure 18-11**), scroll in the bottom row of buttons to the far right, then tap Print.

3. In the Printer Options dialog that appears (see **Figure 18-15**), tap an available printer in the list or Select Printer. iPhone presents you with a list of any compatible wireless printers on your local network.

Tap to select a printer

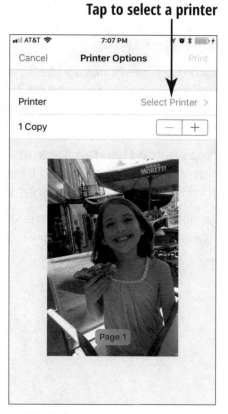

FIGURE 18-15

4. Tap the plus or minus symbols in the Copy field to set the number of copies to print.

5. Tap the Print button, and your photo is sent to the printer.

Run a Slideshow

You can run a slideshow of your images in Photos and even play music and choose transition effects for the show.

1. Tap the Photos app on the Home screen.

2. Display an individual photo in an album that contains more than one photo.

3. Tap the Share button, then tap Slideshow to run the slideshow.

4. Tap the screen, then tap Options in the lower-right corner to see the Slideshow Options dialog, shown in **Figure 18-16**.

5. If you want to play music along with the slideshow, tap Music, then tap a music selection in the list that appears (see **Figure 18-17**). Tap Back in the upper left to not make changes and return to the Slideshow Options screen.

6. In the Slideshow Options dialog, tap Theme, then tap the transition effect that you want to use for your slideshow. Tap Back in the upper left to not make changes and return to the Slideshow Options screen.

7. Tap Done and the slideshow plays with the music and theme you selected. Tap the screen to stop the slideshow at any time.

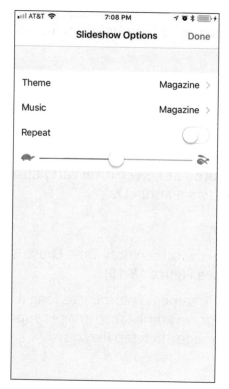

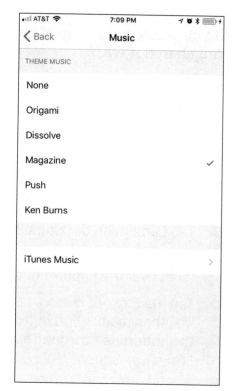

FIGURE 18-16

FIGURE 18-17

Delete Photos

You might find that it's time to get rid of some of those old photos of the family reunion or the last community center project. If the photos weren't transferred from your computer, but instead were taken, downloaded, or captured as screenshots on the iPhone, you can delete them.

1. Tap the Photos app icon on the Home screen.

2. Tap the Albums tab, then tap an album to open it.

3. Locate and tap on a photo that you want to delete, then tap the Trash icon. In the confirming dialog that appears, tap the Delete Photo button to finish the deletion.

WARNING

If you delete a photo in Photo Sharing, it is deleted on all devices that you shared it with.

Create Time-Lapse Videos from Photos

The Time Lapse feature of Camera allows you to create a time-lapse photo show. iPhone captures photos at select intervals, allowing the capture of a dynamic scene (such as a sunset).

1. Tap Camera on the Home screen.

2. Swipe the listing at the bottom of the screen until Time Lapse is centered over the Capture button (see **Figure 18-18**).

3. Tap the Capture button. Leave the camera recording as long as you like, then tap the End button. Your new time-lapse images appear in the bottom-left corner. Tap the image, then tap Play.

FIGURE 18-18

Chapter **19**

Creating and Watching Videos

U sing the TV app (formerly known as Videos in earlier iOS versions), you can watch downloaded movies or TV shows, as well as media that you've synced from iCloud on your Mac or PC, and even media that's provided from other content providers, such as cable and streaming video services. The TV app aims to be your one-stop shop for your viewing pleasure.

In addition, newer iPhone models sport both a front and rear video camera that you can use to capture your own videos, and by downloading the iMovie app for iPhone (a more limited version of the longtime mainstay on Mac computers), you add the capability to edit those videos. A 12MP camera can record high-definition video. With these latest models, you also get 4K video, which produces rich detail with 8 million pixels per frame.

A few other features of video in newer iPhone models include image stabilization to avoid the shakes when recording, more frames shot per second for smoother video, and Cinematic Video Stabilization, which means that your iPhone continually autofocuses as you're recording.

In this chapter, I explain all about shooting and watching video content from a variety of sources. For practice, you might want to refer to Chapter 15 first to find out how to purchase or download one of many available TV shows or movies from the iTunes Store.

Capture Your Own Videos with the Built-In Cameras

The camera lens that comes on newer iPhones has perks for photographers, including a large aperture and highly accurate sensor, which make for better images all around. In addition, auto image stabilization makes up for any shakiness in the hands holding the phone, and autofocus has sped up thanks to the fast processors being used. For videographers, you'll appreciate a fast frames-per-second capability as well as a slow-motion feature.

1. To capture a video, tap the Camera app on the Home screen. In iPhone, two video cameras are available for capturing video, one from the front and one from the back of the device. (See more about this topic in the next task.)

2. The Camera app opens (see **Figure 19-1**). Tap and slide the camera-type options above the red Record button until Video rests above the button; this is how you switch from the still camera to the video camera.

3. If you want to switch between the front and back cameras, tap the Switch Camera button in the top-right corner of the screen (refer to **Figure 19-1**).

4. Tap the red Record button to begin recording the video. (The red dot in the middle of this button turns into a red square when the camera is recording.) When you're finished, tap the Record button again. Your new video is now listed in the bottom-left corner of the screen. Tap the video to play it, share it, or delete it. In the future, you can find and play the video in your Camera Roll when you open the Photos app.

Record button

FIGURE 19-1

TIP

Before you start recording, remember where the camera lens is —
while holding the iPhone and panning, you can easily put your fingers
directly over the lens! Also, you can't pause your recording; when you
stop, your video is saved, and when you start recording, you're creating a new video file.

Play Movies or TV Shows with TV

Open the TV app for the first time and you'll be greeted with a
Welcome screen; tap Continue. You'll be asked to sign in to your
television provider, as seen in **Figure 19-2**.

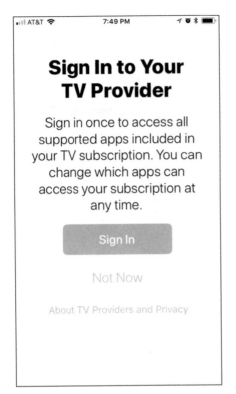

FIGURE 19-2

Signing in will allow you to use the TV app to access content in other apps (like ESPN or Disney), if such services are supported by your TV provider. This way, you only need to use the TV app to access content and sign in, as opposed to having multiple apps to juggle and sign in to.

TIP

Should you decide to skip signing in to your TV provider and worry about it later (or if you've already opened the TV app and cruised right past this part), you can access the same options by going to Settings⇨TV Provider, tapping the name of your provider (a partial list of which is shown in **Figure 19-3**), then entering your account information.

The TV app offers a couple of ways to view movies and TV shows: via third-party providers or items you've purchased or rented from the iTunes Store.

To access content from third-party providers like NBC, ABC, PBS, and more, tap the Watch Now button in the bottom-left of your screen (**Figure 19-4**). Swipe to see hit shows and browse by genres like Comedy, Action, and others.

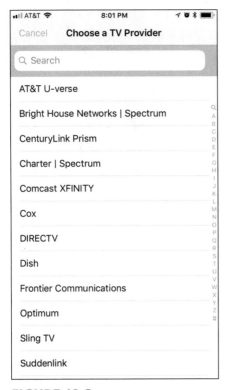

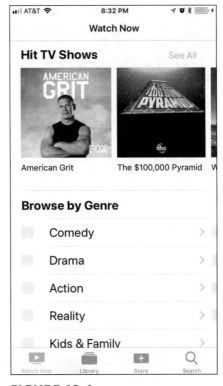

FIGURE 19-3

FIGURE 19-4

Tap on a show that interests you, then tap an episode to see a description, like I've done in **Figure 19-5**. Tap Play; if you have the app that supports the video, the video will open automatically in the correct app. If you don't have the app installed, you'll be asked if you'd like to download and install it, as shown in **Figure 19-6**.

TIP

If your iPhone is on the same Wi-Fi network as your computer and both are running iTunes, with the iPhone and iTunes set to use the same Home Sharing account, you see the Shared List. With this setup, you can stream videos from iTunes on your computer to your iPhone.

FIGURE 19-5

FIGURE 19-6

To access video you've purchased or rented from the iTunes Store, follow these steps:

1. Tap the TV app icon on the Home screen to open the application, then tap Library at the bottom of the screen.

2. On a screen like the one in **Figure 19-7**, tap the appropriate category at the top of the screen (TV Shows or Movies, depending on the content you've downloaded), then tap the video you want to watch.

   Information about the movie or TV show episodes appears, as shown in **Figure 19-8.**

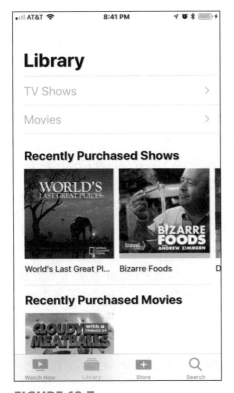

FIGURE 19-7

FIGURE 19-8

3. For TV Shows, tap the episode that you'd like to play; for Movies, the Play button appears on the description screen. Tap the Play button and the movie or TV show begins playing (see **Figure 19-9**). (If you see a small, cloud-shaped icon instead of a Play button, tap it and the content is downloaded from iCloud.)

FIGURE 19-9

The progress of the playback is displayed on the Progress bar showing how many minutes you've viewed and how many remain. If you don't see the bar, tap the screen once to display it briefly, along with a set of playback tools at the bottom of the screen.

4. With the playback tools displayed, take any of these actions:

- Tap the Pause button to pause playback.

- Tap either Go to Previous Chapter or Go to Next Chapter to move to a different location in the video playback.

If a video has chapter support, another button called Scenes appears here for displaying all chapters so that you can move more easily from one to another.

- Tap the circular button on the Volume slider and drag the button left or right to decrease or increase the volume, respectively.

If your controls disappear during playback, just tap the screen and they'll reappear.

5. To stop the video and return to the information screen, tap the Done button to the left of the Progress bar.

If you've watched a video and stopped it before the end, it opens by default to the last location where you were viewing. To start a video from the beginning, tap and drag the circular button (the *playhead*) on the Progress bar all the way to the left.

Turn On Closed-Captioning

iTunes and iPhone offer support for closed-captioning and subtitles. Look for the CC logo on media that you download to use this feature.

Video you record won't have this capability.

If a movie has either closed-captioning or subtitles, you can turn on the feature in iPhone.

1. Begin by tapping the Settings icon on the Home screen.

2. Tap General ⇨ Accessibility. On the screen that appears, scroll down and tap Subtitles & Captioning.

3. On the menu that displays (see **Figure 19-10**), tap the Closed Captions + SDH switch to turn on the feature. Now when you play a movie with closed-captioning, you can tap the Audio and Subtitles button to the left of the playback controls to manage these features.

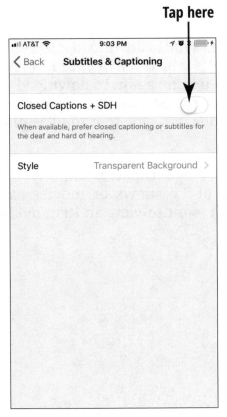

Tap here

FIGURE 19-10

Delete a Video from the iPhone

You can buy videos directly from your iPhone, or you can sync via iCloud or iTunes to place content you've bought or created on another device on your iPhone.

When you want to get rid of video content on your iPhone because it's a memory hog, you can delete it:

1. Open the TV app, then go to the TV show or movie you want to delete.

2. Tap the Downloaded button.

3. Tap Remove Download in the options that appear. The downloaded video will be deleted from your iPhone.

If you buy a video using iTunes and sync to download it to your iPhone, then delete it from your iPhone, it's still saved in your iTunes Library. You can sync your computer and iPhone again to download the video again. Remember, however, that rented movies, when deleted, are gone with the wind. Also, video doesn't sync to iCloud as photos and music do.

TIP

iPhone has a much smaller storage capacity than your typical computer, so downloading lots of TV shows or movies can fill its storage area quickly. If you don't want to view an item again, delete it to free space.

Chapter **20**

Playing Games

The iPhone is super for playing games, with its bright screen, portable size, and ability to rotate the screen as you play and track your motions. You can download game apps from the App Store and play them on your device.

In this chapter, you get an overview of game playing on your iPhone, including purchasing and downloading games the new App Store's dedicated Games section, and playing games solo or against friends.

Purchase and Download Games

Time to get your game on!

TIP

Although a few games have versions for both Mac and iOS users, the majority are either macOS-version only (macOS is the name of the Mac's operating system) or iOS-version only — something to be aware of when you buy games.

1. Open the App Store.
2. Tap the Games button at the bottom of the screen (see **Figure 20-1**).

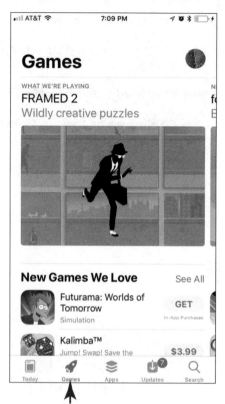

Games button

FIGURE 20-1

3. Navigating the Games screen is simple:

    - Swipe from right to left to see featured apps in such categories as "What We're Playing" and "Editors' Choice."

    - Swipe down to find the Top Paid and Free games or to shop by categories (tap See All to view all of the available categories), as shown in **Figure 20-2**.

4. Explore the list of games in the type you selected until you find something you like; tap the game to see its information screen.

5. To buy a game, tap the button labeled with either the word Get or the price (such as $2.99).

6. When the dialog opens appears at the bottom of the screen (as illustrated in **Figure 20-3**), tap Enter Password, type your password in the Password field on the next screen, then tap Done to download the game.

Tap to view all categories

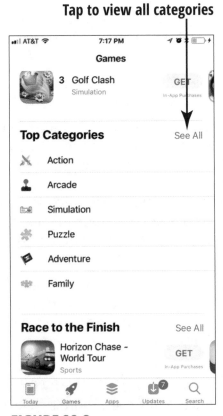

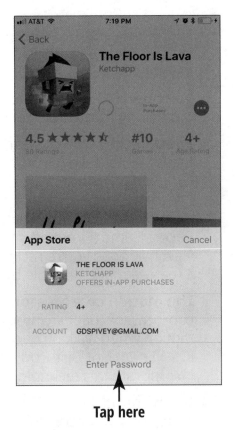

Tap here

FIGURE 20-2   FIGURE 20-3

7. The game downloads. Tap the Open button to go to the downloaded game or find the games icon on your Home screen and tap to open it.

8. Have fun!

Master iPhone Game-Playing Basics

It's almost time to start playing games. For many reasons, iPhone is a good, smaller–screen gaming device because of the following:

» **Fantastic-looking screen:** The iPhone screen offers bright colors for great gaming. In-Plane Switching (IPS) technology lets you hold your iPhone at almost any angle (it has a 178-degree viewing angle) and still see good color and contrast.

- » **Faster processor:** The super-fast processor chips that appeared in the iPhone 6s and 6s Plus and later models are ideal for gaming.

- » **Long battery life:** A device's long battery life means that you can tap energy from it for many hours of gaming fun.

- » **Specialized game-playing features:** Some newer games have features that take full advantage of the iPhone's capabilities. For example, Nova (from Gameloft) features Multiple Target Acquisition, which lets you to target multiple bad guys in a single move to blow them out of the water with one shot. In Real Racing Game (Firemint), for example, you can look in your rearview mirror as you're racing to see what's coming up behind you, a feature made possible by the iPhone's large screen.

- » **The motion coprocessor:** iPhone contains a motion-detecting coprocessor that can interpret data from a sensor about your motion when walking or driving. Many fitness apps, and even iOS 11's Do Not Disturb While Driving feature (see Chapter 5), incorporate this technology.

- » **Great sound:** The built-in iPhone speaker is a powerful little item, but if you want an experience that's even more up close and personal, you can plug in a headphone, some speaker systems, or a microphone using the built-in Lightning connector. (You may need to use the Lightning-to-3.5mm adapter that comes with newer iPhone models for products that incorporate standard 3.5mm headphone jacks.)

TIP

In addition to the motion coprocessor, most later iPhone models have a built-in motion sensor — the three-axis accelerometer — as well as a gyroscope. These features provide lots of fun for people developing apps for the iPhone because they make the automatically rotating screen part of the gaming experience for you to enjoy. For example, a built-in compass reorients itself automatically as you switch your iPhone from landscape to portrait orientation. In some racing games, you can grab the iPhone as though it were a steering wheel and rotate the device to simulate the driving experience.

Play against Yourself

Many games allow you to play a game all on your own. Each has different rules and goals, so you'll have to study a game's instructions and Help to learn how to play it, but here's some general information about these types of games:

» Often, a game can be played in two modes: with others or in a solitaire version, in which you play yourself or the computer.

» Many games you may be familiar with in the offline world, such as Carcassonne or Scrabble, have online versions. For these, you already know the rules of play, so you simply need to figure out the execution. For example, in the online Carcassonne game, you tap to place a tile on the board, tap the placed tile to rotate it, and tap the check mark to complete your turn and reveal another tile.

» All the games you play on your own record your scores in Game Center so that you can track your progress.

Challenge Friends in Game Center

If you and a friend have both downloaded the same games, you can challenge your friend to beat your scores and even join you in a game, if the game supports Game Center interaction. You'll have to consult the developer's game information to find out if that's the case.

If it turns out that the game developer does support Game Center features in the game you'd like to play with a friend, you'll need to make sure your Apple ID information is registered for Game Center interaction. To do so:

1. Open the Settings app.

2. Scroll down a bit and tap Game Center, seen in **Figure 20-4.**

FIGURE 20-4

Tap Game Center

3. Tap to toggle the Game Center switch to On (green), then click Continue if prompted. You will be logged in using your Apple ID and password.

4. When signed in, toggle the Nearby Players switch to On (green) if it isn't already. This option enables you to find and invite nearby players who connect with you over Wi-Fi or Bluetooth, assuming the game you want to play supports this functionality.

Chapter **21**

Navigating with Maps

The Maps app has lots of useful functions. You can find directions with alternative routes from one location to another. You can bookmark locations to return to them again. And the Maps app delivers information about locations, such as phone numbers and web links to businesses. You can even add a location to your Contacts list or share a location link with your buddy using Mail, Messages, Twitter, or Facebook. The Nearby feature helps you explore local attractions and businesses, and the Transit view lets you see public transit maps for select cities around the world. iOS 11 also introduces some great new features, such as lane guidance (helps you get in the correct lane for upcoming turns), speed limit indicators for many roads, and maps of such indoor locations as shopping centers and airports.

You're about to have some fun exploring Maps in this chapter.

Go to Your Current Location

iPhone can figure out where you are at any time and display your current location.

1. From the Home screen, tap the Maps icon. Tap the Current Location button (the small arrow in the upper-right corner; see **Figure 21-1**). A map is displayed with your current location indicated (refer to **Figure 21-1**).

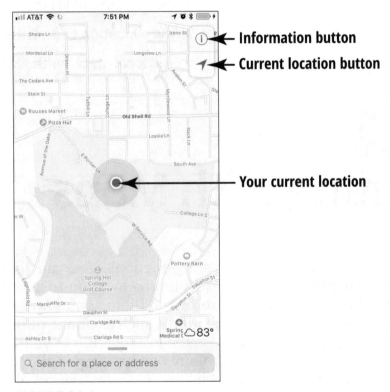

FIGURE 21-1

TECHNICAL STUFF

Depending on your connection, Wi-Fi or 3G/4G (sometimes noted as LTE in Maps), a pulsating circle may appear around the marker, indicating the area surrounding your location is based on cell tower triangulation. Your exact location can be anywhere within the area of the circle, and the location service is likely to be less accurate using a Wi-Fi connection than your phone's 3G or 4G connection.

2. Double-tap the screen to zoom in on your location. (Additional methods of zooming in and out are covered in the "Zoom In and Out" section in this chapter.)

As mentioned previously, if you access maps via a Wi-Fi connection, your current location is a rough estimate based on a triangulation method. Your iPhone can more accurately pinpoint where you are by using your 3G or 4G/LTE data connection, your iPhone's global positioning system (GPS), and Bluetooth. But you can get pretty accurate results with just a Wi-Fi–connected iPhone if you type a starting location and an ending location to get directions.

Change Views

The Maps app offers three views: Map, Transit, and Satellite. iPhone displays the Map view (refer to **Figure 21-1**) by default the first time you open Maps.

1. To change views, with Maps open, tap the Information button in the upper right of the screen (refer to **Figure 21-1**) to reveal the Maps Settings dialog, shown in **Figure 21-2.**

In the Maps Settings dialog, you can also access a Traffic overlay feature. If you live in a large metropolitan area (this feature doesn't really work in small towns or rural settings), turn on this feature by toggling the Traffic switch to On (green).

2. Tap the Transit button, then tap the Close button (looks like a white X within a gray circle) in the upper right of the Maps Setting dialog. In Transit view, if you have a major city for which Transit information is available, you'll see data about public transit.

3. Tap the Information button again in the upper right, tap the Satellite button, then tap the Close button. The Satellite view (shown in **Figure 21-3**) appears.

You can also toggle the Labels switches in the Maps Settings dialog to see street names superimposed on maps while in Satellite view.

4. You can display a 3D effect on any view by tapping the Show 3D map option in the Maps menu.

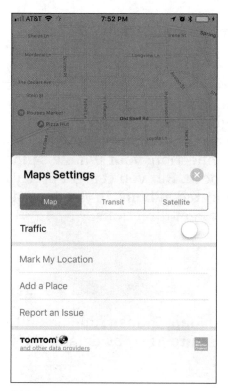

FIGURE 21-2   **FIGURE 21-3**

 Maps displays a weather icon in the lower-right corner of a map to indicate the weather conditions in the area.

TIP

Zoom In and Out

You'll appreciate the Zoom feature because it gives you the capability to zoom in and out to see more or less detailed maps and to move around a displayed map.

1. With a map displayed, double-tap with a single finger to zoom in (see **Figure 21-4;** the image on the left shows the map before zooming in, and the image on the right shows the map after zooming).

2. Double-tap with two fingers to zoom out, revealing less detail.

3. Place two fingers positioned together on the screen and move them apart to zoom in.

FIGURE 21-4

4. Place two fingers apart on the screen, then pinch them together to zoom out.

5. A new option in iOS 11 called one-handed zoom allows you to zoom in and out with just one finger. To start it, double-tap on the screen, but on the second tap hold your finger on the screen. Now, drag your finger up or down the screen to zoom in or out.

6. Press your finger to the screen and drag the map in any direction to move to an adjacent area.

TIP

It can take a few moments for the map to redraw itself when you enlarge, reduce, or move around it, so be patient. Areas that are being redrawn look like blank grids but are filled in eventually. Also, if you're in Satellite view, zooming in may take some time; wait it out. The blurred image resolves itself and looks quite nice, even tightly zoomed.

Go to Another Location or a Favorite

1. With Maps open, tap in the Search field (see **Figure 21-5**). The keyboard opens.

Search field

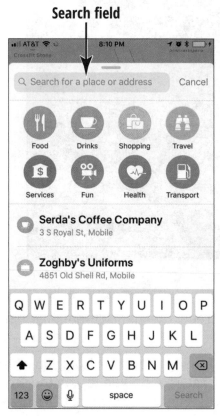

FIGURE 21-5

2. Type a location, using either a street address with city and state, a stored contact name, or a destination (such as Empire State Building or Lincoln Memorial). Maps may make suggestions as you type if it finds any logical matches. Tap the result you prefer. The location appears with a marker on it (the marker depends on which kind of establishment the location is, such as restaurant or landmark) and an information dialog with the location name and a Directions button (see **Figure 21-6**).

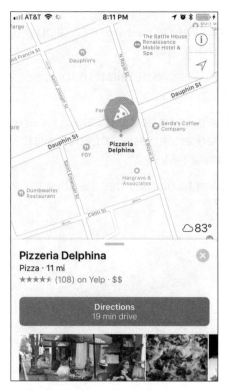
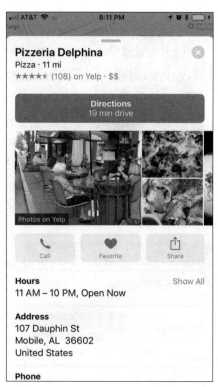

FIGURE 21-6

TIP

Swipe up on the information dialog and more information is displayed, such as pictures of the location, address and phone information, and more.

3. Swipe down on the information dialog. You move back to the map, where you can tap the screen and drag in any direction to move to a nearby location.

Drop a Marker (or Pin)

Markers and pins are the same thing, but the iOS 11 version of Maps leans toward using markers as the default term. I felt that this part of the chapter was the best place to mark that difference, in case you've used iOS devices in the past and have always referred to marked locations as pins and were wondering what all this marker business was all about.

1. Display a map that contains a spot where you want to drop a marker to help you find directions to or from that site.

2. If you need to, you can zoom in to a more detailed map to see a better view of the location you want to mark.

3. Press and hold your finger on the screen at the location where you want to place the marker. The marker appears, together with an information dialog (refer to **Figure 21-6**).

4. Swipe up on the information dialog to display details about the marker location (see **Figure 21-7**).

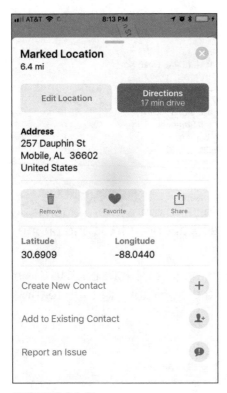

FIGURE 21-7

TIP

If a location has associated reviews on sites, such as the restaurant and travel review site Yelp (www.yelp.com), you can display details about the location and scroll down to read the reviews.

Find Directions

You can get directions in a couple of different ways.

1. Tap a marker on your map, then tap the Directions button in the information dialog. A blue line appears, showing the route between your current location and the chosen marker (see **Figure 21-8**). Sometimes alternate routes will display as well (in a lighter shade of blue), allowing you to select which you'd rather take; just tap the alternate route if you deem it's best for you. Tap the Close button to return to the Maps main screen.

2. You can enter two locations to get directions from one to the other. Tap the Search field to open the keyboard and type the location you'd like to get to, then select the location from the list. In the information dialog that appears, you see the destination at the top and From just below it (shown in **Figure 21-9**).

FIGURE 21-8

FIGURE 21-9

3. My Location is the default, but if you want to change it to a different location, just tap My Location, type in the new starting point, then tap Route in the upper-right corner (see **Figure 21-10**).

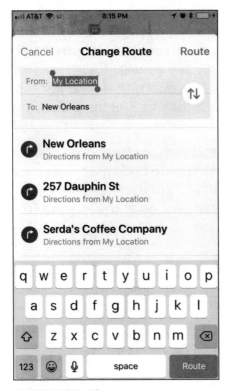

FIGURE 21-10

At the bottom of the information dialog you have buttons called Walk, Transit, and Ride (along with the default Drive). Tap one of them to see directions that are optimized for that particular mode of transportation.

TIP

4. Tap the Go button when you're ready to start on your route.

Get Turn-by-Turn Navigation Help

1. After you've found directions, tap the Go button to get started.

The narration begins and text instructions are displayed at the top of the screen, as you can see in **Figure 21-11**. Estimated arrival time and distance are shown at the bottom of the screen in the collapsed information dialog. Continue on your way according to the route until the next instruction is spoken.

2. For an overview of your route (as shown in **Figure 21-12**) at any time, swipe up on the information dialog, then tap the Overview button that appears in the lower-left corner. Swipe up on the information dialog again and tap Turn-by-turn to continue on your way.

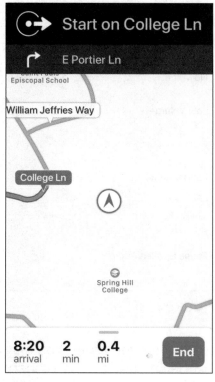

FIGURE 21-11   **FIGURE 21-12**

3. To see the details of your route (seen in **Figure 21-13**), swipe up on the information dialog, then tap the Details button. Tap Done when you're ready to resume turn-by-turn navigation.

4. To adjust the volume of the spoken navigation aid, swipe up on the information dialog, then tap the Audio button. Adjust the audio settings to either No Voice, Low Volume, Normal Volume, or Loud Volume (as seen in **Figure 21-14**). Toggle the Pause Spoken Audio

switch to On if you want to pause other audio that you may be listening to when Maps needs to give you directions. Tap Done to get back to your route.

FIGURE 21-13   **FIGURE 21-14**

5. Maps will end the route automatically after you arrive. You may also end the route manually by tapping the End button, then confirming by tapping the End Route button, shown in **Figure 21-15** (tap Resume to continue along your merry way).

TIP

It's no problem if you need to perform another task while in the middle of getting directions. Press the Home button to get out of Maps and you'll notice a blue bar appearing at the top of your screen. Simply tap that blue bar to get back to your navigation in Maps after the other task is complete.

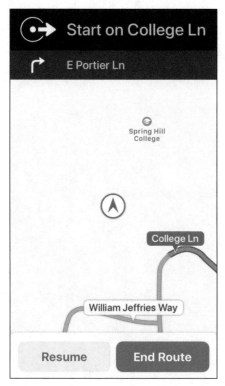

FIGURE 21-15

View and Share Information about a Location

1. Go to a location and tap its marker.

2. Swipe up on the information dialog that appears at the bottom of the screen.

3. In the expanded information dialog (refer to **Figure 21-16**), tap the Website icon to visit the location's web page, if one is associated with it.

4. You can also tap the Call icon to instantly place a call to the location, or tap the Share icon to share the location's information with someone else via Messages, Mail, and other means.

5. Swipe down on the information dialog to return to the Map view.

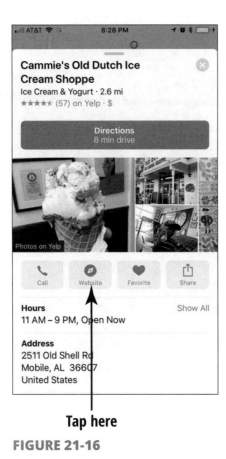

Tap here

FIGURE 21-16

Add a Location to a Contact

1. Tap a marker or location and swipe up on the information dialog to expand it.

2. Scroll down to the bottom of the information dialog and tap Create New Contact or Add to Existing Contact, as shown in **Figure 21-17**.

3. The New Contact dialog appears (see **Figure 21-18**).

TIP

If you choose Add to an Existing Contact here, you can choose a contact from your Contacts list to add the location information to.

4. Whatever information was available about the location has already been entered. Enter any additional information you need, such as a name, phone number, or email address.

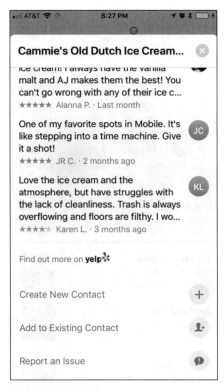

FIGURE 21-17

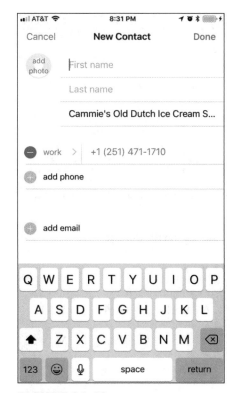

FIGURE 21-18

5. Tap Done in the upper-right corner. The information is stored in your Contacts address book.

Find Local Places with Nearby

As you can see in **Figure 21-19**, when you perform a search, a row of buttons is displayed across the top of the results.

These take you to Nearby results; that is, businesses and services that are near your current location.

1. Begin a search and tap one of these buttons, such as Food. Results for the Food category are shown in **Figure 21-20**.

2. Tap an item in the list or on the map to see more information or tap one of the other Food-related icons to narrow your search categories (for example, Coffee Shops or Bakeries).

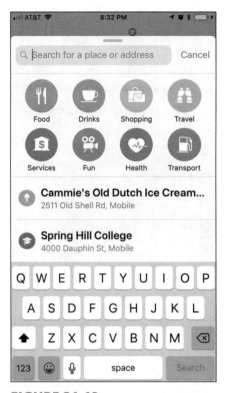

FIGURE 21-19

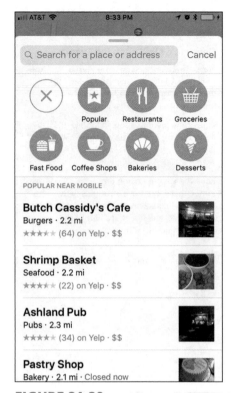

FIGURE 21-20

5

Living with Your iPhone

IN THIS PART . . .

Scheduling your life

Recording your day

Maintaining your iPhone

Chapter **22**

Keeping On Schedule with Calendar and Clock

Whether you're retired or still working, you have a busy life full of activities (even busier if you're retired, for some unfathomable reason). You may need a way to keep on top of all those activities and appointments. The Calendar app on your iPhone is a simple, elegant, electronic daybook that helps you do just that.

In addition to being able to enter events and view them in a list or by the day, week, or month, you can set up Calendar to send alerts to remind you of your obligations and search for events by keywords. You can even set up repeating events, such as birthdays, monthly get-togethers with the girls or guys, or weekly babysitting appointments with your grandchild. To help you coordinate calendars on multiple devices, you can also sync events with other calendar accounts. And by taking advantage of the Family Sharing feature, you can create a Family calendar that everybody in your family can view and add events to.

Another preinstalled app that can help you stay on schedule is Clock. Though simple to use, Clock helps you view the time in multiple locations, set alarms, check yourself with a stopwatch feature, and use a timer.

In this chapter, you master the simple procedures for getting around your calendar, creating a Family calendar, entering and editing events, setting up alerts, syncing, and searching. You also learn the simple ins and outs of using Clock.

View Your Calendar

Calendar offers several ways to view your schedule.

1. Start by tapping the Calendar app icon on the Home screen to open it. Depending on what you last had open and the orientation in which you're holding your iPhone, you may see today's calendar, List view, the year, the month, the week, an open event, or the Search screen with search results displayed.

TIP

If you're lucky enough to own one of the Plus iPhone models (iPhone 7 Plus, for example), because of their wider screens, when you hold them horizontally and you're in the Calendar app, you see more information on the screen than you see on other iPhone models. For example, in Monthly view, you see the entire month on the left and detailed information on events for the selected day.

2. Tap the Today button at the bottom of the screen to display Today's view (if it isn't already displayed), then tap the List View button to see all scheduled events for that day. The List view, shown in **Figure 22-1,** displays your daily appointments for every day in a list, with times listed on the left. Tap an event in the list to get more event details, or tap the Add button (the + symbol) to add an event.

TIP

If you'd like to display events only from a particular calendar, such as the Birthday or US Holidays calendars, tap the Calendars button at the bottom of the List view and select a calendar to base the list on.

3. Tap the current month in the upper-left corner to display months; in the Month view, the List View button changes to a Combined View button. Tap this to show the month calendar at the top and a scrollable list of events at the bottom, as shown in **Figure 22-2.** Tap the button again to return to the Month view.

New Event button

List View button

Combined view button

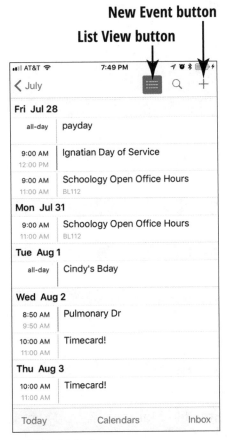

FIGURE 22-1

FIGURE 22-2

4. Tap a date in the Month calendar and you'll see that week at the top and the selected day's events below.

TECHNICAL STUFF

The Week view can't display combined lists.

5. In the Month view, note the year displayed at the top left of the screen; tap the arrow to its left to get a yearly display (see **Figure 22-3**), then tap another month to display it. In the Year view, you see the calendar for the entire year with a red circle around the current day.

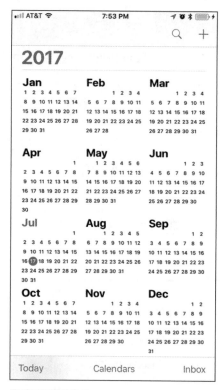

FIGURE 22-3

6. To move from one month to the next in Month view, you can also scroll up or down the screen with your finger.

7. To jump back to today, tap the Today button in the bottom-left corner of Calendar. The month containing the current day is displayed.

TIP

To view any invitation that you accepted, which placed an event on your calendar, tap Inbox in the lower-right corner and a list of invitations is displayed. You can use text within emails (such as a date, flight number, or phone number) to add an event to Calendar. Tap Done to return to the calendar.

Add Calendar Events

1. With any view displayed, tap the Add button (which looks like a plus symbol) in the upper-right corner of the screen to add an event (refer to **Figure 22-3**). The New Event dialog appears.

2. Enter a title for the event and, if you want, a location.

3. Tap the All-day switch to turn it on for an all-day event. Tap the Starts or Ends field; the scrolling setting for day, hour, and minute appears (see **Figure 22-4**).

FIGURE 22-4

4. Place your finger on the date, hour, minute, or AM/PM column and move your finger to scroll up or down.

5. If you want to add notes, use your finger to scroll down in the New Event dialog and tap in the Notes field. Type your note, then tap the Add button to save the event.

You can edit any event at any time by simply tapping it in any view of your calendar and, when the details are displayed, tap Edit in the upper-left corner. The Edit Event dialog appears, offering the same settings as the New Event dialog. Tap the Done button to save your changes or Cancel to return to your calendar without saving any changes.

Create Repeating Events

If you want an event to repeat, such as a weekly or monthly appointment, you can set a repeating event.

1. With any view displayed, tap the Add button to add an event. The New Event dialog (refer to **Figure 22-4**) appears.

2. Enter a title and location for the event and set the start and end dates and times, as shown in the preceding task, "Add Calendar Events."

3. Scroll down the page if necessary, then tap the Repeat field; the Repeat dialog, shown in **Figure 22-5,** is displayed.

4. Tap a preset time interval: Every Day, Week, 2 Weeks, Month, or Year and you return to the New Event dialog. Tap Custom and make the appropriate settings if you want to set any other interval, such as every two months on the 6th of the month.

5. Tap Done. You return to the Calendar.

Other calendar programs may give you more control over repeating events; for example, you might be able to make a setting to repeat an event the fourth Tuesday of every month. If you want a more robust calendar feature, you might consider setting up your appointments in an application such as Outlook, Google Calendar, or the macOS version of Calendar and syncing it to iPhone. But if you want to create a simple repeating event in iPhone's Calendar app, simply add the first event on a Tuesday and make it repeat every week. Easy, huh?

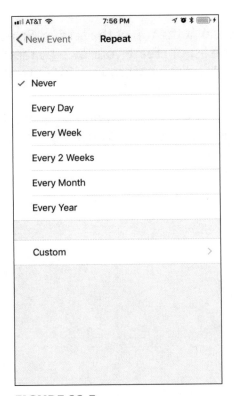

FIGURE 22-5

Add Alerts

If you want your iPhone to alert you when an event is coming up, you can use the Alert feature.

1. Tap the Settings icon on the Home screen and choose Sounds.

2. Scroll down to Calendar Alerts and tap it; then tap any Alert Tone, which causes iPhone to play the tone for you. After you've chosen the alert tone you want, tap Sounds to return to Sounds settings. Press the Home button, then tap Calendar and create an event in your calendar or open an existing one for editing, as covered in earlier tasks in this chapter.

TIP

You can also set your iPhone to alert you of a Calendar event with a vibration for times when you have your sound muted and can't hear an alert (the vibrations can also act as a secondary alert to the alert tones). Tap the Settings icon on the Home screen, tap Sounds, tap

Calendar Alerts, then tap Vibration at the top of the screen. Select a vibration pattern from one in the list or create your own by tapping Create New Vibration. You can also disable vibrations for Calendar alerts by tapping None at the very bottom of the screen.

3. In the New Event (refer to **Figure 22-4**) or Edit Event dialog, tap the Alert field. The Event Alert dialog appears, as shown in **Figure 22-6.**

FIGURE 22-6

4. Tap any preset interval, from 5 Minutes to 2 Days Before or At Time of Event and tap New Event to return to the New Event dialog. (You can scroll down in the Event Alert dialog to see more options.)

The Alert setting is shown in the New Event or Edit dialog (see **Figure 22-7**).

TECHNICAL STUFF

5. Tap Done in the Edit Event dialog or Add in the New Event dialog to save all settings.

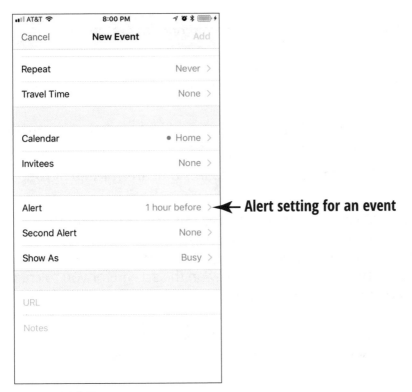

FIGURE 22-7

TIP

If you work for an organization that uses a Microsoft Exchange account, you can set up your iPhone to receive and respond to invitations from colleagues in your company. When somebody sends an invitation that you accept, it appears on your calendar. Check with your company network administrator (who will jump at the chance to get her hands on your iPhone) or the iPhone User Guide to set up this feature if it sounds useful to you.

TIP

iCloud offers individuals functionality similar to Microsoft Exchange.

Create a Calendar Account

If you use a calendar available from an online service, such as Yahoo! or Google, you can subscribe to that calendar to read events saved there on your iPhone.

1. Tap the Settings icon on the Home screen to get started.

2. Tap the Accounts & Passwords option.

3. Tap Add Account and the Add Account options, shown in **Figure 22-8,** appear.

4. Tap a selection, such as Outlook.com, Gmail, or Yahoo!, depending on the calendar service you'd like to use.

TIP

Turn on Calendars for other accounts that aren't listed by tapping Other.

5. In the next screen that appears (see **Figure 22-9**), enter your account information for the service (the screen you see will vary, depending on the service you selected in Step 4). If you don't yet have an account for the service, there will be a way on the screen for you to create a new account.

FIGURE 22-8

FIGURE 22-9

6. Tap Next. iPhone verifies your address.

7. On the following screen (see **Figure 22-10**), tap the On/Off switch for the Calendars field; your iPhone retrieves data from your calendar at the interval you have set to fetch data. Tap the back arrow in the top-left corner. To review these settings for data fetching, tap the Fetch New Data option in the Accounts dialog.

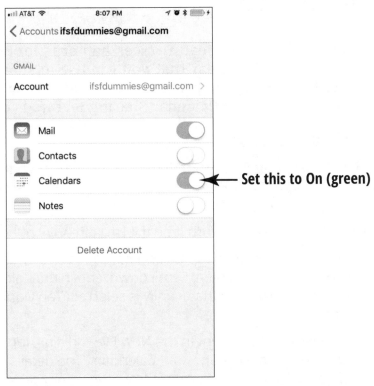

Set this to On (green)

FIGURE 22-10

8. In the Fetch New Data dialog that appears, be sure that the Push option's On/Off switch reads On (green), then scroll down to choose the option you prefer for how frequently data is pushed to your iPhone: every 15 minutes; every 30 minutes; hourly; or manually. If you have multiple accounts, you can choose how to retrieve event information for them individually.

WARNING

Though you can have calendar events pushed to you or synced from multiple email accounts, having data pushed to your iPhone may drain your battery more quickly. It's not a major concern, but one to be aware of if you notice your battery draining quickly over an extended period of time.

Use a Family Calendar

If you set up the Family Sharing feature (see Chapter 15 for how to do this), you create a Family calendar that you can use to share family events with up to five other people. After you set up Family Sharing, you have to make sure that the Calendar Sharing feature is on.

1. Tap Settings on the Home screen.

2. Tap iCloud and check that Family Sharing is set up in the second line of the dialog (see **Figure 22-11**). You will see Family Sharing rather than Set Up Family Sharing if it has been set up.

3. Tap the switch for Calendars to turn it on if it isn't already on.

4. Now tap the Home button, then tap Calendars. Tap the Calendars button at the bottom of the screen. Scroll down, and in the Calendars dialog that appears, make sure that Family is selected. Tap Done in the upper-right corner.

5. Now when you create a new event in the New Event dialog, tap Calendar and choose Family or Show All Calendars. The details of events contain a notation that an event is from the Family calendar.

TIP

If you store birthdays for people in the Contacts app, by default the Calendar app then displays these when the day comes around so that you won't forget to pass on your congratulations! You can turn off this feature by tapping Calendars in the Calendar app and deselecting Birthday Calendar.

Click to set up Family Sharing if it's not already in use

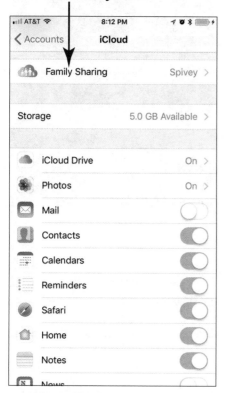

FIGURE 22-11

Delete an Event

When an upcoming luncheon or meeting is canceled, you should delete the appointment.

1. With Calendar open, tap an event (see **Figure 22-12**).

2. Tap Delete Event at the bottom of the screen.

3. If this is a repeating event, you have the option to delete this instance of the event or this and all future instances of the event (see **Figure 22-13**). Tap the button for the option you prefer. The event is deleted, and you return to Calendar view.

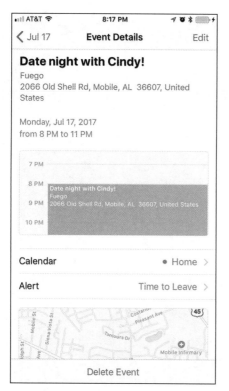

FIGURE 22-12   **FIGURE 22-13**

TIP

If an event is moved but not canceled, you don't have to delete the old one and create a new one. Simply edit the existing event to change the day and time in the Event dialog.

Display Clock

Clock is a preinstalled app that resides on the Home screen along with other preinstalled apps, such as iBooks and Camera.

1. Tap the Clock app to open it. If this is the first time you've opened Clock, you'll see the World Clock tab (see **Figure 22-14**).

2. You can add a clock for many (but not all) locations around the world. With Clock displayed, tap the Add button (looks like a plus symbol) in the upper-right corner.

3. Tap a city on the list or tap a letter on the right side to display locations that begin with that letter (see **Figure 22-15**), then tap a city. You can also tap in the Search field and begin to type a city name to find and tap a city. The clock appears in the last slot at the bottom.

FIGURE 22-14

FIGURE 22-15

Delete a Clock

1. To remove a location, tap the Edit button in the top-left corner of the World Clock screen.

2. Tap the minus symbol next to a location, then tap Delete (see **Figure 22-16**).

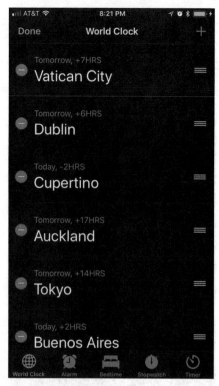

FIGURE 22-16

Set an Alarm

1. With the Clock app displayed, tap the Alarm tab.

2. Tap the Add button, the + in the upper-right corner. In the Add Alarm dialog shown in **Figure 22-17,** take any of the following actions, tapping Back after you make each setting to return to the Add Alarm dialog:

   - Tap Repeat if you want the alarm to repeat at a regular interval, such as every Monday or every Sunday.

   - Tap Label if you want to name the alarm, such as "Take Pill" or "Call Glenn."

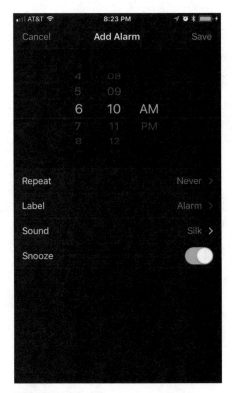

FIGURE 22-17

- Tap Sound to choose the tune the alarm will play.

- Tap the On/Off switch for Snooze if you want to use the Snooze feature.

3. Place your finger on any of the three columns of sliding numbers at the top of the dialog and scroll to set the time you want the alarm to occur; then tap Save. The alarm appears on the calendar on the Alarm tab.

To delete an alarm, tap the Alarm tab and tap Edit. All alarms appear. Tap the red circle with a minus in it, then tap the Delete button.

TIP

Set Bedtime and Waking Alerts

The Clock can also help you develop better sleeping habits by allow-ing you to set bedtime and wake alerts and keeping track of your sleep habits.

1. Tap the Bedtime button at the bottom of the Clock app screen.

2. If this is your first time to open the Bedtime feature, tap Get Started and answer the questions you're asked to help configure the Bedtime settings.

3. When you've completed the initial configuration, you will see a screen displaying your bedtime and waking hours (see **Figure 22-18**).

FIGURE 22-18

4. You can manually change the bedtime by pressing the button that looks like a moon and dragging it around the clock face. You can do the same for the wake time by pressing and dragging the button that looks like a bell. To keep the same amount of sleep time you can press and drag the orange band.

5. Tap the Options button in the upper-left corner to reconfigure the settings for Bedtime (refer to **Figure 22-19**). You can adjust the days

the Bedtime feature is used, the reminder time, the Wake Up Sound, and the volume for the Wake Up Sound. Tap Done when finished (or Cancel if you didn't make any changes).

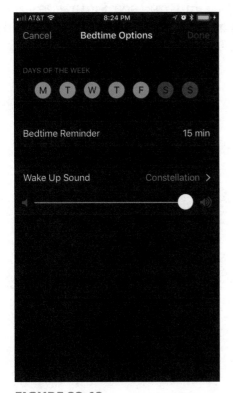

FIGURE 22-19

6. Tap the Bedtime toggle switch to Off to disable or On to enable.

Swipe down on the Bedtime screen to see a history of your sleep patterns.

Use Stopwatch and Timer

Sometimes life seems like a countdown or a ticking clock counting the minutes you've spent on a certain activity. You can use the Timer and Stopwatch tabs of the Clock app to do a countdown to a specific time, such as the moment when your chocolate chip cookies are done cooking or to time an activity, such as a walk.

These two work very similarly: Tap the Stopwatch or Timer tab from Clock's screen, then tap the Start button (see **Figure 22-20**). When you set the Timer, iPhone uses a sound to notify you when time's up. When you start the Stopwatch, you have to tap the Stop button when the activity is done.

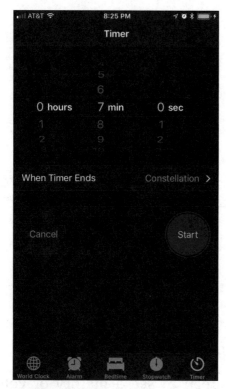

FIGURE 22-20

TIP

Stopwatch allows you to log intermediate timings, such as a lap around a track or the periods of a timed game. With Stopwatch running, just tap the Lap button and the first interval of time is recorded. Tap Lap again to record a second interval, and so forth.

Chapter **23**

Working with Reminders and Notifications

The Reminders app and Cover Sheet (formerly known as Notification Center) features warm the hearts of those who need help remembering all the details of their lives.

Reminders is a kind of to-do list that lets you create tasks and set reminders so that you don't forget important commitments.

You can even be reminded to do things when you arrive at or leave a location. For example, you can set a reminder so that, when your iPhone detects that you've left the location of your golf game, an alert reminds you to pick up your grandchildren, or when you arrive at your cabin, iPhone reminds you to turn on the water . . . you get the idea.

Cover Sheet allows you to review all the things you should be aware of in one place, such as mail messages, text messages, calendar appointments, and alerts.

If you occasionally need to escape all your obligations, try the Do Not Disturb feature. Turn this feature on, and you won't be bothered with alerts until you're ready to be.

In this chapter, you discover how to set up and view tasks in Reminders and how Cover Sheet can centralize all your alerts in one easy-to-find place.

Create a Reminder

Creating an event in Reminders is pretty darn simple:

1. Tap Reminders on the Home screen.

2. On the screen that appears, tap Reminders, then tap a blank slot with a plus sign to the left of it in the displayed list to add a task (see **Figure 23-1**). The onscreen keyboard appears.

3. Enter a task name or description using the onscreen keyboard, then tap Done.

TIP

The following task shows how to add more specifics about an event for which you've created a reminder.

Tap here to add a task

FIGURE 23-1

Edit Reminder Details

TIP

1. Tap a reminder, then tap the Details button (an i in a circle) that appears to the right of it to open the Details dialog shown in **Figure 23-2.**

   I deal with reminder settings in the following task.

2. Tap a Priority: None, Low (!), Medium (!!), or High (!!!) from the choices that appear.

3. Tap Notes and enter any notes about the event using the onscreen keyboard (see **Figure 23-3**).

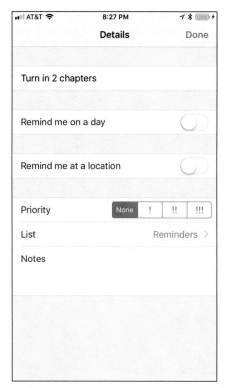

FIGURE 23-2

FIGURE 23-3

4. Tap List, then tap which list you want the reminder saved to, such as your calendar, iCloud, Exchange, or a category of reminders that you've created. Tap Details to return to the Details screen.

5. Tap Done to save the task.

TIP

With this version of the app, priority settings now display the associated number of exclamation points on a task in a list to remind you of its importance.

Schedule a Reminder by Time or Location

One of the major purposes of Reminders is to remind you of upcoming tasks. To set a reminder, follow these steps:

1. Tap a task, then tap the Details button that appears to the right of the task.

2. In the dialog that appears (refer to **Figure 23-2**), toggle the Remind Me on a Day switch to turn the feature On (green).

3. Tap the Alarm field that appears below this setting (see **Figure 23-4**) to display date settings.

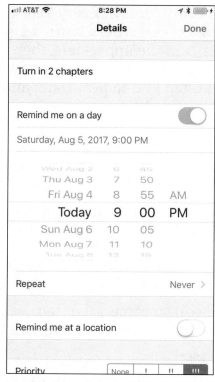

FIGURE 23-4

4. Tap and flick the day, hour, and minutes fields to scroll to the date and time for the reminder.

5. Tap Remind Me at a Location, then tap the Location field. If prompted, tap Allow to let Reminders use your current location.

   You have to be in range of a GPS signal for the location reminder to work properly.

TIP

6. Use the field labeled Current Location to find your location or enter a location in the Search field. Tap Details in the upper-left corner to return to the task detail screen.

7. Tap Done to save the settings for the reminder.

TIP

If you want a task to repeat with associated reminders, tap the Repeat field in the Details dialog (the Remind Me on a Day option must be On for this to appear), and from the dialog that appears, tap Every Day, Every Week, Every 2 Weeks, Every Month, Every Year (for those annual meetings or great holiday get-togethers with the gang), or create a Custom interval. Tap Details in the upper-left, then tap Done in the upper-right to save details for the task. To stop the task from repeating, tap the End Repeat field, tap End Repeat Date, and select a date from the scrolling calendar.

Create a List

You can create your own lists of tasks to help you keep different parts of your life organized and even edit the tasks on the list in List view.

1. Tap Reminders on the Home screen to open it. If a particular list is open, tap its name to return to the List view.

2. Tap New (the + symbol in the upper-right corner), then tap List in the resulting dialog to display the New List form shown in **Figure 23-5.**

3. Tap New List, then enter a name for the list.

4. Tap a color; the list name will appear in that color in List view.

5. Tap Done to save the list. Tap a blank line to enter a task, or tap the list name to return to the List view.

FIGURE 23-5

Sync with Other Devices and Calendars

To make all these settings work, you should set up your default Calendar in the Settings⇨Calendar settings and set up your iCloud account to enable Reminders (Settings⇨Apple ID [top of the screen]⇨iCloud).

TIP

Your default Calendar account is also your default Reminders account.

1. To determine which tasks are brought over from other calendars (such as Outlook), tap the Settings button on the Home screen.

2. Tap your Apple ID, then tap iCloud. In the dialog that appears, be sure that Reminders is set to On (green).

3. Tap Settings to return to the main settings list, swipe up to scroll down a bit, then tap Reminders.

4. Tap the Sync button, then choose how far back to sync Reminders (shown in **Figure 23-6**).

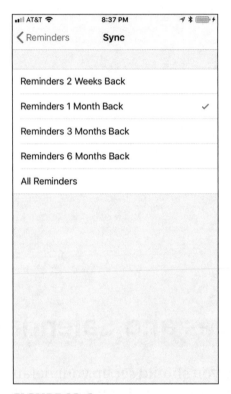

FIGURE 23-6

Mark as Complete or Delete a Reminder

You may want to mark a task as completed or just delete it entirely.

1. With Reminders open and a list of tasks displayed, tap the circle to the left of a task to mark it as complete. When you tap Show

Completed, the task now appears as completed; when you next open Reminders, it will have been removed from the Reminders category.

2. To delete more than one reminder, with the list of tasks displayed, tap Edit, and in the screen shown in **Figure 23-7,** tap the red minus icon to the left of any task and tap Delete; or tap Delete List at the bottom of the screen and tap Delete in the confirming dialog to delete all the events on the list.

Red minus icon

FIGURE 23-7

3. Tap Done when finished marking or deleting reminders.

Set Notification Types

Cover Sheet is a list of various alerts and scheduled events; it even provides information (such as stock quotes) that you can display by swiping down from the top of your iPhone screen. Cover Sheet is on by default, but you don't have to include every type of notification there if you don't want to; for example, you may never want to be notified of incoming messages but always want to have reminders listed here — it's up to you. Some Cover Sheet settings let you control what types of notifications are included:

1. Tap Settings, then tap Notifications.

2. In the settings that appear (see **Figure 23-8**), you see a list of items to be included in Cover Sheet. You can view the state of an item by reading it directly under the item's name. For example, under Accuweather in Figure 23-8, you read "Badges, Sounds, Banners," indicating the methods of notifications that are enabled for that app.

3. Tap any item. In the settings that appear, set an item's Allow Notifications switch (see **Figure 23-9**) to On or Off, to include or exclude it from Cover Sheet.

4. Tap an Alert Style to choose to have no alert, view a banner across the top of the screen, or have a boxed alert appear.

TIP

If you enable Banners, it will appear, then disappear automatically if you tap the Temporary style. If you choose Persistent, you have to take an action to dismiss the alert when it appears (such as swiping it up to dismiss it or tapping to view it).

5. If you want to be able to view alerts when the lock screen is displayed, turn on the Show on Cover Sheet setting.

6. Tap Notifications in the upper-left corner to return to the main Notifications settings screen. When you've finished making settings, press the Home button.

TIP

You can drag across or tap an alert displayed in Cover Sheet to go to its source, such as the Reminders app, to see more details about it.

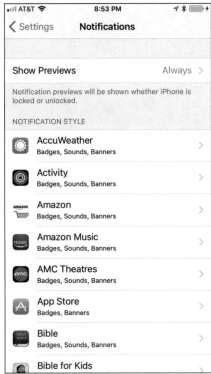

FIGURE 23-8

FIGURE 23-9

View Cover Sheet

After you've made settings for what should appear in Cover Sheet, you'll regularly want to take a look at those alerts and reminders.

1. From any screen, tap and hold your finger at the top of the screen and drag down to display Cover Sheet (see **Figure 23-10**).

TIP

Swipe from left-to-right on the date at the top of the Cover Sheet to view other notifications such as weather, reminders, Siri app suggestions, and more. Swipe from right-to-left on the date at the top to return to app notifications.

2. To close Cover Sheet, swipe upward from the bottom of the screen.

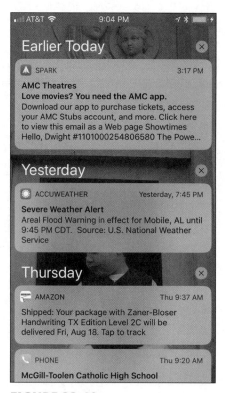

FIGURE 23-10

TIP

To determine what is displayed in Cover Sheet, see the previous task.

There are two sections in Cover Sheet for you to play with: Notifications and Today.

1. Swipe down from the top of the screen to open Cover Sheet. Notifications is displayed by default.

2. Swipe from left to right on the date/time at the top of Cover Sheet to access the Today tab to view information in widgets that pertain to today, such as Reminders, weather, stock prices, Calendar items, and other items you've selected to display in Cover Sheet (see the preceding task).

TIP

You select which widgets appear in the Today tab by tapping the Edit button at the bottom of the Today screen, then selecting the items you want to see. Tap Done to return to the Today screen.

3. Swipe from right to left on the date/time at the top of Cover Sheet to visit the Notifications section to see all notifications that you set up in the Settings app. You'll see only notifications that you haven't responded to, deleted in the Notifications section, or haven't viewed in their originating app.

Work with Notifications in Cover Sheet

You will receive notifications on Cover Sheet when a message has been received or you've missed a phone call, for example. There are several ways to respond to notifications; you'll need to begin by swiping down from the top of your screen to open Cover Sheet.

TIP

You don't have to unlock your phone if you're viewing your lock screen; just tap and drag down from the Status bar to view Cover Sheet.

» Tap an item, and you're taken to the originating app, where you can take the appropriate action: create and send a return message, initiate a phone call, or whatever. Swiping from left to right on a notification and tapping the Open button produces the same effect.

TIP

If you're on the lock screen, you'll have to use Touch ID or enter your passcode to view the notification in its app.

» Swiping from right to left will yield two options: Clear and View.

  • Tap Clear to remove the notification from Cover Sheet. No worries, though. The item is still available for viewing in its originating app.

  • Tap View to open a window in Cover Sheet offering an expanded view of the notification, as shown in **Figure 23-11.** Tap the X to clear the notification, tap the notification window to open the notification in its app, or tap outside the notification window to return to Cover Sheet.

FIGURE 23-11

Get Some Rest with Do Not Disturb

Do Not Disturb is a simple but useful setting you can use to stop any alerts, phone calls, text messages, and FaceTime calls from appearing or making a sound. You can make settings to allow calls from certain people or several repeat calls from the same person in a short time period to come through. (The assumption here is that such repeat calls may signal an emergency situation or urgent need to get through to you.)

1. Tap Settings, then tap Do Not Disturb.

2. Set the Do Not Disturb switch to On (green) to enable the feature.

3. In the other settings shown in **Figure 23-12,** do any of the following:

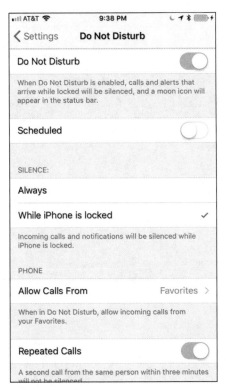

FIGURE 23-12

- Toggle the Scheduled switch to On (green) to allow alerts during a specified time period to appear.

- Tap Allow Calls From, then from the next screen select Everyone, No One, Favorites, or Groups such as All Contacts.

- Toggle the Repeated Calls switch to On to allow a second call from the same person in a three-minute time period to come through.

- Choose to silence incoming calls and notifications Always or Only while iPhone is locked.

4. Press the Home button to return to the Home screen.

> » **Extend your iPhone's battery life**
>
> » **Fix a nonresponsive iPhone**
>
> » **Update the iOS software**
>
> » **Get support**
>
> » **Find and back up your iPhone**

Chapter **24**

Troubleshooting and Maintaining Your iPhone

Phones don't grow on trees — they cost a pretty penny, especially with phone equipment subsidies and two-year contracts disappearing. That's why you should learn how to take care of your iPhone and troubleshoot any problems it might have so that you get the most out of it.

In this chapter, I provide some advice about the care and maintenance of your iPhone, as well as tips about how to solve common problems, update iPhone system software, and even reset the iPhone if something goes seriously wrong. In case you lose your iPhone, I even tell you about a feature that helps you find it, activate it remotely, or even disable it if it has fallen into the wrong hands. Finally, you get information about backing up your iPhone settings and content using iCloud and the fingerprint reader feature, Touch ID.

Keep the iPhone Screen Clean

If you've been playing with your iPhone, you know (despite Apple's claim that the iPhone has a fingerprint–resistant screen) that it's a fingerprint magnet. Here are some tips for cleaning your iPhone screen:

» **Use a dry, soft cloth.** You can get most fingerprints off with a dry, soft cloth, such as the one you use to clean your eyeglasses or a cleaning tissue that's lint and chemical free. Or try products used to clean lenses in labs, such as Kimwipes (which you can get from several major retailers, such as Amazon).

» **Use a slightly dampened soft cloth.** This may sound counter-intuitive to the previous tip, but to get the surface even cleaner, very (and I stress, very) slightly dampen the soft cloth. Again, make sure that whatever cloth material you use is free of lint.

» **Remove the cables.** Turn off your iPhone and unplug any cables from it before cleaning the screen with a moistened cloth, even a very slightly moistened one.

» **Avoid too much moisture.** Avoid getting too much moisture around the edges of the screen, where it can seep into the unit. It isn't so much the glass surface you should worry about, as it is the Home button and the speaker holes on the top and bottom of the iPhone.

» **Don't use your fingers!** That's right, by using a stylus rather than your finger, you entirely avoid smearing oil from your skin or cheese from your pizza on the screen. There are a number of top-notch styluses out there; just search Amazon for "iPhone stylus" and you'll be greeted with a multitude of them (most have a very reasonable price).

» **Never use household cleaners.** They can degrade the coating that keeps the iPhone screen from absorbing oil from your fingers. Plus, there's just simply no need to go that far since the screen cleans quite easily with little or no moisture at all.

WARNING Don't use premoistened lens-cleaning tissues to clean your iPhone screen! Most brands of wipes contain alcohol, which can damage the screen's coating.

Protect Your Gadget with a Case

Your screen isn't the only element on the iPhone that can be damaged, so consider getting a case for it so that you can carry it around the house or around town safely. Besides providing a bit of padding if you drop the device, a case makes the iPhone less slippery in your hands, offering a better grip when working with it.

Several types of covers and cases are available, but be sure to get one that will fit your model of iPhone because their dimensions and button placements may differ, and some models have slightly different thicknesses. There are differences between covers and cases:

» **Covers tend to be more for decoration than overall protection.** While they do provide some protection, they're generally thin and not well-padded.

» **Cases are more solid and protect most, if not all, of your iPhone.** They're usually a bit bulky and provide more padding than covers.

You can choose covers from such manufacturers as Griffin (www.griffintechnology.com), or you can also check out Apple's range of silicone and leather covers (www.apple.com/shop/iphone/iphone-accessories/cases-protection).

Cases range from a few dollars to $70 or more for leather (with some outrageously expensive designer cases costing upward of $500). Some provide protection for the screen, back, and sides; others protect only the back and sides. If you carry your iPhone around much, consider a case with a screen cover to provide better protection for the screen or use a screen overlay, such as InvisibleShield from Zagg (www.zagg.com/us/en_us/invisibleshield). If you're the literary type, try the BookBook case that looks like a well-worn leather book (www.twelvesouth.com/product/family/bookbook).

Extend Your iPhone's Battery Life

The much-touted battery life of the iPhone is a wonderful feature, but you can do some things to extend it even further. Here are a few tips to consider:

» **Keep tabs on remaining battery life.** You can estimate the amount of remaining battery life by looking at the Battery icon on the far-right end of the Status bar, at the top of your screen.

» **Use standard accessories to charge your iPhone most effectively.** When connected to a recent-model Mac or Windows computer for charging, the iPhone can slowly charge; however, the most effective way to charge your iPhone is to plug it into a wall outlet using the Lightning to USB Cable and the 5W USB power adapter that come with your iPhone.

TIP

Third-party charging cables usually work just fine, but some are less reliable than others. If you use a third-party cable and notice that your iPhone is taking longer than usual to charge, it's a good idea to try another cable.

» **Use a case with an external battery pack.** These cases are very handy when you're traveling or unable to reach an electrical outlet easily. However, they're also a bit bulky and can be cumbersome in smaller hands.

» **The fastest way to charge iPhone is to turn it off while charging it.** If turning your iPhone completely off doesn't sound like the best idea for you, you can disable Wi-Fi or Bluetooth to facilitate a faster recharge.

TIP

Activate Airplane Mode to turn both Wi-Fi and Bluetooth off at the same time.

» **The Battery icon on the Status bar indicates when the charging is complete.**

TIP

Your iPhone battery is sealed in the unit, so you can't replace it yourself the way you can with many laptops or other cellphones. If the battery is out of warranty, you have to fork over about $79 to have Apple install a new one with AppleCare coverage. See the "Get Support" task, later in this chapter, to find out where to get a replacement battery.

TIP

Apple offers AppleCare+. For $99, you get two years of coverage, which even covers you if you drop or spill liquids on your iPhone (Apple covers up to two incidents of accidental damage). If your iPhone has to be replaced, it will cost you only $49, rather than the $250 it used to cost with garden-variety AppleCare. You can purchase AppleCare+ when you buy your iPhone or within 60 days of the date of purchase. See www.apple.com/support/products/iphone.html for more details.

Find Out What to Do with a Nonresponsive iPhone

If your iPhone goes dead on you, it's most likely a power issue, so the first thing to do is to plug the Lightning to USB Cable into the USB power adapter, plug the USB power adapter into a wall outlet, plug the other end of the cable into your iPhone, and charge the battery.

Another thing to try — if you believe that an app is hanging up the iPhone — is to press the Sleep/Wake button for a couple of seconds, then press and hold the Home button. The app you were using should close.

You can always try the tried-and-true reboot procedure: On the iPhone, you press the Sleep/Wake button on the right until the red slider appears. Drag the slider to the right to turn off your iPhone. After a few moments, press the Sleep/Wake button to boot up the little guy again.

If the situation seems drastic and none of these ideas works, try to force restart your iPhone. To do this, press the Sleep/Wake button and the Home button at the same time until the Apple logo appears onscreen. This may take at least ten seconds, so be patient.

TIP

If your phone has this problem often, try closing out some active apps that may be running in the background and using up too much memory. To do this, press the Home button twice, then from the screen showing active apps, tap and drag an app upward. Also check to see that you haven't loaded up your iPhone with too much content, such as videos, which could be slowing down its performance.

Update the iOS Software

Apple occasionally updates the iPhone system software, known as iOS, to fix problems or offer enhanced features. You should occasionally check for an updated version (say, every month). You can check by connecting your iPhone to a recognized computer (that is, a computer that you've used to sign into your Apple account before) with iTunes installed, but it's even easier to just update from your iPhone Settings, though it's a tad slower:

1. Tap Settings from the Home screen.

2. Tap General, then tap Software Update (see **Figure 24-1**).

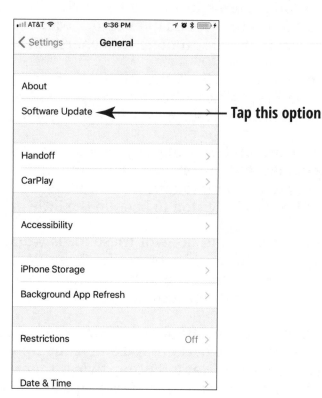

FIGURE 24-1

3. A message tells you whether your software is up-to-date. If it's not, tap Download and Install and follow the prompts to update to the latest iOS version.

TIP

If you're having problems with your iPhone, you can use the Update feature to try to restore the current version of the software. Follow the preceding set of steps, then tap the Restore button instead of the Software Update button in Step 2.

Restore the Sound

My wife frequently has trouble with the sound on her iPhone, and subsequently we've learned quite a bit about troubleshooting sound issues, enabling us to pass our knowledge on to you. Make sure that:

WARNING

» **You haven't touched the volume control buttons on the side of your iPhone.** They're on the left side of the phone.

Be sure not to touch the volume decrease button and inadvertently lower the sound to a point where you can't hear it. Pushing the volume buttons will have no effect if the iPhone is sleeping, so don't worry about this happening while the iPhone is just sitting in your pocket or purse.

» **You haven't flipped the Ringer/Silent switch.** Moving the switch located on the left side above the volume buttons mutes sound on the iPhone.

WARNING

This switch can be moved if you drop your iPhone — so don't do that!

» **The speaker isn't covered up.** No, really — it may be covered in a way that muffles the sound.

» **A headset isn't plugged in.** Sound doesn't play over the speaker and the headset at the same time.

» **The volume limit is set to On.** You can set up the volume limit for the Music app to control how loudly your music can play (which is useful if you have teenagers around). Tap Settings on the Home screen and then, on the screen that displays, tap Music, then tap Volume Limit under the Playback section if it is set to On. Use the slider that appears (see **Figure 24-2**) to set the volume limit. If the slider button is all the way to the left, you've set your volume limit too low (all the way down, as a matter of fact).

Drag the slider to set the volume limit

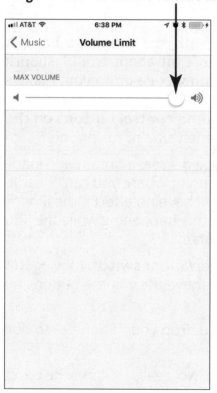

FIGURE 24-2

TIP

When all else fails, reboot. This strategy worked for us — just press the Sleep/Wake button until the red slider appears, then drag the slider to the right. After the iPhone turns off, press the Sleep/Wake button again until the Apple logo appears, and you may find yourself back in business, sound-wise.

Get Support

Every single new iPhone comes with a year's coverage for repair of the hardware and 90 days of free technical support. Apple is known for its high level of customer support, so if you're stuck, I definitely recommend that you try it. Here are a few options that you can explore for getting help:

» **The Apple Store:** Go to your local Apple Store (if one is handy) to see what the folks there might know about your problem. Call first and make an appointment at the Genius Bar to be sure to get prompt service.

» **The Apple support website:** It's at support.apple.com/iphone. You can find online manuals, discussion forums, and downloads, and you can use the Apple Expert feature to contact a live support person by phone.

» **The iPhone User Guide:** You can download the free manual that is available through iBooks from the iBooks Store. See Chapter 16 for more about iBooks.

» **The Apple battery replacement service:** If you need repair or service for your battery, visit www.apple.com/batteries/service-and-recycling and scroll down to the iPhone Owners section. Note that your warranty provides free battery replacement if the battery level dips below 50 percent and won't go any higher during the first year you own it. If you purchase the AppleCare+ service agreement, this is extended to two years.

 Apple recommends that you have your iPhone battery replaced only by an Apple Authorized Service Provider.

WARNING

Find a Missing iPhone

You can take advantage of the Find My iPhone feature to pinpoint the location of your iPhone. This feature is extremely handy if you forget where you left your iPhone or someone steals it. Find My iPhone not only lets you track down the critter but also lets you wipe out the data contained in it if you have no way to get the iPhone back.

You must have an iCloud account to use the Find My iPhone feature. If you don't have an iCloud account, see Chapter 4 to find out how to set one up.

If you're using Family Sharing, someone in your family can find your device and play a sound. This works even if the ringer on the iPhone is turned off. See Chapter 15 for more about Family Sharing. Also, see Apple's support article on "Family Sharing and location" at https:// support.apple.com/en-us/HT201087 (as of this writing) for help with this service.

Follow these steps to set up the Find My iPhone feature:

1. Tap Settings on the Home screen.

2. In Settings, tap your Apple ID at the top of the screen, then tap iCloud.

3. In the iCloud settings, tap Find My iPhone, then tap the On/Off switch for Find My iPhone to turn the feature on (see **Figure 24-3**).

4. From now on, if your iPhone is lost or stolen, you can go to www.icloud.com from your computer, iPad, or another iPhone and enter your Apple ID and password.

5. In your computer's browser, the iCloud Launchpad screen appears. Click the Find My iPhone button to display a map of its location and some helpful tools (see **Figure 24-4**).

6. Click the green circle representing your iPhone, then click the Information button (the small "i"). In the window that appears, choose one of three options:

   • To wipe information from the iPhone, click the Erase iPhone button.

   • To lock the iPhone from access by others, click the Lost Mode button.

   • Tap Play Sound to have your phone play a sound that might help you locate it if you're in its vicinity.

Set this to On

FIGURE 24-3

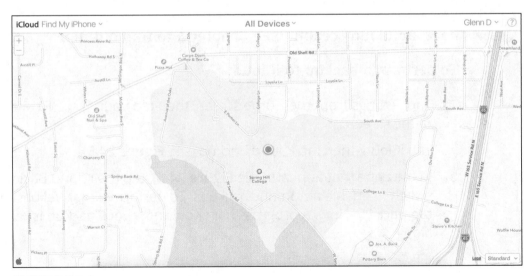

FIGURE 24-4

TIP

Erase iPhone will delete all data from your iPhone, including contact information and content (such as music). However, even after you've erased your iPhone, it will display your phone number on the lock screen along with a message so that any Good Samaritan who finds it can contact you. If you've created an iTunes or iCloud backup, you can restore your iPhone's contents from those sources.

TIP

The Lost Mode feature allows you to send whomever has your iPhone a note saying how to return it to you. If you choose to play a sound, it plays for two minutes, helping you track down your iPhone in case it fell under a couch cushion or somebody holding your iPhone is within earshot.

Back Up to iCloud

You used to be able to back up your iPhone content using only iTunes, but since Apple's introduction of iCloud with iOS 5, you can back up via a Wi-Fi network to your iCloud storage. You get 5GB of storage for free or you can pay for increased storage (a total of 50GB for $.99 per month, 200GB for $2.99 per month, or 1TB for $9.99 per month).

TIP

You must have an iCloud account to back up to iCloud. If you don't have an iCloud account, see Chapter 4 to find out more.

To perform a backup to iCloud:

1. Tap Settings from the Home screen, then tap your Apple ID at the top of the screen.

2. Tap iCloud, then tap iCloud Backup (see **Figure 24-5**).

3. In the pane that appears (see **Figure 24-6**), tap the iCloud Backup switch to enable automatic backups. To perform a manual backup, tap Back Up Now. A progress bar shows how your backup is moving along.

Set this to On

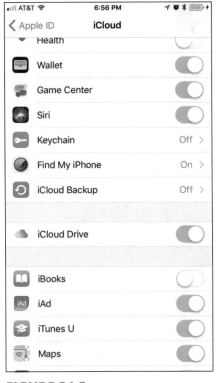

FIGURE 24-5

FIGURE 24-6

TIP

If you get your iPhone back after it wanders and you've erased it, just enter your Apple ID and password and you can reactivate it.

TIP

You can also back up your iPhone using iTunes. This method actually saves more types of content than an iCloud backup, and if you have encryption turned on in iTunes, it can save your passwords as well. However, this method does require that you connect to a computer to perform the backup. Unfortunately, you can't back up to both iTunes and iCloud. However, if you do back up and get a new iPhone down the line, you can restore all your data to the new phone easily.

Index

E

F

About the Author

Dwight Spivey has been a technical author and editor for a decade, but has been a bona fide technophile for more than three of them. He's the author of *iPhone for Seniors For Dummies,* 6th Edition (Wiley), *Idiot's Guide to Apple Watch* (Alpha), *Home Automation For Dummies* (Wiley), *How to Do Everything Pages, Keynote & Numbers* (McGraw-Hill), and many more books covering the tech gamut. Dwight is also the Educational Technology Specialist at Spring Hill College. His technology experience is extensive, consisting of macOS, iOS, Android, Linux, and Windows operating systems in general, educational technology, desktop publishing software, laser printers and drivers, color and color management, and networking. Dwight lives on the Gulf Coast of Alabama with his wife, Cindy, and their four children, Victoria, Devyn, Emi, and Reid.

Oh, and their dog, Rocky, and parakeet, Samwise.

Dedication

Again, this one goes out to my parents, Glenn and Glinda, who allowed me to dive deep into my geeky side from an early age, and now I've finally written some books they might find a use for other than decorating their shelves. They're truly the most selfless people I've ever known — what a blessing it's been to be their son.

I love you both.

Author's Acknowledgments

Sincerest thanks to my agent, Carole Jelen of Waterside, for continuing to find stellar projects like this one for me!

I've heard it said that a book's author is only as good as the team that's behind him. In my case, the incredible team behind me are the real stars of the show. The wonderful editing and beautiful graphic design are two elements that set For Dummies books apart from the crowd, not simply the words of the author. The crew behind this book was truly critical to its completion, and I want every single one of them to know how grateful I am for their professionalism, dedication, hard work, and their patience in working with me. Thank you to the following wonderful people, from the bottom of my heart: Amy Fanrei, Pat O'Brien, and Matthew Fecher.

Publisher's Acknowledgments

Project Manager: Pat O'Brien

Technical Editor: Matthew Fecher

Sr. Editorial Assistant: Cherie Case

Production Editor: Siddique Shaik

Cover Image: © g-stockstudio/ iStockphoto